W9-APG-135

Core Knowledge Sequence

Content Guidelines for Grades K-8

Core Knowledge Foundation

ART DIRECTION AND DESIGN: Bill Womack
COVER: Pino Trogu and Bill Womack

PHOTO CREDITS: Shakespeare, Corbis-Bettman; Nefertiti, Charles & Josette Lenars/Corbis

Core Knowledge Foundation
801 East High Street
Charlottesville, VA 22902
telephone: (804) 977-7550
fax: (804) 977-0021
e-mail: coreknow@coreknowledge.org
home page: www.coreknowledge.org

Contents

CONTENT

GUIDELINES

FOR

GRADES

K-8

WHAT IS THE CORE KNOWLEDGE SEQUENCE?

The Core Knowledge Sequence is a detailed outline of specific content to be taught in language arts, history, geography, mathematics, science, and the fine arts. As the core of a school's curriculum, it can provide a solid, coherent foundation of learning, while allowing flexibility to meet local needs.

The Sequence represents a first and ongoing attempt to state specifically a core of shared knowledge that children should learn in American schools. It should be emphasized that the Core Knowledge Sequence is not a list of facts to be memorized. Rather, it is a guide to coherent content from grade to grade, designed to encourage steady academic progress as children build their knowledge and skills from one year to the next.

The Core Knowledge Sequence is distinguished by its specificity. While most state or district curricula provide general guidelines concerning skills, they typically offer little help in deciding specific content. The specific content in the Sequence provides a solid foundation on which to build skills instruction. Moreover, because the Sequence offers a coherent plan that builds year by year, it helps prevent the many repetitions and gaps in instruction that can result from vague curricular guidelines (for example, repeated units on "Pioneer Days" or "Saving the Rain Forest"; or, inadequate attention to the Bill of Rights, or to adding fractions with unlike denominators, or to African geography).

THE CONSENSUS BEHIND THE CORE KNOWLEDGE SEQUENCE

The Core Knowledge Sequence is the result of a long process of research and consensus-building undertaken by the Core Knowledge Foundation, an independent, nonpartisan, nonprofit organization dedicated to excellence and fairness in early education.

Here is how we achieved the consensus behind the Core Knowledge Sequence. First, we analyzed the many reports issued by state departments of education and by professional organizations—such as the National Council of Teachers of Mathematics and the American Association for the Advancement of Science—which recommend general outcomes for elementary and secondary education. We also tabulated the knowledge and skills specified in the successful educational systems of several other countries, including France, Japan, Sweden, and West Germany.

In addition, we formed an advisory board on multiculturalism that proposed a core knowledge of diverse cultural traditions that American children should all share as part of their school-based common culture. We sent the resulting materials to three independent groups of teachers, scholars, and scientists around the country, asking them to create a master list of the core knowledge children should have by the end of grade six. About 150 teachers (including college professors, scientists, and administrators) were involved in this initial step.

These items were amalgamated into a draft master plan, and further groups of teachers and specialists were asked to agree on a grade-by-grade sequence of the items. That draft sequence was then sent to some one hundred educators and specialists who participated in a national conference that was called to hammer out a working agreement on core knowledge for the first six grades.

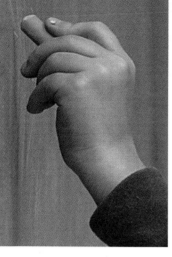

This important meeting took place in March 1990. The conferees were elementary school teachers, curriculum specialists, scientists, science writers, officers of national organizations, representatives of ethnic groups, district superintendents, and school principals from across the country. A total of twenty-four working groups decided on revisions to the draft sequence. The resulting provisional sequence was further fine-tuned during a year of implementation at a pioneering school, Three Oaks Elementary in Lee County, Florida. Also, the Visual Arts and Music sections of the Sequence were further developed based on the research of the Core Knowledge Foundation, with the assistance of advisors and teachers.

As more and more schools use the Sequence, it has been periodically updated and revised based on the principle of learning from experience. In general, there is more stability than change in the Sequence. (See E. D. Hirsch's *Cultural Literacy* for a discussion of the inherent stability of the content of literate culture.)

THE SEQUENCE AS THE CORE OF THE CURRICULUM

The Core Knowledge Sequence is not meant to outline the whole of a school's curriculum, but rather to provide a coherently organized plan for the content that should make up at least 50% of the curriculum, with the remainder of instruction devoted to skills and local requirements.

The content in the Sequence is compatible with a variety of instructional methods and additional subject matters. Teachers may choose to teach only the content specified in the Sequence or to supplement as they see fit. For example, a fifth grade teacher could teach a coherent unit on the Civil War based solely on the topics specified in the Sequence. Or the teacher might choose to go into greater depth and detail by adding, for example, more attention to particular battles, specific leaders, songs, poems, historical fiction, letters, videos, and field trips. In short, while the Sequence specifies a coherent core of knowledge, the teacher remains free to decide when to go beyond what is in the Sequence.

Because the Core Knowledge Sequence describes the fundamentals of a good education only in the elementary and middle grades, some apparently relevant items may not be included. For example, while the Sequence specifies that students in the fourth grade learn about the three branches of American government, it does not require that they learn about the electoral college. A teacher who wants to present the electoral college is free to do so, but should keep in mind that students will revisit these subjects later in high school.

CORE KNOWLEDGE PROMOTES EXCELLENCE AND FAIRNESS

Excellence: All the most successful educational systems in the world teach a core of knowledge in the early grades. They do this because as both research and common sense demonstrate, we learn new knowledge by building on what we already know. It is important to begin building foundations of knowledge in the early grades because that is when children are most receptive, and because academic deficiencies in the first six grades can permanently impair the quality of later schooling.

Fairness: Only by specifying the knowledge that all children should share can we guarantee equal access to that knowledge. In our current system, disadvantaged children especially suffer from low expectations that translate into watered-down curricula. In schools using the Core Knowledge Sequence, however, disadvantaged children, like all children, are exposed to a coherent core of challenging, interesting knowledge. This knowledge not only provides a foundation for later learning, but also makes up the common ground for communication in a diverse society.

A NOTE ON MULTICULTURALISM

Respect for the diversity in our population is fostered by the knowledge specified in the Core Knowledge Sequence, which has been reviewed by distinguished scholars in the field of

multicultural studies. Some people have urged the Foundation to make a separate listing of multicultural entries in this Sequence, but to do so would contradict our embrace of an inclusive, rather than divisive, multiculturalism. As Professor James Comer of Yale University has written (in a review of E. D. Hirsch's *Cultural Literacy*),

> *. . . respect for cultural diversity is important but is best achieved when young people have adequate background knowledge of mainstream culture. In order for a truly democratic and economically sound society to be maintained, young people must have access to the best knowledge available so that they can understand the issues, express their viewpoints, and act accordingly.*

The Core Knowledge Sequence is designed to provide "access to the best knowledge available," including significant knowledge of diverse peoples and cultures. For a more detailed discussion of these issues, write or call the Foundation and request a copy of E. D. Hirsch's essay called "Toward a Centrist Curriculum: Two Kinds of Multiculturalism in Elementary School."

THE ARTS IN THE CURRICULUM

The arts are not a peripheral part of the curriculum, but an essential part of the knowledge children should learn in the early grades.

Early instruction in the arts should be non-competitive, and provide many opportunities to sing, dance, listen to music, play act, read and write poetry, draw, paint, and make objects. Equally important, when children are young and receptive, they should be exposed to fine paintings, great music, and other inspiring examples of art. As children progress in their knowledge and competencies, they can begin to learn more about the methods and terminology of the different arts, and become familiar with an ever wider range of great artists and acknowledged masterworks.

Through attaining a basic knowledge of the arts, children are not only better prepared to understand and appreciate works of art, but also to communicate their ideas, feelings, and judgments to others. A good understanding of the arts grows out of at least three modes of knowledge—creative (i.e., directly making artworks), historical, and analytical. Early study of the arts should embrace all three modes with special emphasis on creativity and active participation.

The arts guidelines in the Core Knowledge Sequence are organized into two main sections: the Visual Arts and Music. While the Sequence does not present other arts such as dance or drama as separate disciplines, we acknowledge their importance and have incorporated them in other disciplines in the Sequence (for example, dance is in Music; drama, in Language Arts).

CORE KNOWLEDGE SCHOOLS

Core Knowledge schools are dedicated to teaching solid academic content and skills to all children. To implement Core Knowledge, many people involved with the school's operations, including both staff and parents, need to engage in a great deal of thoughtful discussion and cooperative planning. Teachers make a commitment to teach all the topics in the Core Knowledge Sequence at the assigned grade levels. This commitment ensures consistency, and it helps avoid serious gaps in knowledge, as well as needless repetitions in instruction, as students progress through the grades.

The Sequence serves as the planning document in each classroom. Its high level of specificity proves useful not only when planning but also when communicating among staff members and with parents. Core Knowledge schools develop a schoolwide plan to teach all of the topics in the Sequence. Typically this plan is developed over a period of two to three years, either by phasing in topics and subjects, or by adding additional grade levels each year.

The Core Knowledge Foundation serves as the hub of a nationwide network for hundreds of Core Knowledge schools. Presentations and workshops are available to introduce Core Knowledge and to assist schools in the implementation of the Sequence. Each year the Foundation holds a national conference to provide opportunities for networking with other Core Knowledge schools and obtaining new ideas for teaching the topics in the Sequence.

For more information on implementing a Core Knowledge program and the recommended training, call or write the Director of School Programs at the Core Knowledge Foundation.

CORE KNOWLEDGE RESOURCES

For a good first resource, teachers and parents may wish to consult the books in the Core Knowledge Series, titled *What Your Kindergartner-Sixth Grader Needs to Know*, edited by E. D. Hirsch, Jr. The books should be available at bookstores nationwide, or they may be ordered from the Core Knowledge Foundation by calling 1-800-238-3233. (Earnings from sales of the Core Knowledge Series go to the non-profit Core Knowledge Foundation. E. D. Hirsch, Jr. receives no remuneration for editing the Series, nor any other remuneration from the Core Knowledge Foundation.)

Other resources that may be purchased from the Foundation include:

- *Books to Build On: A Grade-by-Grade Resource Guide for Parents and Teachers*, an annotated listing of a variety of resources relevant to the topics specified in the Sequence.
- Core Classics: Illustrated literary classics abridged for young readers while remaining faithful in style and substance to the original works, including *Gulliver's Travels, Robinson Crusoe, Sherlock Holmes, Pollyanna, Treasure Island,* and more.
- Core Chronicles: History books written in a lively narrative style for young readers.
- Core Knowledge Preschool Sequence: Content and Skill Guidelines for Young Children
- Lesson plans developed and shared by teachers in Core Knowledge schools. Some of these lessons are available on the Core Knowledge home page at www.coreknowledge.org.

For a list of current resources and prices, call or write the Core Knowledge Foundation, or visit the Core Knowledge home page at www.coreknowledge.org.

Core Knowledge Foundation
801 East High Street
Charlottesville, VA 22902
telephone: (804) 977-7550
fax: (804) 977-0021
e-mail: coreknow@coreknowledge.org
home page: www.coreknowledge.org

Grade K

Overview of Topics   KINDERGARTEN

Language Arts
I. Reading and Writing
   A. Book and Print Awareness
   B. Phonemic Awareness
   C. Decoding and Encoding
   D. Reading and Language Comprehension
   E. Writing and Spelling
II. Poetry
   A. Mother Goose and Other Traditional Poems
   B. Other Poems, Old and New
III. Fiction
   A. Stories
   B. Aesop's Fables
   C. American Legends and Tall Tales
   D. Literary Terms
IV. Sayings and Phrases

History and Geography
World:
I. Geography: Spatial Sense
II. An Overview of the Seven Continents

American:
I. Geography
II. Native American Peoples, Past and Present
III. Early Exploration and Settlement
   A. The Voyage of Columbus in 1492
   B. The Pilgrims
   C. July 4, "Independence Day"
IV. Presidents, Past and Present
V. Symbols and Figures

Visual Arts
I. Elements of Art
   A. Color
   B. Line
II. Sculpture
III. Looking at and Talking about Works of Art

Music
I. Elements of Music
II. Listening and Understanding
III. Songs

Mathematics
I. Patterns and Classification
II. Numbers and Number Sense
III. Money
IV. Computation
V. Measurement
VI. Geometry

Science
I. Plants and Plant Growth
II. Animals and Their Needs
III. The Human Body
IV. Introduction to Magnetism
V. Seasons and Weather
VI. Taking Care of the Earth
VII. Science Biographies

Language Arts: Kindergarten

I. Reading and Writing

A. BOOK AND PRINT AWARENESS
- Know parts of a story (for example, title, beginning, end) and their functions.
- Know that print goes from left to right across the page and from top to bottom down the page, and that words are separated by spaces.
- Follow print, pointing to each word from left to right, when listening to familiar stories or other texts read aloud.

B. PHONEMIC AWARENESS
TEACHERS: Phonemic awareness is the understanding that the sound of a word consists of a sequence of smaller, individual sounds. These basic speech sounds that make up words are called phonemes. For example, there are three phonemes in the word "mat": /m/ /a/ /t/. Phonemes are written within back slashes: for example, when you see /b/, you should say neither "bee" nor "buh," but instead a short, clipped "bh" sound. To *segment* is to take words apart into separate syllables or phonemes. To *blend* is to put together separate syllables or phonemes.

NOTE: See Appendix A, Sample Phoneme Sequence.

- Given a spoken word, produce another word that rhymes with the given word.
- Orally segment words into syllables and demonstrate understanding of syllable breaks by such means as, for example, clapping hands on each syllable or placing a different colored marker to represent each syllable.
  Example: "muffin" ➔ "muf" *[clap]* + "fin" *[clap]*
- Orally blend syllables into words.
  Example: "muf" + "fin" ➔ "muffin"

NOTE: The technical term "rime" is not the same as "rhyme" in poetry.

- Orally blend onsets (any initial consonant or consonant cluster) and rimes (the vowel and any following consonants) in spoken words.
  Example: /c/ - / at/ ➔ cat
  /s/ - /it/ ➔ sit
- Orally blend isolated sounds into a spoken one-syllable word.
  Example: /c/ - /u/ - /p/ ➔ cup

NOTE: Some programs insist upon using only the letter sounds and not the letter names. This may be a useful practice in the early stages of learning, in order to avoid confusion between the names of the letters and the speech sounds they represent. For instance, h ("aitch") does not sound like /h/, and w ("double-u") does not sound like /w/. But outside the classroom, most adults will use the letter names, and most children "learn their ABCs"—that is, the letter names—very early. The important goal is to make sure the child understands through consistent performance the difference between speech sounds and their letter names.

- Given prompting with a picture, isolate and repeat the initial or final sound of a one-syllable spoken word.
  Example: bat ➔ /b/   bird ➔ /d/

C. DECODING AND ENCODING
TEACHERS: Decoding is the act of turning the letters into the speech sounds they represent. Encoding is the act of turning the sounds of spoken language into the corresponding written letters. Children need to understand that the sequence of sounds in a spoken word is represented by a left-to-right sequence of letters in a written or printed word. The goal is, through regular and systematic practice, for decoding and encoding to become automatic, and so allow the child to focus attention instead on meaning.

In abbreviations such as CVC, C stands for "consonant" and V stands for "vowel." A CVC word is a consonant-vowel-consonant word, such as "cat" or "mop." An example of a CCVC word is "frog." An example of a CVCC word is "tent."

- Recognize and name all uppercase and lowercase letters of the alphabet. [See Note]
- Match a letter to a spoken phoneme.
  Example: *Teacher says* /b/. *Child points to letter card with* b.
- Decode a letter into the phoneme it represents.
  Example: *Teacher shows letter card* b. *Child says* /b/.

- Write the correct letters to represent a sound or sequence of sounds, up to three consonants or two consonants and a short vowel sound.

  Example: *Spoken by teacher:* /s/   *Written by child:* s

  Spoken by teacher: /m/ /b/ /m/   *Written by child:* m b m

  Spoken by teacher: /b/ /i/ /b/   *Written by child:* b i b

- Read any three-sound CVC word (for example, cat, sit) or nonsense word (for example, mup, fap).
- Read simple phrases or sentences made up of the phonemes mastered so far.

  Example: "Cat ran up." "Sam sat."

- Begin to read VCC, CVCC, and CCVC words with adjacent consonants and short vowel sounds (for example, ant, milk, frog).
- Begin to recognize common words by sight, including *a, the, I, my, you, is, are.*

D. READING AND LANGUAGE COMPREHENSION

- Understand and follow oral directions.
- Tell in his or her own words what happened in stories or parts of stories, and predict what will happen next in stories.
- Distinguish fantasy from realistic text.
- Listen to and understand a variety of texts, both fiction and nonfiction.

E. WRITING AND SPELLING

- Write his or her own name (first and last).
- Write all uppercase and lowercase letters of the alphabet.
- Use letter-sound knowledge to write simple words and messages, consistently representing initial and final consonant sounds (for example, writing "boat" as "bot").

II. Poetry

TEACHERS: Children should be introduced to a varied selection of poetry with strong rhyme and rhythm. Children should hear these rhymes read aloud, and should say some of them aloud. Some rhymes may also be sung to familiar melodies. The poems listed here represent some of the most popular and widely anthologized titles; children may certainly be introduced to more Mother Goose rhymes beyond the selection below. Whereas children are not expected to memorize the following rhymes, they will delight in knowing their favorites by heart, and will experience a sense of achievement and satisfaction in being able to recite some of the rhymes.

A. MOTHER GOOSE AND OTHER TRADITIONAL POEMS

A Diller, A Dollar
Baa, Baa, Black Sheep
Diddle, Diddle, Dumpling
Early to Bed
Georgie Porgie
Hey Diddle Diddle
Hickory, Dickory, Dock
Hot Cross Buns
Humpty Dumpty
It's Raining, It's Pouring
Jack and Jill
Jack Be Nimble
Jack Sprat
Ladybug, Ladybug
Little Bo Peep
Little Boy Blue
Little Jack Horner
Little Miss Muffet
London Bridge Is Falling Down

Mary, Mary, Quite Contrary
Old King Cole
Old Mother Hubbard
One, Two, Buckle My Shoe
Pat-a-Cake
Rain, Rain, Go Away
Ride a Cock-Horse
Ring Around the Rosey
Rock-a-bye, Baby
Roses Are Red
See-Saw, Margery Daw
Simple Simon
Sing a Song of Sixpence
Star Light, Star Bright
There Was a Little Girl
There Was an Old Woman Who Lived in a Shoe
This Little Pig Went to Market
Three Blind Mice

NOTE: Children should read aloud with someone outside of school at least 10 minutes daily.

NOTE REGARDING PRESCHOOL CONTENT: Some of the poems and stories specified here are appropriate for preschoolers. Indeed, one would hope that most preschoolers would come to kindergarten having heard, for example, some Mother Goose rhymes or the story of "Goldilocks and the Three Bears." However, as not all children attend preschool, and as home preparation varies, the Core Knowledge Sequence offers a core of familiar rhymes and stories for all kindergarten children. See also the Core Knowledge Preschool Sequence, available from the Core Knowledge Foundation.

NOTE: The poems listed here constitute a selected core of poetry for this grade. You are encouraged to expose children to more poetry, old and new. To bring children into the spirit of poetry, read it aloud and encourage them to speak it aloud so they can experience the music in the words.

B . OTHER POEMS, OLD AND NEW

April Rain Song (Langston Hughes)
Happy Thought (Robert Louis Stevenson)
I Do Not Mind You, Winter Wind (Jack Prelutsky)
Mary Had a Little Lamb (Sara Josepha Hale)
The More It Snows (A. A. Milne)
My Nose (Dorothy Aldis)
Rain (Robert Louis Stevenson)
Three Little Kittens (Eliza Lee Follen)
Time to Rise (Robert Louis Stevenson)
Tommy (Gwendolyn Brooks)
Twinkle Twinkle Little Star (Jane Taylor)

III. Fiction

TEACHERS: While the following works make up a strong core of literature, the content of the language arts includes not only stories, fables, and poems, but also the well-practiced, operational knowledge of how written symbols represent sounds, and how those sounds and symbols convey meaning. Thus, the stories specified below are meant to complement, not to replace, materials designed to help children practice decoding skills (see above, I. Reading and Writing).

The following works constitute a core of stories for this grade. In kindergarten, these stories are meant to be read-aloud selections. Expose children to many more stories, including classic picture books and read-aloud books. (In schools, teachers across grade levels should communicate their choices in order to avoid undue repetition.) Children should also be exposed to non-fiction prose: biographies, books on science and history, books on art and music, etc. And, children should be given opportunities to tell and write their own stories.

A. STORIES

The Bremen Town Musicians (Brothers Grimm)
Chicken Little (also known as "Henny-Penny")
Cinderella (Charles Perrault)
Goldilocks and the Three Bears
How Many Spots Does a Leopard Have? (African folk tale)
King Midas and the Golden Touch
The Legend of Jumping Mouse (Native American: Northern Plains legend)
The Little Red Hen
Little Red Riding Hood
Momotaro: Peach Boy (Japanese folk tale)
Snow White and the Seven Dwarfs
The Three Billy Goats Gruff
The Three Little Pigs
A Tug of War (African folk tale)
The Ugly Duckling (Hans Christian Andersen)
The Velveteen Rabbit (Margery Williams)
selections from *Winnie-the-Pooh* (A. A. Milne)
The Wolf and the Kids (Brothers Grimm)

B. AESOP'S FABLES

The Lion and the Mouse
The Grasshopper and the Ants
The Dog and His Shadow
The Hare and the Tortoise

Note: Children will read more American legends and tall tales in grade 2.

C. AMERICAN FOLK HEROES AND TALL TALES
Johnny Appleseed
Casey Jones

D. LITERARY TERMS
Teachers: As children become familiar with stories, discuss the following:

author
illustrator

IV. Sayings and Phrases

Teachers: Every culture has phrases and proverbs that make no sense when carried over literally into another culture. For many children, this section may not be needed; they will have picked up these sayings by hearing them at home and among friends. But the sayings have been one of the categories most appreciated by teachers who work with children from home cultures that differ from the standard culture of literate American English.

A dog is man's best friend.
April showers bring May flowers.
Better safe than sorry.
Do unto others as you would have them do unto you.
The early bird gets the worm.
Great oaks from little acorns grow.
Look before you leap.
A place for everything and everything in its place.
Practice makes perfect.
[It's] raining cats and dogs.
Where there's a will there's a way.

History and Geography: Kindergarten

<u>TEACHERS:</u> In kindergarten, children often study aspects of the world around them: the family, the school, the community, etc. The following guidelines are meant to broaden and complement that focus. The goal of studying selected topics in World History in Kindergarten is to foster curiosity and the beginnings of understanding about the larger world outside the child's locality, and about varied civilizations and ways of life. This can be done through a variety of means: story, drama, art, music, discussion, and more.

The study of geography embraces many topics throughout the Core Knowledge Sequence, including topics in history and science. Geographic knowledge includes a spatial sense of the world, an awareness of the physical processes that shape life, a sense of the interactions between humans and their environment, an understanding of the relations between place and culture, and an awareness of the characteristics of specific regions and cultures.

WORLD HISTORY AND GEOGRAPHY

I. Geography: Spatial Sense (working with maps, globes, and other geographic tools)

<u>TEACHERS:</u> Foster children's geographical awareness through regular work with maps and globes. Have students regularly locate themselves on maps and globes in relation to places they are studying. Children should make and use a simple map of a locality (such as classroom, home, school grounds, "treasure hunt").

- Maps and globes: what they represent, how we use them
- Rivers, lakes, and mountains: what they are and how they are represented on maps and globes
- Locate the Atlantic and Pacific Oceans.
- Locate the North and South Poles.

II. An Overview of the Seven Continents

<u>TEACHERS:</u> Help children gain a beginning geographic vocabulary and a basic sense of how we organize and talk about the world by giving names to some of the biggest pieces of land. Introduce children to the seven continents through a variety of media (tracing, coloring, relief maps, etc.), and associate the continents with familiar wildlife, landmarks, etc. (for example, penguins in Antarctica; the Eiffel Tower in Europe). Throughout the school year, reinforce names and locations of continents when potential connections arise in other disciplines (for example, connect Grimm's fairy tales to Europe; voyage of Pilgrims to Europe and North America; story of "Momotaro—Peach Boy" to Asia [Japan]; study of Native Americans to North America).

<u>NOTE:</u> In later grades, children will continue to learn about all the continents as well as specific countries and peoples.

- Identify and locate the seven continents on a map and globe:
  Asia
  Europe
  Africa
  North America
  South America
  Antarctica
  Australia

TEACHERS: The study of American history begins in grades K-2 with a brief overview of major events and figures, from the earliest days to recent times. A more in-depth, chronological study of American history begins again in grade 3 and continues onward. The term "American" here generally, but not always, refers to the lands that became the United States. Other topics regarding North, Central, and South America may be found in the World History and Geography sections of this Sequence.

I. Geography
- Name and locate the town, city, or community, as well as the state where you live.
- Locate North America, the continental United States, Alaska, and Hawaii.

II. Native American Peoples, Past and Present

TEACHERS: As children progress through the grades of the Core Knowledge Sequence, they will learn about many different Native American peoples in many different regions. In kindergarten, study at least one specific group of Native Americans: explore how they lived, what they wore and ate, the homes they lived in, their beliefs and stories, etc., and also explore the current status of the tribe or nation. You might explore a local or regional tribe or nation, and compare it with one far away.

- Become familiar with the people and ways of life of at least one Native American tribe or nation, such as:
    Pacific Northwest: Kwakiutl, Chinook
    Plateau: Nez Perce
    Great Basin: Shoshone, Ute
    Southwest: Dine [Navajo], Hopi, Apache
    Plains: Blackfoot, Comanche, Crow, Kiowa, Dakota, Cheyenne, Arapaho, Lakota (Sioux)
    Northeast: Huron, Iroquois
    Eastern Woodlands: Cherokee, Seminole, Delaware, Susquehanna, Mohican,
        Massachusett, Wampanoag, Powhatan

III. Early Exploration and Settlement
A. THE VOYAGE OF COLUMBUS IN 1492
- Queen Isabella and King Ferdinand of Spain
- The Niña, Pinta, and Santa Maria
- Columbus's mistaken identification of "Indies" and "Indians"
- The idea of what was, for Europeans, a "New World"

B. THE PILGRIMS
- The Mayflower
- Plymouth Rock
- Thanksgiving Day celebration

C. JULY 4, "INDEPENDENCE DAY"
- The "birthday" of our nation
- Democracy (rule of the people): Americans wanted to rule themselves instead of being ruled by a faraway king.
- Some people were not free: slavery in early America

IV. Presidents, Past and Present

<u>TEACHERS:</u> Introduce children to famous presidents, and discuss with them such questions as: What is the president? How does a person become president? Who are some of our most famous presidents, and why?

See below, Symbols and Figures: Mount Rushmore; the White House.

- George Washington
    The "Father of His Country"
    Legend of George Washington and the cherry tree
- Thomas Jefferson, author of Declaration of Independence
- Abraham Lincoln
    Humble origins
    "Honest Abe"
- Theodore Roosevelt
- Current United States president

V. Symbols and Figures

- Recognize and become familiar with the significance of
    American flag
    Statue of Liberty
    Mount Rushmore
    The White House

Visual Arts: Kindergarten

SEE PAGE 3, "The Arts in the Curriculum."

TEACHERS: In schools, lessons on the visual arts should illustrate important elements of making and appreciating art, and emphasize important artists, works of art, and artistic concepts. When appropriate, topics in the visual arts may be linked to topics in other disciplines. While the following guidelines specify a variety of artworks in different media and from various cultures, they are not intended to be comprehensive. Teachers are encouraged to build upon the core content and expose children to a wide range of art and artists.

I. Elements of Art

TEACHERS: The generally recognized elements of art include line, shape, form, space, light, texture, and color. In kindergarten, introduce children to line and color. Engage students in recognizing and using different kinds of lines and colors, and point out lines and colors in nature. (You may also wish to observe shapes in art and nature—see Math: Geometry.)

A. COLOR
- Observe how colors can create different feelings and how certain colors can seem "warm" (red, orange, yellow) or "cool" (blue, green, purple)
- Observe the use of color in
  Pieter Bruegel, *The Hunters in the Snow*
  Helen Frankenthaler, *Blue Atmosphere*
  Paul Gauguin, *Tahitian Landscape*
  Pablo Picasso, *Le Gourmet*

B. LINE
- Identify and use different lines: straight, zigzag, curved, wavy, thick, thin
- Observe different kinds of lines in
  Katsushika Hokusai, *Tuning the Samisen*
  Henri Matisse, *The Purple Robe*
  Joan Miró, *People and Dog in the Sun*

II. Sculpture

See also American History K, Native Americans, *re* totem pole.

- Recognize and discuss the following as sculptures:
  Northwest American Indian totem pole
  Statue of Liberty
- Mobiles: Alexander Calder's *Lobster Trap and Fish Tail*

III. Looking at and Talking about Works of Art

TEACHERS: After children have been introduced to some elements of art and a range of artworks and artists, engage them in looking at pictures and talking about them. Ask the children about their first impressions—what they notice first, and what the picture makes them think of or feel. Go on to discuss the lines and colors, details not obvious at first, why they think the artist chose to depict things in a certain way, etc.

- Observe and talk about
  Pieter Bruegel, *Children's Games*
  Mary Cassatt, *The Bath*
  Winslow Homer, *Snap the Whip*
  Diego Rivera, *Mother's Helper*
  Henry O. Tanner, *The Banjo Lesson*

Music

Music: Kindergarten

SEE PAGE 3, "The Arts in the Curriculum."

TEACHERS: In schools, lessons on music should feature activities and works that illustrate important musical concepts and terms, and should introduce important composers and works. When appropriate, topics in music may be linked to topics in other disciplines.

The following guidelines focus on content, not performance skills, though many concepts are best learned through active practice (singing, clapping rhythms, playing instruments, etc.).

I. Elements of Music

- Through participation, become familiar with some basic elements of music (rhythm, melody, harmony, form, timbre, etc.).

    Recognize a steady beat; begin to play a steady beat.

    Recognize that some beats have accents (stress).

    Move responsively to music (marching, walking, hopping, swaying, etc.).

    Recognize short and long sounds.

    Discriminate between fast and slow.

    Discriminate between obvious differences in pitch: high and low.

    Discriminate between loud and quiet.

    Recognize that some phrases are the same, some different.

    Sing unaccompanied, accompanied, and in unison.

II. Listening and Understanding

TEACHERS: To encourage listening skills and the beginnings of understanding, play various kinds of music often and repeatedly. In the kindergarten classroom, music can be played for enjoyment, to accompany activities, to inspire creative movement, etc. Expose children to a wide range of music, including children's music, popular instrumental music, and music from various cultures.

Music

NOTE: Grieg's "In the Hall of the Mountain King" is a good work to illustrate dynamics (loud and quiet), as well as tempo (slow and fast).

- Recognize the following instruments by sight and sound: guitar, piano, trumpet, flute, violin, drum.
- Become familiar with the following works:

    Edvard Grieg, "Morning" and "In the Hall of the Mountain King" from *Peer Gynt*

    Victor Herbert, "March of the Toys" from *Babes in Toyland*

    Richard Rodgers, "March of the Siamese Children" from *The King and I*

    Camille Saint-Saëns, *Carnival of the Animals*

III. Songs

TEACHERS: See also Language Arts, Mother Goose poems. A number of the poems may be sung to familiar melodies.

The Bear Went Over the Mountain

Bingo

The Farmer in the Dell

Go In and Out the Window

Go Tell Aunt Rhody

Here We Go Round the Mulberry Bush

The Hokey Pokey

Hush Little Baby

If You're Happy and You Know It

Jingle Bells

John Jacob Jingleheimer Schmidt
Kumbaya
London Bridge
Old MacDonald Had a Farm
Row, Row, Row Your Boat
This Old Man
Twinkle Twinkle Little Star
The Wheels on the Bus

TEACHERS: You may wish to supplement the songs listed above with songs from the Core Knowledge Preschool Sequence, as follows:

A Tisket, A Tasket
Are You Sleeping?
Blue-Tail Fly (Jimmie Crack Corn)
Do Your Ears Hang Low?
Did You Ever See a Lassie?
Eensy, Weensy Spider
Five Little Ducks That I Once Knew
Five Little Monkeys Jumping On the Bed
Happy Birthday to You
Head and Shoulders, Knees and Toes
Here is the Beehive
I Know an Old Lady
I'm a Little Teapot
Kookaburra
Lazy Mary
Looby Loo
Oats, Peas, Beans and Barley Grow
Oh, Do You Know the Muffin Man?
Oh Where, Oh Where, Has My Little Dog Gone?
One Potato, Two Potato
Open, Shut Them
Pop Goes the Weasel
Teddy Bear, Teddy Bear, Turn Around
Teddy Bears Picnic
Where is Thumbkin?
Who Stole the Cookie from the Cookie Jar?
You Are My Sunshine

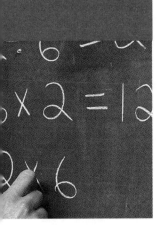

Mathematics: Kindergarten

TEACHERS: Mathematics has its own vocabulary and patterns of thinking. It is a discipline with its own language and conventions. Thus, while some lessons may offer occasional opportunities for linking mathematics to other disciplines, it is critically important to attend to math as math. From the earliest years, mathematics requires incremental review and steady practice: not only the diligent effort required to master basic facts and operations, but also thoughtful and varied practice that approaches problems from a variety of angles, and gives children a variety of opportunities to apply the same concept or operation in different types of situations. While it is important to work toward the development of "higher-order problem-solving skills," it is equally important—indeed, it is prerequisite to achieving "higher order" skills—to have a sound grasp of basic facts, and an automatic fluency with fundamental operations.

I. Patterns and Classification

- Establish concepts of likeness and difference by sorting and classifying objects according to various attributes: size, shape, color, amount, function, etc.
- Define a set by the common property of its elements.
- In a given set, indicate which item does not belong.
- Moving from concrete objects to pictorial representations, recognize patterns and predict the extension of a pattern.
- Extend a sequence of ordered concrete objects.

II. Numbers and Number Sense

- Using concrete objects and pictorial representations, compare sets:
  same as (equal to)
  more than
  less than
  most
  least
- Count
  forward from 1 to 31, first beginning with 1, and later from any given number
  backward from 10
  from 1 to 10 by twos
  by fives and tens to 50
- Recognize and write numbers 1 to 31 (with special attention to the difference between certain written symbols, such as: 6 and 9; 2 and 5; 1 and 7; 12 and 21, etc.).
- Count and write the number of objects in a set.
- Given a number, identify one more, one less.
- Identify ordinal position, first (1st) through sixth (6th).
- Identify pairs.
- Interpret simple pictorial graphs.
- Identify $\frac{1}{2}$ as one of two equal parts of a region or object; find $\frac{1}{2}$ of a set of concrete objects.

III. Money

- Identify pennies, nickels, dimes, and quarters.
- Identify the one-dollar bill.
- Identify the dollar sign ($) and cents sign (¢).
- Write money amounts using the cents sign (¢).

IV. Computation

- Add and subtract to ten, using concrete objects.
- Recognize the meaning of the plus sign (+).
- Subtraction: the concept of "taking away"; recognize the meaning of the minus sign (-).

V. Measurement

- Identify familiar instruments of measurement, such as ruler, scale, thermometer.
- Compare objects according to:
    Linear measure
        long and short; longer than, shorter than
        measure length using non-standard units
        begin to measure length in inches
        height: taller than, shorter than
    Weight (mass)
        heavy, light
        heavier than, lighter than
    Capacity (volume)
        full and empty
        less full than, as full as, fuller than
    Temperature: hotter and colder
- Time
    Sequence events: before and after; first, next, last.
    Compare duration of events: which takes more or less time.
    Read a clock face and tell time to the hour.
    Know the days of the week and the months of the year.
    Orientation in time: today, yesterday, tomorrow; morning, afternoon; this morning
        vs. yesterday morning, etc.

VI. Geometry

- Identify left and right hand.
- Identify top, bottom, middle.
- Know and use terms of orientation and relative position, such as:
    closed, open
    on, under, over
    in front, in back (behind)
    between, in the middle of
    next to, beside
    inside, outside
    around
    far from, near
    above, below
    to the right of, to the left of
    here, there
- Identify and sort basic plane figures: square, rectangle, triangle, circle.
- Identify basic shapes in a variety of common objects and artifacts (windows, pictures, books, buildings, cars, etc.).
- Recognize shapes as the same or different.
- Make congruent shapes and designs.
- Compare size of basic plane figures (larger, smaller).

Science: Kindergarten

TEACHERS: Effective instruction in science requires hands-on experience and observation. In the words of the 1993 report from the American Association for the Advancement of Science, Benchmarks for Science Literacy, "From their very first day in school, students should be actively engaged in learning to view the world scientifically. That means encouraging them to ask questions about nature and to seek answers, collect things, count and measure things, make qualitative observations, organize collections and observations, discuss findings, etc."

While experience counts for much, book learning is also important, for it helps bring coherence and order to a child's scientific knowledge. Only when topics are presented systematically and clearly can children make steady and secure progress in their scientific learning. The child's development of scientific knowledge and understanding is in some ways a very disorderly and complex process, different for each child. But a systematic approach to the exploration of science, one that combines experience with book learning, can help provide essential building blocks for deeper understanding at a later time.

I. Plants and Plant Growth

TEACHERS: Through reading aloud, observation, and activities such as growing plants from seeds in varying conditions, explore the following with children:

- What plants need to grow: sufficient warmth, light, and water
- Basic parts of plants: seed, root, stem, branch, leaf
- Plants make their own food.
- Flowers and seeds: seeds as food for plants and animals (for example, rice, nuts, wheat, corn)
- Two kinds of plants: deciduous and evergreen
- Farming
  How some food comes from farms as crops
  How farmers must take special care to protect their crops from weeds and pests
  How crops are harvested, kept fresh, packaged, and transported for people to buy and consume

II. Animals and Their Needs

TEACHERS: Through reading aloud, observation, and activities, explore with children the common characteristics and needs of animals, including:

- Animals, like plants, need food, water, and space to live and grow.
- Plants make their own food, but animals get food from eating plants or other living things.
- Offspring are very much (but not exactly) like their parents.
- Most animal babies need to be fed and cared for by their parents; human babies are especially in need of care when young.
- Pets have special needs and must be cared for by their owners.

III. The Human Body

- The five senses and associated body parts:
  Sight: eyes
  Hearing: ears
  Smell: nose
  Taste: tongue
  Touch: skin
- Taking care of your body: exercise, cleanliness, healthy foods, rest

IV. Introduction to Magnetism

TEACHERS: Through reading aloud, observation, and experiments with magnets, introduce children to the idea that there are forces we cannot see that act upon objects. Children should:

- Identify familiar everyday uses of magnets (for example, in toys, in cabinet locks, in "refrigerator magnets," etc.).
- Classify materials according to whether they are or are not attracted by a magnet.

V. Seasons and Weather

TEACHERS: The emphasis in kindergarten should be on observation and description; technical explanations of meteorological phenomena should be taken up in later grades; see grades 2 and 4 for more detailed study of Meteorology.

- The four seasons
- Characteristic local weather patterns during the different seasons
- The sun: source of light and warmth
- Daily weather changes
   Temperature: thermometers are used to measure temperature
   Clouds
   Rainfall: how the condition of the ground varies with rainfall; rainbows
   Thunderstorms: lightning and thunder, hail, safety during thunderstorms
   Snow and snowflakes, blizzard

VI. Taking Care of the Earth

- Conservation: Some natural resources are limited, so people must be careful not to use too much of them (example: logging and reforestation).
- Practical measures for conserving energy and resources (for example, turning off unnecessary lights, tightly turning off faucets, etc.)
- Some materials can be recycled (for example, aluminum, glass, paper).
- Pollution (for example, littering, smog, water pollution) can be harmful, but if people are careful they can help reduce pollution.

VII. Science Biographies

   George Washington Carver
   Jane Goodall
   Wilbur and Orville Wright

Overview of Topics Grade 1

Language Arts
I. Reading and Writing
   A. Phonemic Awareness
   B. Decoding, Word Recognition, and Oral Reading
   C. Reading Comprehension and Response
   D. Writing
   E. Spelling, Grammar, and Usage
II. Poetry
III. Fiction
   A. Stories
   B. Aesop's Fables
   C. Different Lands, Similar Stories
   D. Literary Terms
IV. Sayings and Phrases

History and Geography
World:
I. Geography
   A. Spatial Sense
   B. Geographical Terms and Features
II. Early Civilizations
   A. Mesopotamia: The "Cradle of Civilization"
   B. Ancient Egypt
   C. History of World Religions
III. Modern Civilization and Culture: Mexico
   A. Geography
   B. Culture

American:
I. Early People and Civilizations
   A. The Earliest People: Hunters and Nomads
   B. Maya, Inca, and Aztec Civilizations
II. Early Exploration and Settlement
   A. Columbus
   B. The Conquistadors
   C. English Settlers
III. From Colonies to Independence: The American Revolution
IV. Early Exploration of the American West
V. Symbols and Figures

Visual Arts
I. Art from Long Ago
II. Elements of Art
   A. Color
   B. Line
   C. Shape
   D. Texture
III. Kinds of Pictures: Portrait and Still Life

Music
I. Elements of Music
II. Listening and Understanding
   A. Musical Terms and Concepts
   B. Music Can Tell a Story
   C. American Musical Traditions (Jazz)
III. Songs

Mathematics
I. Patterns and Classification
II. Numbers and Number Sense
III. Money
IV. Computation
   A. Addition
   B. Subtraction
   C. Solving Problems and Equations
V. Measurement
VI. Geometry

Science
I. Living Things and Their Environments
   A. Habitats
   B. Oceans and Undersea Life
   C. Environmental Change and Habitat Destruction
   D. Special Classifications of Animals
II. The Human Body
   A. Body Systems
   B. Germs, Diseases, and Preventing Illness
III. Matter
IV. Properties of Matter: Measurement
V. Introduction to Electricity
VI. Astronomy
VII. The Earth
   A. Geographical Features of the Earth's Surface
   B. What's Inside the Earth
VIII. Science Biographies

1

Language Arts: Grade 1

I. Reading and Writing

TEACHERS: Many of the following sub-goals are designed to help children achieve the overall goal for reading in first grade: to be able to read (both aloud and silently), with fluency, accuracy, and comprehension any story or other text appropriately written for first grade, such as E. H. Minarik's *Little Bear* books, Syd Hoff's *Danny and the Dinosaur* and *Sammy and the Seal*, and Arnold Lobel's *Frog and Toad* books, among many others.

A.   PHONEMIC AWARENESS

TEACHERS: Phonemic awareness is the understanding that the sound of a word consists of a sequence of smaller, individual sounds. These basic speech sounds that make up words are called phonemes. For example, there are three phonemes in the word "mat": /m/ /a/ /t/. Phonemes are written within back slashes: for example, when you see /b/, you should say neither "bee" nor "buh," but instead a short, clipped "bh" sound. To segment is to take words apart into separate syllables or phonemes. To blend is to put together separate syllables or phonemes.

NOTE: See Appendix A, Sample Phoneme Sequence.

- Count the number of syllables in a word.
- Isolate the initial or final consonant sound, or the medial vowel sound, of a one-syllable word.
  Example: sad ➜ /s/ - /ad/ ➜ /s/
                     sad ➜ /sa/ - /d/ ➜ /d/
                     sad ➜ /s/ - /a/ - /d/ ➜ /a/
- Orally segment one-syllable words into phonemes.
  Example: red ➜ /r/ - /e/ - /d/
                     coat ➜ /k/ - /ō/ - /t/
- Orally blend the phonemes of a one-syllable word.
  Example: /c/ - /a/ - /t/ ➜ cat
- Orally delete initial and final phonemes in one-syllable words.
  Example: *delete initial phoneme:* gold ➜ old
                     delete final phoneme: barn ➜ bar
- Orally substitute the initial or final consonant sound, or the medial vowel sound, in one-syllable words.
  Example: *Say* bat. *Change* /b/ to /s/. ➜ sat
                     Say mop. *Change* /p/ to /m/. ➜ mom
                     Say map. *Change* /a/ to /o/. ➜ mop

B.   DECODING, WORD RECOGNITION, AND ORAL READING

NOTE: See Appendix A, Sample Phoneme Sequence. Note that, as children proceed, they should be presented with simple, decodable stories written in a controlled vocabulary that corresponds to the letter-sound patterns they have been taught.

TEACHERS: Decoding is the act of turning the letters into the speech sounds they represent. Children need to understand that the sequence of sounds in a spoken word is represented by a left-to-right sequence of letters in a written or printed word. The goal is, through regular and systematic practice, for decoding to become automatic, and so allow the child to focus attention instead on meaning. Children who can decode automatically become less dependent on context clues, and thus become more fluent readers.

In abbreviations such as CVC, C stands for "consonant" and V stands for "vowel." A CVC word is a consonant-vowel-consonant word, such as "cat" or "mop." An example of a CCVC word is "frog." An example of a CVCC word is "tent." An example of a CCVCC word is "plant." Examples of one-syllable words ending in -VC-e are "gate" and "fine."

- Accurately decode phonetically regular one-syllable words (for example, cat, pig, farm, boat, team, feet, cake), including one-syllable words ending in VC-e.
- Accurately decode simple one-syllable nonsense words (for example, mup, fap, chim).
- Decode common initial digraphs, such as *ch, qu, th* (as in chin, queen, thin), as well as the ending digraph *ng* (as in sing).

- Decode words with common vowel sounds that can be spelled in different ways (such as boot, blue, few; shout, cow; boil, toy; bed, head), and words with common consonant sounds that can be spelled in different ways (such as jet, gem; sip, cent; kite, cat; rat, write).
- Use letter-sound knowledge to sound out unknown words when reading.
- Recognize a number of common, irregularly spelled words by sight, including *a, the, have, says, said, are, one, once, where, two.*

NOTE: Children should read aloud with someone outside of school at least 10 minutes daily.

C. READING COMPREHENSION AND RESPONSE

- Read and understand simple written instructions.
- Notice his or her own difficulties in understanding text.
- Predict what will happen next in stories, justify his or her predictions, and later discuss whether predictions were confirmed.
- Discuss how, why, and what-if questions about both fiction and non-fiction texts.
- Use complete and detailed sentences to respond to what, when, where, and how questions.

    Example: Q: How did the boy save the town?
             A: He put his finger in the hole in the dike to stop the leak,
                   and he stayed there all night long.

- Demonstrate familiarity with a variety of fiction and non-fiction selections, including both read-aloud works and independent readings.

D. WRITING

- Produce a variety of writings—for example, brief stories, descriptions, journal entries—with spelling sufficient to be able to read the words himself or herself.

E. SPELLING, GRAMMAR, AND USAGE

- Spell words from oral dictation composed of the phonemes studied so far.
- Correctly spell three- and four-letter short vowel words (for example, cat, pig, tent).
- Use knowledge of letter-sound correspondence to spell independently.
- Use correct end punctuation: period, question mark, exclamation point.
- Use capitalization for the first word of a sentence, for names of people, and for the pronoun *I.*
- Form the regular plural of a singular noun by adding *s.*

II. Poetry

NOTE: The poems listed here constitute a selected core of poetry for this grade. You are encouraged to expose children to more poetry, old and new, and to have children write their own poems. To bring children into the spirit of poetry, read it aloud and encourage them to speak it aloud so they can experience the music in the words. Whereas children are not expected to memorize the following rhymes, they will delight in knowing their favorites by heart, and will experience a sense of achievement and satisfaction in being able to recite some of the rhymes.

Hope (Langston Hughes)
I Know All the Sounds the Animals Make (Jack Prelutsky)
My Shadow (Robert Louis Stevenson)
The Owl and the Pussycat (Edward Lear)
The Pasture (Robert Frost)
The Purple Cow (Gelett Burgess)
Rope Rhyme (Eloise Greenfield)
Sing a Song of People (Lois Lenski)
Solomon Grundy (traditional)
The Swing (Robert Louis Stevenson)
Table Manners [also known as "The Goops"] (Gelett Burgess)
Thanksgiving Day ["Over the river and through the wood"] (Lydia Maria Child)
Washington (Nancy Byrd Turner)
Wynken, Blynken, and Nod (Eugene Field)

III. Fiction

<u>Teachers:</u>   While the following works make up a strong core of literature, the "content" of the language arts includes not only stories, fables, and poems, but also the well-practiced, operational knowledge of how written symbols represent sounds, and how those sounds and symbols convey meaning. Thus, the stories specified below are meant to complement, not to replace, materials designed to help children practice decoding skills (see above, I. Reading and Writing).

The titles here constitute a core of stories for this grade. They are available in a variety of editions, some designed for novice readers, and others best for reading aloud to children. In first grade, many of the following titles are likely to be read-aloud selections. It is recommended that you provide a mixture of texts, including some beginning readers, with their necessarily limited vocabulary and syntax, for these can give children the important sense of accomplishment that comes from being able to "read it all by myself."

Expose children to many more stories, including classic picture books and read-aloud books. (In schools, teachers across grade levels should communicate their choices in order to avoid undue repetition.)   Children should also be exposed to non-fiction prose—biographies, books on science and history, books on art and music—and they should be given opportunities to tell and write their own stories.

A.   STORIES
The Boy at the Dike (folktale from Holland)
The Frog Prince
Hansel and Gretel
selections from *The House at Pooh Corner* (A. A.Milne)
How Anansi Got Stories from the Sky God (folktale from West Africa)
It Could Always Be Worse (Yiddish folktale)
Jack and the Beanstalk
The Knee-High Man (African-American folktale)
Medio Pollito (Hispanic folktale)
The Pied Piper of Hamelin
Pinocchio
The Princess and the Pea
Puss-in-Boots
Rapunzel
Rumpelstiltskin
Sleeping Beauty
The Tale of Peter Rabbit (Beatrix Potter)
Tales of Br'er Rabbit (recommended tales: Br'er Rabbit Gets Br'er Fox's Dinner;
      Br'er Rabbit Tricks Br'er Bear; Br'er Rabbit and the Tar Baby)
Why the Owl Has Big Eyes (Native American legend)

B.   AESOP'S FABLES
The Boy Who Cried Wolf
The Dog in the Manger
The Wolf in Sheep's Clothing
The Maid and the Milk Pail
The Fox and the Grapes
The Goose and the Golden Eggs

C.   DIFFERENT LANDS, SIMILAR STORIES

TEACHERS: To give students a sense that people all around the world tell certain stories that, while they differ in details, have much in common, introduce students to similar folk tales from different lands, such as the following:

Lon Po Po (China) and Little Red Riding Hood

Issun Boshi, or One-Inch Boy (Japan); Tom Thumb (England); Thumbelina (by the Danish writer Hans Christian Andersen); Little Finger of the Watermelon Patch (Vietnam)

Some of the many variations on the Cinderella story (from Europe, Africa, China, Vietnam, Egypt, Korea, etc.)

D.   LITERARY TERMS

Characters, heroes, and heroines

Drama

  actors and actresses

  costumes, scenery and props

  theater, stage, audience

NOTE: Children should learn terms relating to drama as part of their participation in a play appropriate for first graders—possibly a dramatized version of one of the stories listed above.

IV. Sayings and Phrases

TEACHERS: Every culture has phrases and proverbs that make no sense when carried over literally into another culture. For many children, this section may not be needed; they will have picked up these sayings by hearing them at home and among friends. But the sayings have been one of the categories most appreciated by teachers who work with children from home cultures that differ from the standard culture of literate American English.

A.M. and P.M.

An apple a day keeps the doctor away.

Do unto others as you would have them do unto you. [also in Kindergarten]

Fish out of water

Hit the nail on the head.

If at first you don't succeed, try, try again.

Land of Nod

Let the cat out of the bag.

The more the merrier.

Never leave till tomorrow what you can do today.

Practice makes perfect. [also in Kindergarten]

Sour grapes

There's no place like home.

Wolf in sheep's clothing

History and Geography: Grade 1

TEACHERS: In first grade, children often study aspects of the world around them: the family, the school, the community, etc. The following guidelines are meant to broaden and complement that focus. The goal of studying selected topics in World History in first grade is to foster curiosity and the beginnings of understanding about the larger world outside the child's locality, and about varied civilizations and ways of life. This can be done through a variety of means: story, drama, art, music, discussion, and more.

The study of geography embraces many topics throughout the Core Knowledge Sequence, including topics in history and science. Geographic knowledge embraces a spatial sense of the world, an awareness of the physical processes that shape life, a sense of the interactions between humans and their environment, an understanding of the relations between place and culture, and an awareness of the characteristics of specific regions and cultures.

World History and Geography

I. Geography

A. SPATIAL SENSE (Working with Maps, Globes, and Other Geographic Tools)

TEACHERS: Foster children's geographical awareness through regular work with maps and globes. Have students regularly locate themselves on maps and globes in relation to places they are studying.

- Name your continent, country, state, and community.
- Understand that maps have keys or legends with symbols and their uses.
- Find directions on a map: east, west, north, south.
- Identify major oceans: Pacific, Atlantic, Indian, Arctic.
- Review the seven continents: Asia, Europe, Africa, North America, South America, Antarctica, Australia.
- Locate: Canada, United States, Mexico, Central America.
- Locate: the Equator, Northern Hemisphere, Southern Hemisphere, North and South Poles.

B. GEOGRAPHICAL TERMS AND FEATURES
- peninsula, harbor, bay, island

II. Early Civilizations

TEACHERS: As you introduce children to early civilizations, keep in mind the question, What is civilization? Help children see recurring features such as settling down, agriculture, building towns and cities, and learning how to write.

A. MESOPOTAMIA: THE "CRADLE OF CIVILIZATION"
- Importance of Tigris and Euphrates Rivers
- Development of writing, why writing is important to the development of civilization
- Code of Hammurabi (early code of laws), why rules and laws are important to the development of civilization

B. ANCIENT EGYPT
- Geography
   Africa
   Sahara Desert
- Importance of Nile River, floods and farming
- Pharaohs
   Tutankhamen
   Hatshepsut, woman pharaoh
- Pyramids and mummies, animal gods, Sphinx
- Writing: hieroglyphics

See also Visual Arts 1,
Art from Long Ago: Art of
Ancient Egypt.

C. HISTORY OF WORLD RELIGIONS

TEACHERS: Since religion is a shaping force in the story of civilization, the Core Knowledge Sequence introduces children in the early grades to major world religions, beginning with a focus on geography and major symbols and figures. The purpose is not to explore matters of theology but to provide a basic vocabulary for understanding many events and ideas in history. The goal is to familiarize, not proselytize; to be descriptive, not prescriptive. The tone should be one of respect and balance: no religion should be disparaged by implying that it is a thing of the past. To the question, "Which one is true?" an appropriate response is: "People of different faiths believe different things to be true. The best people to guide you on this right now are your parents or someone at home."

NOTE: Students will be introduced to Hinduism and Buddhism in grade 2, and examine Islam in more detail in grade 4. They also examine lasting ideas from Judaism and Christianity in grade 6.

NOTE: In older sources you may find these formerly used spellings: Mohammed, Mecca, Koran.

- Judaism
    Belief in one God
    Story of the Exodus: Moses leads the Hebrews out of Egypt
    Israel, Chanukah, Star of David, Torah, synagogue
- Christianity
    Christianity grew out of Judaism
    Jesus, meaning of "messiah"
    Christmas and Easter, symbol of the cross
- Islam
    Originated in Arabia, since spread worldwide
    Followers are called Muslims
    Allah, Muhammad, Makkah, Qur'an, mosque
    Symbol of crescent and star (found on the flags of many mainly Islamic nations)

III. Modern Civilization and Culture: Mexico

NOTE: For historical connections, see American History 1, Maya and Aztec civilizations; Conquistadors, Cortes, Moctezuma. See also Music I, "La Cucaracha"; Language Arts 1, "Medio Pollito," and Visual Arts 1, Diego Rivera, *Piñata* and, *The History of Medicine in Mexico* (mural).

A. GEOGRAPHY
- North American continent, locate Mexico relative to Canada and the United States
- Central America, Yucatan Peninsula
- Pacific Ocean, Gulf of Mexico, Rio Grande
- Mexico City

B. CULTURE
- Indian and Spanish heritage
- Traditions: fiesta, piñata
- National holiday: September 16, Independence Day

American History & Geography

AMERICAN HISTORY AND GEOGRAPHY

TEACHERS: The study of American history begins in grades K-2 with a brief overview of major events and figures, from the earliest days to recent times. A more in-depth, chronological study of American history begins again in grade 3 and continues onward. The term "American" here generally, but not always, refers to the lands that became the United States. Other topics regarding North, Central, and South America may be found in the World History and Geography sections of this Sequence.

I. Early People and Civilizations

A. THE EARLIEST PEOPLE: HUNTERS AND NOMADS
- Crossing the land bridge from Asia to North America
  From hunting to farming
  Gradual development of early towns and cities

B. MAYA, INCA, AND AZTEC CIVILIZATIONS

TEACHERS: Children will study the Maya, Inca, and Aztec civilizations in detail in grade 5. First grade teachers should examine the fifth grade guidelines to see how these topics build in the later grade. Here, introduce children to these civilizations. Though it is historically accurate to note the warlike nature of the Maya and Aztecs, it is recommended that mention of the practice of human sacrifice be left to the fifth grade.

- Maya in Mexico and Central America
- Aztecs in Mexico
  Moctezuma (also called Montezuma)
  Tenochtitlan (Mexico City)
- Inca in South America (Peru, Chile)
  Cities in the Andes, Machu Picchu

NOTE: Early exploration and the colonial years will be studied in greater depth and detail in grade 3. First grade teachers should examine the third grade guidelines to see how these topics build in the later grade.

II. Early Exploration and Settlement

A. COLUMBUS

Teachers: Review from kindergarten the story of Columbus's voyage in 1492.

B. THE CONQUISTADORS
- The search for gold and silver
- Hernán Cortés and the Aztecs
- Francisco Pizarro and the Inca
- Diseases devastate Native American population

NOTE: The now-familiar name "Powhatan" was used by English settlers for the leader whose name was Wahunsonacock.

C. ENGLISH SETTLERS
- The story of the Lost Colony
  Sir Walter Raleigh
  Virginia Dare
- Virginia
  Jamestown
  Captain John Smith
  Pocahontas and Powhatan
- Slavery, plantations in Southern colonies
- Massachusetts
  Pilgrims, Mayflower, Thanksgiving Day
  Massachusetts Bay Colony, the Puritans

III. From Colonies to Independence: The American Revolution

TEACHERS: The American Revolution will be studied in greater depth and detail in grade 4. First grade teachers should examine the fourth grade guidelines to see how these topics build in the later grade. It is recommended that first grade teachers focus on the topics specified here, and leave for fourth grade the more detailed study of the Revolution.   In first grade, emphasize the *story* of how we went from colonies to an independent nation.

See below, Symbols and Figures: Liberty Bell.

See also Music 1, "Yankee Doodle."

- Locate the original thirteen colonies.
- The Boston Tea Party
- Paul Revere's ride, "One if by land, two if by sea"
- Minutemen and Redcoats, the "shot heard round the world"
- Thomas Jefferson and the Declaration of Independence, "We hold these truths to be self-evident, that all men are created equal. . . ."
- Fourth of July
- Benjamin Franklin: patriot, inventor, writer
- George Washington: from military commander to our first president
  Martha Washington
  Our national capital city named Washington
- Legend of Betsy Ross and the flag

IV. Early Exploration of the American West

TEACHERS: America's westward growth will be studied in grade 2 and in greater depth and detail in grade 5. First grade teachers should examine the second and fifth grade guidelines to see how these topics build in later grades.

- Daniel Boone and the Wilderness Road
- The Louisiana Purchase
  Explorations of Lewis and Clark
  Sacagawea
- Geography: Locate the Appalachian Mountains, the Rocky Mountains, and the Mississippi River.

V.   Symbols and Figures

- Recognize and become familiar with the significance of
  Liberty Bell
  Current United States president
  American flag
  Eagle

Visual Arts: Grade 1

SEE PAGE 3, "The Arts in the Curriculum."

TEACHERS: In schools, lessons on the visual arts should illustrate important elements of making and appreciating art, and emphasize important artists, works of art, and artistic concepts. When appropriate, topics in the visual arts may be linked to topics in other disciplines. While the following guidelines specify a variety of artworks in different media and from various cultures, they are not intended to be comprehensive. Teachers are encouraged to build upon the core content and expose children to a wide range of art and artists.

I. Art from Long Ago

TEACHERS: Help children see how art has been an important human activity since early times.

See also World History 1, Ancient Egypt.

- Look at and discuss
    Cave paintings
    Art of Ancient Egypt
        Great Sphinx
        Mummy cases: Tutankhamen's coffin
        Bust of Queen Nefertiti

II. Elements of Art

TEACHERS: The generally recognized elements of art include line, shape, form, space, light, texture, and color. In first grade, focus on the following:

A. COLOR
TEACHERS: Review from Kindergarten the idea of "warm" and "cool" colors.

- Know that red, yellow, and blue are commonly referred to as the "primary colors," and that
    blue + yellow = green
    blue + red = purple
    red + yellow = orange
- Observe the use of color in
    Claude Monet, *Tulips in Holland*
    James A. McNeill Whistler, *Arrangement in Black and Gray* (also known as
        Whistler's Mother)
    Diego Rivera, *Piñata*

See also World History 1, Mexico, *re Piñata.*

B. LINE
- Identify and use different lines: straight, zigzag, curved, wavy, spiral, thick, thin
- Observe how different lines are used in
    Jacob Lawrence, *Parade*
    Henri Matisse, *The Swan*
    Georgia O' Keeffe, one of her *Shell* paintings

C. SHAPE
- Recognize basic geometric shapes—square, rectangle, triangle, circle, oval—in nature, man-made objects, and artworks, including
    Jacob Lawrence, *Parade*
    Grant Wood, *Stone City, Iowa*

D. TEXTURE

D. TEXTURE

TEACHERS: Provide opportunities for children to experience both tactile and visual texture (these terms are for your reference only) by having them describe qualities of texture in natural objects (tactile texture) and in works of art (visual texture).

- Describe qualities of texture (as, for example, rough, smooth, bumpy, scratchy, slippery, etc.) in
  American Indian masks
  Edgar Degas, *Little Fourteen-Year-Old Dancer* (also known as *Dressed Ballet Dancer*)
  Albrecht Dürer, *Young Hare*

III. Kinds of Pictures: Portrait and Still Life

TEACHERS: Introduce children to the terms we use to describe different kinds of paintings, discuss examples, and provide opportunities for children to create their own works in different genres. When you look at the specified works, ask the children about their first impressions—what they notice first, and what the picture makes them think of or feel. Go on to discuss lines, shapes, colors, and textures; details not obvious at first; why they think the artist chose to depict things in a certain way, etc.

- Recognize as a portrait or self-portrait:
  Leonardo da Vinci, *Mona Lisa*
  Francisco Goya, *Don Manuel Osorio Manrique de Zuñiga*
  Vincent van Gogh, *Self-portrait* [1889]
- Recognize as a still life:
  Vincent van Gogh, *Irises*
  Paul Cézanne, studies with fruit, such as *Apples and Oranges*
- Recognize as a mural (a painting on a wall):
  Diego Rivera, *The History of Medicine in Mexico*

See also World History 1, Mexico, *re* murals of Diego Rivera.

Music: Grade 1

SEE PAGE 3, "The Arts in the Curriculum."

TEACHERS: In schools, lessons on music should feature activities and works that illustrate important musical concepts and terms, and should introduce important composers and works. When appropriate, topics in music may be linked to topics in other disciplines.

The following guidelines focus on content, not performance skills, though many concepts are best learned through active practice (singing, clapping rhythms, playing instruments, etc.).

I. Elements of Music

- Through participation become familiar with basic elements of music (rhythm, melody, harmony, form, timbre, etc.).
    Recognize a steady beat; moving to a beat; play a steady beat; recognize accents.
    Move responsively to music (marching, walking, hopping, swaying, etc.).
    Recognize short and long sounds.
    Discriminate between fast and slow.
    Discriminate between obvious differences in pitch: high and low.
    Discriminate between loud and quiet.
    Understand that melody can move up and down.
    Hum the melody while listening to music.
    Echo short rhythms and melodic patterns.
    Play simple rhythms and melodies.
    Recognize like and unlike phrases.
    Recognize that music has timbre or tone color.
    Sing unaccompanied, accompanied, and in unison.
- Understand that music is written down in a special way and become familiar with the following notation:

    ○ whole note   ♩ half note   ♪ quarter note

II. Listening and Understanding

TEACHERS: Expose children to a wide range of music, including children's music, popular instrumental music, and music from various cultures.

A. MUSICAL TERMS AND CONCEPTS
- Composers
    Know that a composer is someone who writes music.
    Become familiar with Wolfgang Amadeus Mozart as a composer who wrote what is known as classical music, and listen to the Allegro (first movement) from *A Little Night Music (Eine kleine Nachtmusik)*.
- Orchestra
    Become familiar with the families of instruments in the orchestra: strings, brass, woodwinds, percussion.
    Know that the leader of the orchestra is called the conductor.
    Listen to Sergei Prokofiev, *Peter and the Wolf.*

NOTE: Children will review families of instruments and specific instruments in later grades.

NOTE: If resources are available, read aloud to students the story behind Tchaikovsky's *Nutcracker*, and either attend a performance or show scenes from the ballet, which is available on videotape. You may also wish to introduce children to the Suite from Tchaikovsky's *Sleeping Beauty*, in relation to the story in Language Arts 1, "Sleeping Beauty."

B. MUSIC CAN TELL A STORY
- Opera
  Understand that opera combines music, singing, and acting.
  Listen to selections from Humperdinck's *Hansel and Gretel:* "Brother, Come Dance with Me," "I Am the Little Sandman," "Children's Prayer."
- Instrumental Music
  Listen to Paul Dukas, *The Sorcerer's Apprentice.*
- Ballet
  Understand that ballet combines music and movement, often to tell a story.
  Listen to Tchaikovsky's *Nutcracker Suite.*

TEACHERS: Familiarize children with other types of dance, such as square dancing and tap dancing.

C. AMERICAN MUSICAL TRADITIONS
- Jazz
  Understand that jazz is a kind of music that developed in America, with African and African American roots, and that jazz musicians improvise.
  Recognize Louis Armstrong as a great early jazz musician.

III. Songs

TEACHERS: You may also wish to teach children the song "Brother, Come Dance with Me" in connection with their introduction to the opera *Hansel and Gretel.* And you may wish to teach the poem "Thanksgiving Day" ("Over the river and through the wood") as a song (see Language Arts 1: Poetry).

America the Beautiful
Billy Boy
Dry Bones
For He's a Jolly Good Fellow
Frère Jacques
La Cucaracha
Make New Friends
Michael, Row the Boat Ashore
Oh, Dear, What Can the Matter Be?
Oh, John the Rabbit
Oh! Susanna
On Top of Old Smokey
She'll Be Comin' 'Round the Mountain
Skip to My Lou
Take Me Out to the Ball Game
There's a Hole in the Bucket
When the Saints Go Marching In
Yankee Doodle

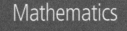

Mathematics: Grade 1

TEACHERS: Mathematics has its own vocabulary and patterns of thinking. It is a discipline with its own language and conventions. Thus, while some lessons may offer occasional opportunities for linking mathematics to other disciplines, it is critically important to attend to math as math. From the earliest years, mathematics requires incremental review and steady practice: not only the diligent effort required to master basic facts and operations, but also thoughtful and varied practice that approaches problems from a variety of angles, and gives children a variety of opportunities to apply the same concept or operation in different types of situations. While it is important to work toward the development of "higher-order problem-solving skills," it is equally important—indeed, it is prerequisite to achieving "higher order" skills—to have a sound grasp of basic facts, and an automatic fluency with fundamental operations.

I. Patterns and Classification

- Establish concepts of likeness and difference by sorting and classifying objects according to various attributes: size, shape, color, amount, function, etc.
- Define a set by the common property of its elements.
- In a given set, indicate which item does not belong.
- Recognize patterns and predict the extension of a pattern.

II. Numbers and Number Sense

TEACHERS: Review and build on topics from kindergarten.

- Recognize and write numbers 0 - 100.
- Count from 0 - 100 by ones; twos; fives; tens.
- Count by tens from a given single-digit number.
- Count forward and backwards.
- Use tallies.
- Identify ordinal position, 1st to 10th.
- Identify dozen; half-dozen; pair.
- Recognize place value: ones, tens, hundreds.
- Identify more and less; counting how many more or less.
- Given a number, identify one more and one less; ten more and ten less.
- Compare quantities using the signs <, >, and = .
- Recognize fractions as part of a whole: $\frac{1}{2}$, $\frac{1}{3}$, $\frac{1}{4}$
- Create and interpret simple pictorial graphs and bar graphs.

III. Money

- Identify and recognize relative value of penny, nickel, dime, quarter.
- Recognize and use dollar ($) and cents (¢) signs.
- Show how different combinations of coins equal the same amounts of money.

IV. Computation

A. ADDITION (using concrete objects, and paper and pencil)

- Know the meaning of the plus (+) sign.
- Know what a "sum" is.
- Know addition facts to 10 + 10 (untimed mastery).
- Add in any order.
- Know what happens when you add zero.
- Know how to write addition problems horizontally and vertically.
- Know that when you add 3 numbers, you get the same sum regardless of grouping of addends.
- Solve two-digit addition problems with and without regrouping.

B. SUBTRACTION (using concrete objects, and paper and pencil)
- Understand subtraction as "taking away."
- Know the meaning of the minus sign (-).
- Know what a "difference" is.
- Know subtraction facts corresponding to addition facts (untimed mastery).
- Know how to write subtraction problems horizontally and vertically.
- Solve two-digit subtraction problems with and without regrouping.
- Mentally subtract 10 from a two-digit number.

C. SOLVING PROBLEMS AND EQUATIONS
- Write an addition or subtraction equation to solve basic one-step story and picture problems.
- Solve simple equations in the form of ___ - 2 = 7; 5 + ___ = 7.

V. Measurement

- Identify familiar instruments of measurement, such as ruler, scale, thermometer.
- Compare objects according to:
  Linear measure
  > Measure length using non-standard units.
  > Measure length in inches and feet, and in centimeters.
  > Measure and draw line segments in inches and centimeters.
  Weight (mass)
  > Compare weights of objects using a balance scale.
  > Measure weight in non-standard units and in pounds.
  Capacity (volume)
  > Estimate and measure capacity in cups.
  > Identify quart, gallon.
  Temperature: associate temperature in degrees Fahrenheit with weather.
- Time
  Sequence events: before and after; first, next, last.
  Compare duration of events: which takes more or less time.
  Read a clock face and tell time to the half-hour.
  Know the days of the week and the months of the year, both in order and out of sequence.
  Orientation in time: today, yesterday, tomorrow; morning, afternoon, evening, night; this morning vs. yesterday morning, etc.

VI. Geometry

- Identify left and right hand.
- Identify top, bottom, middle.
- Know and use terms of orientation and relative position, such as:

closed, open	around
on, under, over	far from, near
in front, in back (behind)	above, below
between, in the middle of	to the right of, to the left of
next to, beside	here, there
inside, outside	

- Identify and draw basic plane figures: square, rectangle, triangle, circle.
- Describe square, rectangle, triangle according to number of sides.
- Identify basic solid figures: sphere, cube, cone.
- Identify basic shapes in a variety of common objects and artifacts (balls, cans, windows, pictures, books, buildings, cars, etc.).
- Make congruent shapes and designs.

Science

Science: Grade 1

TEACHERS: Effective instruction in science requires hands-on experience and observation. In the words of the 1993 report from the American Association for the Advancement of Science, *Benchmarks for Science Literacy*, "From their very first day in school, students should be actively engaged in learning to view the world scientifically. That means encouraging them to ask questions about nature and to seek answers, collect things, count and measure things, make qualitative observations, organize collections and observations, discuss findings, etc."

While experience counts for much, book learning is also important, for it helps bring coherence and order to a child's scientific knowledge. Only when topics are presented systematically and clearly can children make steady and secure progress in their scientific learning. The child's development of scientific knowledge and understanding is in some ways a very disorderly and complex process, different for each child. But a systematic approach to the exploration of science, one that combines experience with book learning, can help provide essential building blocks for deeper understanding at a later time.

I. Living Things and Their Environments

TEACHERS: Introduce the idea of interdependence between living things and their environment.

A. HABITATS
- Living things live in environments to which they are particularly suited.
- Specific habitats and what lives there, for example:
    Forest [oak trees, squirrels, raccoons, snails, mice]
    Meadow and prairie [wildflowers, grasses, prairie dogs]
    Underground [fungi, moles, worms]
    Desert [cactus, lizard, scorpion]
    Water [fish, oysters, starfish]
- The food chain: a way of picturing the relationships between living things
    Animals: big animals eat little ones, big animals die and are eaten by little ones.
    Plants: nutrients, water, soil, air, sunlight

NOTE: The food chain will be studied again in grade 3.

B. OCEANS AND UNDERSEA LIFE
- Most of the earth is covered with water.
- Locate oceans: Pacific, Atlantic, Indian, Arctic.
- Oceans are salt water (unlike fresh water rivers and lakes).
- Coast, shore, waves, tides (high and low)
- Currents, the Gulf Stream
- Landscape of the ocean floor: mountain peaks and deep valleys (trenches)
- Diversity of ocean life: from organisms too small for the eye to see (plankton), to giant whales
- Dangers to ocean life (for example, overfishing, pollution, oil spills)

C. ENVIRONMENTAL CHANGE AND HABITAT DESTRUCTION
- Environments are constantly changing, and this can sometimes pose dangers to specific habitats, for example:
    Effects of population and development
    Rainforest clearing, pollution, litter

D. SPECIAL CLASSIFICATIONS OF ANIMALS
- Herbivores: plant-eaters (for example, elephants, cows, deer)
- Carnivores: flesh-eaters (for example, lions, tigers)
- Omnivores: plant and animal-eaters (for example, bears)
- Extinct animals (for example, dinosaurs)

Science

II. The Human Body

A. BODY SYSTEMS

TEACHERS: Introduce the idea of body systems, and have children identify basic parts of the following body systems:

NOTE: Major body systems will be studied in greater detail in grades 2-6.

- Skeletal system: skeleton, bones, skull
- Muscular system: muscles
- Digestive system: mouth, stomach
- Circulatory system: heart and blood
- Nervous system: brain, nerves

B. GERMS, DISEASES, AND PREVENTING ILLNESS

- Taking care of your body: exercise, cleanliness, healthy foods, rest
- Vaccinations

III. Matter

TEACHERS: Introduce children to the idea that everything is made of matter, and that all matter is made up of parts too small to see.

NOTE: Children are likely to have a notion of atoms that, in absolute scientific terms, is inaccurate. There is no need to be concerned with this inaccuracy at this grade level, since the goal here is simply to introduce concepts and terms that, over time, will be more precisely defined.

- Basic concept of atoms
- Names and common examples of three states of matter:
    solid (for example, wood, rocks)
    liquid (for example, water)
    gas (for example, air, steam)
- Water as an example of changing states of matter of a single substance

IV. Properties of Matter: Measurement

TEACHERS: Have children describe and classify objects according to what they are made of, and according to their physical properties (color, shape, size, weight, texture, etc.).

- Units of measurement:
    Length: centimeter, inch, foot
    Volume: gallon, quart
- Temperature: degrees Fahrenheit

V. Introduction to Electricity

TEACHERS: Through reading aloud, observation and experiment, explore with children basic principles of electricity and electrical safety rules.

NOTE: Electricity will be studied in more detail in grade 4.

- Static electricity
- Basic parts of simple electric circuits (for example, batteries, wire, bulb or buzzer, switch)
- Conductive and nonconductive materials
- Safety rules for electricity (for example, never put your finger, or anything metallic, in an electrical outlet; never touch a switch or electrical appliance when your hands are wet or when you're in the bathtub; never put your finger in a lamp socket; etc.)

VI. Astronomy: Introduction to the Solar System

- Sun: source of energy, light, heat
- Moon: phases of the moon (full, half, crescent, new)
- The nine planets (Mercury, Venus, Earth, Mars, Jupiter, Saturn, Uranus, Neptune, Pluto)
- Stars
    Constellations, Big Dipper
    The sun is a star.
- Earth and its place in the solar system
    The earth moves around the sun; the sun does not move.
    The earth revolves (spins); one revolution takes one day (24 hours).
    Sunrise and sunset
    When it is day where you are, it is night for people on the opposite side of the earth.

VII. The Earth

See also World History and Geography I. A. Spatial Sense.

A. GEOGRAPHICAL FEATURES OF THE EARTH'S SURFACE
- The shape of the earth, the horizon
- Oceans and continents
- North Pole and South Pole, Equator

NOTE: Topics in geology will be studied in more detail in grade 4.

B. WHAT'S INSIDE THE EARTH
- Inside the earth
    Layers: crust, mantle, core
    High temperatures
- Volcanoes and geysers
- Rocks and minerals
    Formation and characteristics of different kinds of rocks: metamorphic, igneous, sedimentary
    Important minerals in the earth (such as quartz, gold, sulfur, coal, diamond, iron ore)

See above, Environmental Change and Habitat Destruction, *re* Rachel Carson; Electricity, *re* Thomas Edison; Human Body: Vaccinations, *re* Edward Jenner; Human Body: germs, diseases, *re* Louis Pasteur.

VIII. Science Biographies

Rachel Carson
Thomas Edison
Edward Jenner
Louis Pasteur

Grade 2

Overview of Topics   Grade 2

Language Arts
I. Reading and Writing
   A. Decoding, Word Recognition, and Oral Reading
   B. Reading Comprehension and Response
   C. Writing
   D. Spelling, Grammar, and Usage
II. Poetry
III. Fiction
   A. Stories
   B. Mythology of Ancient Greece
   C. American Tall Tales
   D. Literary Terms
IV. Sayings and Phrases

History and Geography
World:
I. Geography
   A. Spatial Sense
   B. Geographical Terms and Features
II. Early Civilizations: Asia
   A. Geography of Asia
   B. India
   C. China
III. Modern Civilization and Culture: Japan
   A. Geography
   B. Culture
IV. Ancient Greece

American:
I. American Government: The Constitution
II. The War of 1812
III. Westward Expansion
   A. Pioneers Head West
   B. Native Americans
IV. The Civil War
V. Immigration and Citizenship
VI. Civil Rights
VII. Geography of the Americas
   A. North America
   B. South America
VIII. Symbols and Figures

Visual Arts
I. Elements of Art
II. Sculpture
III. Kinds of Pictures: Landscapes
IV. Abstract Art
V. Architecture

Music
I. Elements of Music
II. Listening and Understanding
   A. The Orchestra
   B. Keyboard Instruments
   C. Composers and Their Music
III. Songs

Mathematics
I. Numbers and Number Sense
II. Fractions
III. Money
IV. Computation
   A. Addition
   B. Subtraction
   C. Introduction to Multiplication
   D. Solving Problems and Equations
V. Measurement
   A. Linear Measure
   B. Weight (Mass)
   C. Capacity (Volume)
   D. Temperature
   E. Time
VI. Geometry

Science
I. Cycles in Nature
   A. Seasonal Cycles
   B. Life Cycles
   C. The Water Cycle
II. Insects
III. The Human Body
   A. Cells
   B. Digestive and Excretory Systems
   C. Taking Care of Your Body: A Healthy Diet
IV. Magnetism
V. Simple Machines
VI. Science Biographies

2

Language Arts: Grade 2

**Language
Arts**

I. Reading and Writing

TEACHERS: Many of the following sub-goals are designed to help children achieve the overall goal for reading in second grade: to be able to read (both aloud and silently), with fluency, accuracy, and comprehension any story or other text appropriately written for second grade. Such texts include Peggy Parrish's *Amelia Bedelia* books, Lillian Hoban's *Arthur* books, and second-grade-level volumes in such nonfiction series as *I Can Read* and *Let's Read and Find Out*.

A. DECODING, WORD RECOGNITION, AND ORAL READING

TEACHERS: Decoding is the act of turning the letters into the speech sounds they represent. Children need to understand that the sequence of sounds in a spoken word is represented by a left-to-right sequence of letters in a written or printed word. By the end of second grade, decoding should (with grade-level appropriate texts) become almost automatic, and so allow the child to focus attention instead on meaning. Depending on previous instruction and practice, some children may need to continue work with decoding skills into third grade.

NOTE: See Appendix A, Sample Phoneme Sequence.

- Accurately decode phonetically regular two-syllable words (for example, basket, rabbit).
- Use knowledge of letter-sound patterns to sound out unfamiliar multisyllable words when reading (for example, caterpillar, motorcycle).
- Recognize and compare the sounds that make up words, and segment and blend a variety of sounds in words.
- Accurately read single-syllable words and most two-syllable words, including
    irregularly spelled words (for example, tough, through)
    words with dipthongs (for example the *oy* sound in boy)
    words with special vowel spellings (for example, the *ow* sound in now and clown, the long *i* sound in night)
    words with common beginnings and endings (for example, the *spr* beginning in spring, the *le* ending in apple and riddle)

B. READING COMPREHENSION AND RESPONSE

NOTE: Children should read outside of school at least 15 minutes daily.

- Reread sentences when he or she does not understand the text.
- Recall incidents, characters, facts, and details of stories and other texts.
- Discuss similarities in characters and events across stories.
- Gain answers to specific questions from reading nonfiction materials, and interpret information from simple diagrams, charts, and graphs.
- Pose plausible answers to how, why, and what-if questions in interpreting texts, both fiction and nonfiction.
- Explain and describe new concepts and information in his or her own words.
- Demonstrate familiarity with a variety of fiction and nonfiction selections, including both read-aloud works and independent readings.

C. WRITING

- Produce a variety of types of writing—such as stories, reports, letters, poems, descriptions—and make reasonable judgments about what to include in his or her own written works based on the purpose and type of composition.
- With assistance, produce written work with a beginning, middle, and end, and when appropriate organize material in paragraphs.
- With assistance, revise and edit to clarify and refine his or her meaning in writing, and attend to spelling, mechanics, and presentation in final drafts of selected works.

D. SPELLING, GRAMMAR, AND USAGE

- When spelling independently, represent all the sounds of a word, writing each sound as a letter or combination of letters.

- Correctly spell any word that contains spelling patterns he or she has been taught so far, and begin to use a first dictionary to check and correct spelling in his or her own writings.
- Write legibly on standard-ruled notebook paper.
- Understand what a complete sentence is and identify subject and predicate in simple sentences.
- Identify parts of speech:
   noun (for concrete nouns)
   verb (for active verbs)
   simple adjectives
- Use adjectives to compare by adding -er and -est.
- Change regular verbs from simple present to past tense using -ed.
- Use the correct forms for present and past tense of common irregular verbs (for example, be, have, see, do, go, come, run, give, sing).
- Recognize singular and plural nouns, and
   form the regular plural by adding s
   know to add es to nouns ending in s, ss, sh, ch, x
   know that some nouns change their spelling in plural form (for example, man, men; woman, women; child, children; tooth, teeth; foot, feet)
- Use capital letters for:
   the first word of a sentence
   proper nouns
   the pronoun I
   holidays and months and days of the week
   names of countries, cities, states
   main words in titles
   initials
- Consistently use correct end punctuation: period, question mark, or exclamation point.
- Recognize the comma and how to use it between day and year when writing a date, and between city and state in an address.
- Recognize the apostrophe and how it is used in common contractions (for example, isn't, aren't, can't, don't, I'm, you're).
- Recognize common abbreviations (for example, St., Rd., Mr., Mrs., Ms., Dr.).
- Understand what synonyms and antonyms are, and provide synonyms or antonyms for given words (for example, happy, glad; hot, cold).

II. Poetry

NOTE: The poems listed here constitute a selected core of poetry for this grade. You are encouraged to expose children to more poetry, old and new, and to have children write their own poems. To bring children into the spirit of poetry, read it aloud and encourage them to read it aloud so they can experience the music in the words.

See below, Literary Terms—limerick, re Edward Lear.

Bed in Summer (Robert Louis Stevenson)
Bee! I'm expecting you (Emily Dickinson)
Buffalo Dusk (Carl Sandburg)
Caterpillars (Aileen Fisher)
Discovery (Harry Behn)
Harriet Tubman (Eloise Greenfield)
Hurt No Living Thing (Christina Rossetti)
Lincoln (Nancy Byrd Turner)
The Night Before Christmas (Clement Clarke Moore)
Rudolph Is Tired of the City (Gwendolyn Brooks)
Seashell (Federico Garcia Lorca)
Smart (Shel Silverstein)
Something Told the Wild Geese (Rachel Field)
There Was an Old Man with a Beard (Edward Lear)
Who Has Seen the Wind? (Christina Rossetti)
Windy Nights (Robert Louis Stevenson)

III. Fiction

Language
Arts

TEACHERS: The titles listed below are available in a variety of editions, including both adaptations for novice readers and others that lend themselves to reading aloud to children—for example, *Charlotte's Web* or "How the Camel Got His Hump." It is recommended that you provide a mixture of texts. Editions designed for beginning readers can help children practice decoding skills. Read-aloud texts, which the children may not be capable of reading on their own, can be understood when the words are read aloud and talked about with a helpful adult. Such active listening to vocabulary and syntax that go beyond the limits of grade-level readability formulas is an important part of developing an increasingly sophisticated verbal sense.

The titles below constitute a core of stories for this grade. Expose children to many more stories, including classic picture books, read-aloud books, etc. (In schools, teachers across grade levels should communicate their choices in order to avoid undue repetition.)   Children should also be exposed to nonfiction prose—biographies, books on science and history, books on art and music—and they should be given opportunities to tell and write their own stories.

NOTE: Review Drama from first grade, and engage children in dramatic activities, possibly with one of the stories below in the form of a play.

A. STORIES

Beauty and the Beast
The Blind Men and the Elephant (a fable from India)
A Christmas Carol (Charles Dickens)
Charlotte's Web (E. B. White)
The Emperor's New Clothes (Hans Christian Andersen)
The Fisherman and His Wife (Brothers Grimm)
How the Camel Got His Hump (a "Just-So" story by Rudyard Kipling)
Iktomi stories (legends of the Plains Indian trickster figure, such as Iktomi Lost His Eyes; Iktomi and the Berries; Iktomi and the Boulder)
The Magic Paintbrush (a Chinese folktale)
El Pajaro Cu (a Hispanic folktale)
selections from *Peter Pan* (James M. Barrie)
Talk (a West African folk tale)
The Tiger, the Brahman, and the Jackal (a folk tale from India)
The Tongue-Cut Sparrow (a folk tale from Japan)

NOTE: "The Magic Paintbrush" is also known as "Tye May and the Magic Brush" and "Liang [or Ma Liang] and the Magic Brush."

See also World History 2, India, *re* "The Blind Men and the Elephant" and "The Tiger, the Brahman, and the Jackal."

B. MYTHOLOGY OF ANCIENT GREECE

TEACHERS: See World History and Geography 2: Ancient Greece.

NOTE: Roman names are listed in parentheses because, although children do not study Ancient Rome until third grade in the Core Knowledge Sequence, you are likely to encounter both Greek and Roman names in various books of myths you may use.

- Gods of Ancient Greece (and Rome)

Zeus (Jupiter)	Ares (Mars)
Hera (Juno)	Hermes (Mercury)
Apollo (Apollo)	Athena (Minerva)
Artemis (Diana)	Hephaestus (Vulcan)
Poseidon (Neptune)	Dionysus (Bacchus)
Aphrodite (Venus)	Hades (Pluto)
Eros (Cupid)	

- Mount Olympus: home of the gods
- Mythological creatures and characters
  Atlas (holding the world on his shoulders)
  centaurs
  Cerberus
  Pegasus
  Pan

NOTE: Students will read more myths in third grade; see Language Arts 3.

- Greek Myths
  - Prometheus (how he brought fire from the gods to men)
  - Pandora's Box
  - Oedipus and the Sphinx
  - Theseus and the Minotaur
  - Daedelus and Icarus
  - Arachne the Weaver
  - Swift-footed Atalanta
  - Demeter and Persephone
  - Hercules (Heracles) and the Labors of Hercules

C. AMERICAN FOLK HEROES AND TALL TALES

TEACHERS: Johnny Appleseed and Casey Jones were introduced in kindergarten.

Paul Bunyan
Johnny Appleseed
John Henry
Pecos Bill
Casey Jones

See also Music 2, Songs, "John Henry."

D. LITERARY TERMS

TEACHERS: In the course of their studies, children should learn the following terms:

myth
tall tale
limerick

IV. Sayings and Phrases

TEACHERS: Every culture has phrases and proverbs that make no sense when carried over literally into another culture. For many children, this section may not be needed; they will have picked up these sayings by hearing them at home and among friends. But the sayings have been one of the categories most appreciated by teachers who work with children from home cultures that differ from the standard culture of literate American English.

Back to the drawing board
Better late than never
Cold feet
Don't cry over spilled milk.
Don't judge a book by its cover.
Easier said than done
Eaten out of house and home
Get a taste of your own medicine
Get up on the wrong side of the bed
In hot water
Keep your fingers crossed.
Practice what you preach.
Two heads are better than one.
Turn over a new leaf
Where there's a will there's a way.
You can't teach an old dog new tricks.

History and Geography: Grade 2

TEACHERS: In second grade, children often study aspects of the world around them: the family, the school, the community, etc. The following guidelines are meant to broaden and complement that focus. The goal of studying selected topics in World History in second grade is to foster curiosity and the beginnings of understanding about the larger world outside the child's locality, and about varied civilizations and ways of life. This can be done through a variety of means: story, drama, art, music, discussion, and more.

The study of geography embraces many topics throughout the Core Knowledge Sequence, including topics in history and science. Geographic knowledge includes a spatial sense of the world, an awareness of the physical processes that shape life, a sense of the interactions between humans and their environment, an understanding of the relations between place and culture, and an awareness of the characteristics of specific regions and cultures.

WORLD HISTORY AND GEOGRAPHY

I. Geography

A. SPATIAL SENSE (Working with Maps, Globes, and Other Geographic Tools)

TEACHERS: Review and reinforce topics from grade 1, including:

See also below, American
History and Geography VII.
Geography of the Americas.

- Name your continent, country, state, and community.
- Understand that maps have keys or legends with symbols and their uses.
- Find directions on a map: east, west, north, south.
- Identify major oceans: Pacific, Atlantic, Indian, Arctic.
- The seven continents: Asia, Europe, Africa, North America, South America, Antarctica, Australia.
- Locate: Canada, United States, Mexico, Central America.
- Locate: the Equator, Northern Hemisphere and Southern Hemisphere, North and South Poles.

B. GEOGRAPHICAL TERMS AND FEATURES

TEACHERS: Review terms from grade 1 (peninsula, harbor, bay, island), and add:

- coast, valley, prairie, desert, oasis

II. Early Civilizations: Asia

TEACHERS: Since religion is a shaping force in the story of civilization, the Core Knowledge Sequence introduces children in the early grades to major world religions, beginning with a focus on geography and major symbols and figures. The purpose is not to explore matters of theology but to provide a basic vocabulary for understanding many events and ideas in history. The goal is to familiarize, not proselytize; to be descriptive, not prescriptive. The tone should be one of respect and balance: no religion should be disparaged by implying that it is a thing of the past. To the question, "Which one is true?" an appropriate response is: "People of different faiths believe different things to be true. The best people to guide you on this right now are your parents or someone at home."

A. GEOGRAPHY OF ASIA

- The largest continent, with the most populous countries in the world
- Locate: China, India, Japan

See also Language Arts 2,
"The Tiger, the Brahman, and
the Jackal," and "The Blind
Men and the Elephant,"
re India.

B. INDIA

- Indus River and Ganges River
- Hinduism
  Brahma, Vishnu, Shiva
  Many holy books, including the Rig Veda

See also Visual Arts 2, Architecture: Great Stupa, *re* Buddhism.

- Buddhism
  Prince Siddhartha becomes Buddha, "the Enlightened One"
  Buddhism begins as an outgrowth of Hinduism in India, and then spreads through
  many countries in Asia.
  King Asoka (also spelled Ashoka)

C.   CHINA

See also Language Arts 2, "The Magic Paintbrush."

TEACHERS: Students will study China again in grade 4. Second grade teachers should examine the fourth grade guidelines to see how these topics build in the later grade.

- Yellow (Huang He) and Yangtze (Chang Jiang) Rivers
- Teachings of Confucius (for example, honor your ancestors)
- Great Wall of China
- Invention of paper
- Importance of silk
- Chinese New Year

III. Modern Civilization and Culture: Japan

NOTE: Students will study feudal Japan in grade 5.
See also Language Arts 2, "The Tongue-Cut Sparrow"; Visual Arts 2, Elements of Art: Hokusai, *The Great Wave*; and, Architecture: Himeji Castle.

A.   GEOGRAPHY
- Locate relative to continental Asia: "land of the rising sun"
- A country made up of islands; four major islands
- Pacific Ocean, Sea of Japan
- Mt. Fuji
- Tokyo

B.   CULTURE
- Japanese flag
- Big modern cities, centers of industry and business
- Traditional craft: origami
- Traditional costume: kimono

IV. Ancient Greece

TEACHERS: Students will study Greece again in grade 6, with a focus on the legacy of ideas from ancient Greece and Rome.

See also Language Arts 2, Greek Myths; Visual Arts 2, Sculpture, Discus Thrower; Architecture, The Parthenon.

NOTE: Suggested topics for learning about Alexander include his tutoring by Aristotle, his horse Bucephalus, and the legend of the Gordian knot.

- Geography: Mediterranean Sea and Aegean Sea, Crete
- Sparta
- Athens as a city-state: the beginnings of democracy
- Persian Wars: Marathon and Thermopylae
- Olympic games
- Worship of gods and goddesses
- Great thinkers: Socrates, Plato, and Aristotle
- Alexander the Great

American
History and
Geography

AMERICAN HISTORY AND GEOGRAPHY

TEACHERS: The study of American history begins in grades K-2 with a brief overview of major events and figures, from the earliest days to recent times. A more in-depth, chronological study of American history begins again in grade 3 and continues onward. The term "American" here generally, but not always, refers to the lands that became the United States. Other topics regarding North, Central, and South America may be found in the World History and Geography sections of this Sequence.

I. American Government: The Constitution

TEACHERS: Through analogies to familiar settings—the family, the school, the community—discuss some basic questions regarding American government, such as: What is government? What are some basic functions of American government? (Making and enforcing laws; settling disputes; protecting rights and liberties, etc.) Only basic questions need to be addressed at this grade level. In fourth grade students will examine in more detail specific issues and institutions of American government, including, for example, the separation of powers, and the relation between state and federal government.

- American government is based on the Constitution, the highest law of our land.
- James Madison, the "Father of the Constitution"
- Government by the consent of the governed: "We the people"

II. The War of 1812

- President James Madison and Dolley Madison
- British impressment of American sailors
- Old Ironsides
- British burn the White House
- Fort McHenry, Francis Scott Key, and "The Star-Spangled Banner"
- Battle of New Orleans, Andrew Jackson

III. Westward Expansion

TEACHERS: Students will study Westward Expansion in greater depth and detail in grade 5. Second grade teachers should examine the fifth grade guidelines to see how these topics build in the later grade. It is recommended that second grade teachers keep their focus on the people and events specified here, and leave for fifth grade the figures and ideas specified for that grade.

A. PIONEERS HEAD WEST
- New means of travel
  - Robert Fulton, invention of the steamboat
  - Erie Canal
  - Railroads: the Transcontinental Railroad
- Routes west: wagon trains on the Oregon Trail
- The Pony Express

B. NATIVE AMERICANS
- Sequoyah and the Cherokee alphabet
- Forced removal to reservations: the "Trail of Tears"
- Some Native Americans displaced from their homes and ways of life by railroads (the "iron horse")
- Effect of near extermination of buffalo on Plains Indians

See also Language Arts 2, Iktomi stories.

IV. The Civil War

TEACHERS: Students will study the Civil War in greater depth and detail in grade 5. Second grade teachers should examine the fifth grade guidelines to see how these topics build in the later grade.

- Controversy over slavery
- Harriet Tubman, the "underground railroad"
- Northern v. Southern states: Yankees and Rebels
- Ulysses S. Grant and Robert E. Lee
- Clara Barton, "Angel of the Battlefield," founder of American Red Cross
- President Abraham Lincoln: keeping the Union together
- Emancipation Proclamation and the end of slavery

V. Immigration and Citizenship

TEACHERS: Students will study Immigration and Urbanization in greater depth and detail in grade 6. Second grade teachers should examine the sixth grade American History guidelines to see how these topics build in the later grade. In second grade, it is recommended that teachers use narrative, biography, and other accessible means to introduce children to the idea that many people have come to America (and continue to come here) from all around the world, for many reasons: to find freedom, to seek a better life, to leave behind bad conditions in their native lands, etc. Discuss with children: What is an immigrant? Why do people leave their home countries to make a new home in America? What is it like to be a newcomer in America? What hardships have immigrants faced? What opportunities have they found?

- America perceived as a "land of opportunity"
- The meaning of "e pluribus unum" (a national motto you can see on the back of coins)
- Ellis Island and the significance of the Statue of Liberty
- Millions of newcomers to America
    - Large populations of immigrants settle in major cities (such as New York, Chicago, Philadelphia, Detroit, Cleveland, Boston, San Francisco)
- The idea of citizenship
    - What it means to be a citizen of a nation
    - American citizens have certain rights and responsibilities (for example, voting, eligible to hold public office, paying taxes)
    - Becoming an American citizen (by birth, naturalization)

VI. Civil Rights

TEACHERS: Through narrative, biography, and other accessible means, introduce students to the idea that while America is a country founded upon "the proposition that all men are created equal," equality has not always been granted to all Americans. Many people, however, have dedicated themselves to the struggle to extend equal rights to all Americans.   Specific figures and issues to study include:

NOTE: In grade 4, students will study, in the historical context of antebellum reform, early pioneers in the women's movement in America, including Elizabeth Cady Stanton, Lucretia Mott, Margaret Fuller, and Sojourner Truth.

NOTE: Students will study the modern American civil rights movement in more depth and detail in grade 8.

- Susan B. Anthony and the right to vote
- Eleanor Roosevelt and civil rights and human rights
- Mary McLeod Bethune and educational opportunity
- Jackie Robinson and the integration of major league baseball
- Rosa Parks and the bus boycott in Montgomery, Alabama
- Martin Luther King, Jr. and the dream of equal rights for all
- Cesar Chavez and the rights of migrant workers

NOTE: In fifth grade the
American Geography
requirements include "fifty
states and capitals."
Teachers in grades two
through four may want to
introduce these incrementally
to prepare for the fifth grade
requirement.

VII. Geography of the Americas

A. NORTH AMERICA
- North America: Canada, United States, Mexico
- The United States
  Fifty states: 48 contiguous states, plus Alaska and Hawaii
  Territories
  Mississippi River
  Appalachian and Rocky Mountains
  Great Lakes
- Atlantic and Pacific Oceans, Gulf of Mexico, Caribbean Sea, West Indies
- Central America

B. SOUTH AMERICA
- Brazil: largest country in South America, Amazon River, rain forests
- Peru and Chile: Andes Mountains
- Locate: Venezuela, Colombia, Ecuador
- Bolivia: named after Simon Bolivar, "The Liberator"
- Argentina: the Pampas
- Main languages: Spanish and (in Brazil) Portuguese

VIII. Symbols and Figures

- Recognize and become familiar with the significance of
  U. S. flag: current and earlier versions
  Statue of Liberty
  Lincoln Memorial

Visual Arts: Grade 2

SEE PAGE 3, "The Arts in the Curriculum."

TEACHERS: In schools, lessons on the visual arts should illustrate important elements of making and appreciating art, and emphasize important artists, works of art, and artistic concepts. When appropriate, topics in the visual arts may be linked to topics in other disciplines. While the following guidelines specify a variety of artworks in different media and from various cultures, they are not intended to be comprehensive. Teachers are encouraged to build upon the core content and expose children to a wide range of art and artists.

I. Elements of Art

TEACHERS: The generally recognized elements of art include line, shape, form, space, light, texture, and color. In second grade, continue when appropriate to discuss qualities of line, shape, color, and texture that children learned about in kindergarten and first grade.

See also World History 2, Japan, re Hokusai.

- Recognize lines as horizontal, vertical, or diagonal.
- Observe the use of line in
    Pablo Picasso, *Mother and Child*
    Katsushika Hokusai, *The Great Wave at Kanagawa Nami-Ura* from *Thirty-six Views of Mt. Fuji*

II. Sculpture

See also World History 2, Ancient Greece, re The Discus Thrower; and China, re Flying Horse.

- Observe shape, mass, and line in sculptures, including
    The Discus Thrower
    Flying Horse (from Wu-Wei, China)
    Auguste Rodin, *The Thinker*

III. Kinds of Pictures: Landscapes

TEACHERS: Briefly review from grade 1: portrait, self-portrait, and still life. In discussing the following works, ask the children about their first impressions—what they notice first, and what the picture makes them think of or feel. Go on to discuss lines, shapes, colors, and textures; details not obvious at first; why they think the artist chose to depict things in a certain way, etc.

- Recognize as landscapes and discuss
    Thomas Cole, *The Oxbow* (also known as *View from Mount Holyoke, Northampton, Massachusetts, after a Thunderstorm*)
    El Greco, *View of Toledo* (also known as *Toledo in a Storm*)
    Henri Rousseau, *Virgin Forest*
    Vincent van Gogh, *The Starry Night*

IV. Abstract Art

NOTE: You may wish to recall from kindergarten, Joan Miró, People and Dog in the Sun.

- Compare lifelike and abstract animals, including
    Paintings of birds by John James Audubon
    Albrecht Dürer, *Young Hare*
    Paul Klee, *Cat and Bird*
    Pablo Picasso, *Bull's Head* (made from bicycle seat and handlebars)
    Henri Matisse, *The Snail* (also known as *Chromatic Composition*)
- Observe and discuss examples of abstract painting and sculpture, including
    Marc Chagall, *I and the Village*
    Constantin Brancusi, *Bird in Space*

V. Architecture

See also World History 2, Ancient Greece, *re* the Parthenon; India, *re* the Great Stupa; Japan, *re* Himeji Castle.

- Understand architecture as the art of designing buildings.
- Understand symmetry and a line of symmetry, and observe symmetry in the design of some buildings (such as the Parthenon).
- Noting line, shape, and special features (such as columns and domes), look at
  The Parthenon
  Great Stupa (Buddhist temple in Sanchi, India)
  Himeji Castle (also known as "White Heron Castle," Japan)
  The Guggenheim Museum (New York City)

Visual Arts

Music: Grade 2

SEE PAGE 3, "The Arts in the Curriculum."

TEACHERS: In schools, lessons on music should feature activities and works that illustrate important musical concepts and terms, and should introduce important composers and works. When appropriate, topics in music may be linked to topics in other disciplines.

The following guidelines focus on content, not performance skills, though many concepts are best learned through active practice (singing, clapping rhythms, playing instruments, etc.).

I. Elements of Music

- Through participation, become familiar with basic elements of music (rhythm, melody, harmony, form, timbre, etc.).
    Recognize a steady beat, accents, and the downbeat; play a steady beat.
    Move responsively to music (marching, walking, hopping, swaying, etc.).
    Recognize short and long sounds.
    Discriminate between fast and slow; gradually slowing down and getting faster.
    Discriminate between differences in pitch: high and low.
    Discriminate between loud and quiet; gradually increasing and decreasing volume.
    Understand that melody can move up and down.
    Hum the melody while listening to music.
    Echo short rhythms and melodic patterns.
    Play simple rhythms and melodies.
    Recognize like and unlike phrases.
    Recognize timbre (tone color).
    Sing unaccompanied, accompanied, and in unison.
    Recognize verse and refrain.
    Recognize that musical notes have names.
    Recognize a scale as a series of notes.
    Sing the C major scale using "do re mi" etc.
- Understand the following notation:

    ≡ staff, 𝄞 treble clef, names of lines and spaces in the treble clef

    ◦ whole note   ♩ half note   ♩ quarter note

    whole rest, half rest, quarter rest

II. Listening and Understanding

TEACHERS: Expose children to a wide range of music, including children's music, popular instrumental music, and music from various cultures.

A. THE ORCHESTRA

- Review families of instruments: strings, brass, woodwinds, percussion.
- Become familiar with instruments in the string family—violin, viola, cello, double bass—and listen to
    Camille Saint-Saëns, from *Carnival of the Animals:* "The Swan" (cello) and "Elephants" (double bass)
    Antonio Vivaldi, *The Four Seasons* (see below, Composers and Their Music)
- Become familiar with instruments in the percussion family—for example, drums (timpani, snare), xylophone, wood block, maracas, cymbals, triangle, tambourine—and listen to
    Carlos Chavez, *Toccata for Percussion*, third movement.

NOTE: In third grade, students will take a closer look at the brass and woodwind families.

NOTE: If you have recordings or other resources, also introduce African drumming and Latin American music with percussion.

B. KEYBOARD INSTRUMENTS

- Recognize that the piano and organ are keyboard instruments, and listen to a variety of keyboard music, including:

See also below, Composers and Their Music, Bach, *Toccata and Fugue in D minor* (organ).

Wolfgang Amadeus Mozart, *Rondo Alla turca* from *Piano Sonata K. 331*
Ludwig van Beethoven, *Für Elise*
Felix Mendelssohn, from *Songs without Words*, "Spring Song"

C. COMPOSERS AND THEIR MUSIC

TEACHERS: Provide brief, child-friendly biographical profiles of the following composers, and listen to representative works:

- Antonio Vivaldi, *The Four Seasons*
- Johann Sebastian Bach, *Minuet in G major* (collected by Bach in the *Anna Magdalena Notebook*); *Jesu, Joy of Man's Desiring*; *Toccata and Fugue in D minor*
- Ludwig van Beethoven, *Symphony No. 6 ("Pastoral")*: first movement and from final movement, "Thunderstorm" to end of symphony

III. Songs

See also Language Arts 2, American tall tales, *re* "Casey Jones" and "John Henry."

See also American History 2, Civil War, *re* "Dixie," "Follow the Drinking Gourd," and "When Johnny Comes Marching Home."

See also American History 2, War of 1812, *re* "The Star-Spangled Banner."

Buffalo Gals
Casey Jones (chorus only)
Clementine
Dixie
Do-Re-Mi
The Erie Canal
Follow the Drinking Gourd
Good Bye Old Paint
Home on the Range
I've Been Working on the Railroad
John Henry
Old Dan Tucker
The Star-Spangled Banner
Swing Low Sweet Chariot
This Land Is Your Land
When Johnny Comes Marching Home

Music

Mathematics: Grade 2

TEACHERS: Mathematics has its own vocabulary and patterns of thinking. It is a discipline with its own language and conventions. Thus, while some lessons may offer occasional opportunities for linking mathematics to other disciplines, it is critically important to attend to math as math. From the earliest years, mathematics requires incremental review and steady practice: not only the diligent effort required to master basic facts and operations, but also thoughtful and varied practice that approaches problems from a variety of angles, and gives children a variety of opportunities to apply the same concept or operation in different types of situations. While it is important to work toward the development of "higher-order problem-solving skills," it is equally important—indeed, it is prerequisite to achieving higher order skills—to have a sound grasp of basic facts, and an automatic fluency with fundamental operations.

I. Numbers and Number Sense

- Recognize and write numbers to 1,000.
- Read and write words for numbers from one to one-hundred.
- Order and compare numbers to 1,000, using the signs <, >, and = .
- Count
    by twos, threes, fives, and tens
    by tens from any given number
    by hundreds to 1,000; by fifties to 1,000
    forward and backward
- Use a number line.
- Use tallies.
- Identify ordinal position, 1st to 20th, and write words for ordinal numbers, first to twentieth.
- Identify even and odd numbers.
- Identify dozen; half-dozen; pair.
- Recognize place value: ones, tens, hundreds, thousands.
- Write numbers up to hundreds in expanded form (for example 64 = 60 + 4; 367 = 300 + 60 + 7).
- Given a number, identify one more and one less; ten more and ten less.
- Round to the nearest ten.
- Create and interpret simple bar graphs.
- Identify and extend numerical and symbolic patterns.
- Record numeric data systematically and find the lowest and highest values in a data set.

II. Fractions

- Recognize these fractions as part of a whole set or region and write the corresponding numerical symbols: $\frac{1}{2}, \frac{1}{3}, \frac{1}{4}, \frac{1}{5}, \frac{1}{6}, \frac{1}{8}, \frac{1}{10}$.
- Recognize fractions that are equal to 1.

III. Money

- Recognize relative values of a penny, nickel, dime, quarter, and dollar.
- Write amounts of money using $ and ¢ signs, and the decimal point.
- Show how different combinations of coins equal the same amounts of money.
- Add and subtract amounts of money.

IV. Computation

A. ADDITION
- Achieve timed mastery of addition facts (2 seconds).
- Recognize what an addend is.
- Know how to write addition problems horizontally and vertically.
- Know how to add in any order and check a sum by changing the order of the addends.
- Estimate the sum.
- Solve two-digit and three-digit addition problems with and without regrouping.
- Find the sum (up to 999) of any two whole numbers.
- Add three two-digit numbers.
- Practice doubling (adding a number to itself).

B. SUBTRACTION
- Understand the inverse relation between addition and subtraction; use addition to check subtraction.
- Know addition and subtraction "fact families."
- Achieve mastery of subtraction facts.
- Estimate the difference.
- Know how to write subtraction problems horizontally and vertically.
- Solve two-digit and three-digit subtraction problems with and without regrouping.
- Given two whole numbers of 999 or less, find the difference.

C. INTRODUCTION TO MULTIPLICATION
- Recognize the "times" sign ($\times$).
- Know what "factor" and "product" mean.
- Understand that you can multiply numbers in any order.
- Multiplication facts: know the product of any single-digit number x 1, 2, 3, 4, 5.
- Know what happens when you multiply by 1, by 0, and by 10.
- Practice simple word problems involving multiplication.

D. SOLVING PROBLEMS AND EQUATIONS
- Solve basic word problems.
- Write and solve simple equations in the form of ___ - 9 = 7; 7 + ___ = 16; 4 x ___ = 8.

V. Measurement

A. LINEAR MEASURE
- Make linear measurements in feet and inches, and in centimeters.
- Know that one foot = 12 inches.
- Know abbreviations: ft., in.
- Measure and draw line segments in inches to 1/2 inch, and in centimeters.
- Estimate linear measurements, then measure to check estimates.

B. WEIGHT (MASS)
- Compare weights of objects using a balance scale.
- Estimate and measure weight in pounds, and know abbreviation: lb.

C. CAPACITY (VOLUME)
- Estimate and measure capacity in cups.
- Measure liquid volumes: cups, pints, quarts, gallons.
- Compare U.S. and metric liquid volumes: quart and liter (one liter is a little more than one quart).

D. TEMPERATURE
- Measure and record temperature in degrees Fahrenheit to the nearest 2 degrees.
- Know the degree sign: °

E. TIME
- Read a clock face and tell time to five-minute intervals.
- Know how to distinguish time as A.M. or P.M.
- Understand noon and midnight.
- Solve problems on elapsed time (how much time has passed?).
- Using a calendar, identify the date, day of the week, month, and year.
- Write the date using words and numbers.

VI. Geometry

TEACHERS: Review and reinforce topics from grade 1 as necessary (left and right, orientation and position, etc.).

- Identify and draw basic plane figures: square, rectangle, triangle, circle.
- Describe square, rectangle, triangle according to number of sides; distinguish between square and rectangle as regards length of sides (a square has sides of equal length).
- Measure perimeter in inches of squares and rectangles.
- Identify solid figures—sphere, cube, pyramid, cone, cylinder—and associate solid figures with planar shapes: sphere (circle), cube (square), pyramid (triangle).
- Make congruent shapes and designs.
- Identify lines as horizontal; vertical; perpendicular; parallel.
- Name lines and line segments (for example, line AB; segment CD).
- Identify a line of symmetry, and create simple symmetric figures.

2

Science: Grade 2

TEACHERS: Effective instruction in science requires hands-on experience and observation. In the words of the 1993 report from the American Association for the Advancement of Science, Benchmarks for Science Literacy, "From their very first day in school, students should be actively engaged in learning to view the world scientifically. That means encouraging them to ask questions about nature and to seek answers, collect things, count and measure things, make qualitative observations, organize collections and observations, discuss findings, etc."

While experience counts for much, book learning is also important, for it helps bring coherence and order to a child's scientific knowledge. Only when topics are presented systematically and clearly can children make steady and secure progress in their scientific learning. The child's development of scientific knowledge and understanding is in some ways a very disorderly and complex process, different for each child. But a systematic approach to the exploration of science, one that combines experience with book learning, can help provide essential building blocks for deeper understanding at a later time.

I. Cycles in Nature

A. SEASONAL CYCLES
- The four seasons and earth's orbit around the sun (one year)
- Seasons and life processes
  Spring: sprouting, sap flow in plants, mating and hatching
  Summer: growth
  Fall: ripening, migration
  Winter: plant dormancy, animal hibernation

B. LIFE CYCLES
- The life cycle: birth, growth, reproduction, death
- Reproduction in plants and animals
  From seed to seed with a plant
  From egg to egg with a chicken
  From frog to frog
  From butterfly to butterfly: metamorphosis (see below: Insects)

NOTE: In fourth grade students will review the water cycle and study other topics in meteorology.

C. THE WATER CYCLE
- Most of the earth's surface is covered by water.
- The water cycle
  Evaporation and condensation
  Water vapor in the air, humidity
  Clouds: cirrus, cumulus, stratus
  Precipitation, groundwater

II. Insects

- Insects can be helpful and harmful to people.
  Helpful: pollination; products like honey, beeswax, and silk; eat harmful insects
  Harmful: destroy crops, trees, wooden buildings, clothes; carry disease; bite or sting
- Distinguishing characteristics
  Exoskeleton, chitin
  Six legs and three body parts: head, thorax and abdomen
  Most but not all insects have wings.
- Life cycles: metamorphosis
  Some insects look like miniature adults when born from eggs, and they molt
      to grow (examples: grasshopper, cricket).
  Some insects go through distinct stages of egg, larva, pupa, adult
      (examples: butterflies, ants).

- Social insects
    Most insects live solitary lives, but some are social (such as ants, honeybees, termites, wasps).
    Ants: colonies
    Honeybees: workers, drones, queen

III. The Human Body

A. CELLS
- All living things are made up of cells, too small to be seen without a microscope.
    Cells make up tissues.
    Tissues make up organs.
    Organs work in systems.

B. THE DIGESTIVE AND EXCRETORY SYSTEMS
TEACHERS: Explore with children what happens to the food we eat by studying body parts and functions involved in taking in food and getting rid of waste. Children should become familiar with the following:

- Salivary glands, taste buds
- Teeth: incisors, bicuspids, molars
- Esophagus, stomach, liver, small intestine, large intestine
- Kidneys, urine, bladder, urethra, anus, appendix

C. TAKING CARE OF YOUR BODY: A HEALTHY DIET
- The "food pyramid"
- Vitamins and minerals

IV. Magnetism

TEACHERS: Magnetism was introduced in kindergarten. Review and introduce new topics in second grade, with greater emphasis on experimentation.

- Magnetism demonstrates that there are forces we cannot see that act upon objects.
- Most magnets contain iron.
- Lodestones: naturally occurring magnets
- Magnetic poles: north-seeking and south-seeking poles
- Magnetic field (strongest at the poles)
- Law of magnetic attraction: unlike poles attract, like poles repel
- The earth behaves as if it were a huge magnet: north and south magnetic poles (near, but not the same as, geographic North Pole and South Pole)
- Orienteering: use of a magnetized needle in a compass, which will always point to the north

V. Simple Machines

<u>Teachers:</u> Examine with children how specific tools are made to perform specific jobs—for example, hammers, screwdrivers, pliers, etc. Through observation and experimentation, examine with children how simple machines help make work easier, and how they are applied and combined in familiar tools and machines.

- Simple machines
  - lever
  - pulley
  - wheel-and-axle
    - gears: wheels with teeth and notches
    - how gears work, and familiar uses (for example, in bicycles)
  - inclined plane
  - wedge
  - screw
- Friction, and ways to reduce friction (lubricants, rollers, etc.)

VI. Science Biographies

See above, Human Body: Cells *re* Anton van Leeuwenhoek; Simple Machines: Friction, *re* Elijah McCoy.

Anton van Leeuwenhoek
Elijah McCoy
Florence Nightingale
Daniel Hale Williams

Science

Grade 3

Overview of Topics — Grade 3

Language Arts
I. Reading and Writing
   A. Reading Comprehension and Response
   B. Writing
   C. Spelling, Grammar, and Usage
   D. Vocabulary
II. Poetry
III. Fiction
   A. Stories
   B. Myths and Mythical Characters
   C. Literary Terms
IV. Sayings and Phrases

History and Geography
World:
I. World Geography
   A. Spatial Sense
   B. Geographical Terms and Features
   C. Canada
   D. Important Rivers of the World
II. Ancient Rome
   A. Geography of the Mediterranean Region
   B. Background
   C. The Empire
   D. The "Decline and Fall" of Rome
   E. The Eastern Roman Empire: Byzantine Civilization
III. The Vikings

American:
I. The Earliest Americans
   A. Crossing the Land Bridge
   B. Native Americans
II. Early Exploration of North America
   A. Early Spanish Exploration and Settlement
   B. Exploration and Settlement of the American
      Southwest
   C. The Search for the Northwest Passage
III. The Thirteen Colonies: Life and Times Before the
      Revolution
   A. Geography
   B. Southern Colonies
   C. New England Colonies
   D. Middle Atlantic Colonies

Visual Arts
I. Elements of Art
   A. Light
   B. Space in Artworks
   C. Design: How the Elements of Art Work Together
II. American Indian Art
III. Art of Ancient Rome and Byzantine Civilization

Music 3
I. Elements of Music
II. Listening and Understanding
   A. The Orchestra
   B. Composers and Their Music
   C. Musical Connections
III. Songs

Mathematics
I. Numbers and Number Sense
II. Fractions and Decimals
III. Money
IV. Computation
   A. Addition
   B. Subtraction
   C. Multiplication
   D. Division
   E. Solving Problems and Equations
V. Measurement
   A. Linear Measure
   B. Weight (Mass)
   C. Capacity (Volume)
   D. Temperature
   E. Time
VI. Geometry

Science
I. Introduction to Classification of Animals
II. The Human Body
   A. The Muscular System
   B. The Skeletal System
   C. The Nervous System
   D. Vision: How the Eye Works
   E. Hearing: How the Ear Works
III. Light and Optics
IV. Sound
V. Ecology
VI. Astronomy
VII. Science Biographies

Language Arts: Grade 3

I.   Reading and Writing

TEACHERS: Many of the following sub-goals are designed to help children achieve the overall goal for reading in third grade: to be able to read (both aloud and silently), with fluency, accuracy, and comprehension any story or other text appropriately written for third grade. Such texts include Beverly Cleary's *Ramona* books, Laura Ingalls Wilder's *Little House in the Big Woods*, and third-grade-level volumes in such nonfiction series as *Let's Read and Find Out* and *New True Books*.

In third grade, children should be competent decoders of most one- and two-syllable words, and they should become increasingly able to use their knowledge of phonemes, syllable boundaries, and prefixes and suffixes to decode multisyllable words. Systematic attention to decoding skills should be provided as needed for children who have not achieved the goals specified for grades 1 and 2.

NOTE: Children should read outside of school at least 20 minutes daily.

A.   READING COMPREHENSION AND RESPONSE
  * Independently read and comprehend longer works of fiction ("chapter books") and nonfiction appropriately written for third grade or beyond.
  * Point to specific words or passages that are causing difficulties in comprehension.
  * Orally summarize main points from fiction and nonfiction readings.
  * Ask and pose plausible answers to how, why, and what-if questions in interpreting texts, both fiction and nonfiction.
  * Use a dictionary to answer questions regarding meaning and usage of words with which he or she is unfamiliar.
  * Know how to use a table of contents and index to locate information.

B.   WRITING
TEACHERS: Children should be given many opportunities for writing, both imaginative and expository, with teacher guidance that strikes a balance between encouraging creativity and requiring correct use of conventions. The following guidelines build on the second grade guidelines: please refer to them and provide review and reinforcement as necessary to ensure mastery.

  * Produce a variety of types of writing—such as stories, reports, poems, letters, descriptions—and make reasonable judgments about what to include in his or her own written works based on the purpose and type of composition.
  * Know how to gather information from basic print sources (such as a children's encyclopedia), and write a short report presenting the information in his or her own words.
  * Know how to use established conventions when writing a friendly letter: heading, salutation (greeting), closing, signature.
  * Produce written work with a beginning, middle, and end.
  * Organize material in paragraphs and understand
    how to use a topic sentence
    how to develop a paragraph with examples and details
    that each new paragraph is indented
  * In some writings, proceed with guidance through a process of gathering information, organizing thoughts, composing a draft, revising to clarify and refine his or her meaning, and proofreading with attention to spelling, mechanics, and presentation of a final draft.

NOTE: Review from grade 2: Capital letters for: the first word of a sentence; proper nouns; the pronoun "I"; holidays and months and days of the week; names of countries, cities, states; main words in titles; initials.

NOTE: Review and reinforce from grade 2: singular and plural nouns; making words plural with *s* or *es*; irregular plurals; correct usage of irregular verbs (be, have, do, go, come, etc.); regular past tense with *-ed* and past tense of irregular verbs.

NOTE: Children should know that a *possessive* noun shows ownership.

NOTE: Teach only words that can be clearly analyzed into prefix and base word; for example, do not teach "discover" or "display" as prefixed words.

NOTE: Review synonyms and antonyms.

C. SPELLING, GRAMMAR, AND USAGE

- Spell most words correctly or with a highly probable spelling, and use a dictionary to check and correct spellings about which he or she is uncertain.
- Use capital letters correctly.
- Understand what a complete sentence is, and
  - identify subject and predicate in single-clause sentences
  - distinguish complete sentences from fragments
- Identify and use different sentence types:
  - declarative (makes a statement)
  - interrogative (asks a question)
  - imperative (gives a command)
  - exclamatory (for example, "What a hit!")
- Know the following parts of speech and how they are used:
  - nouns (for concrete nouns)
  - pronouns (singular and plural)
  - verbs: action verbs and auxiliary (helping) verbs
  - adjectives (including articles: *a* before a consonant, *an* before a vowel, and *the*)
  - adverbs
- Know how to use the following punctuation:
  - end punctuation: period, question mark, or exclamation point
  - comma: between day and year when writing a date; between city and state in an address; in a series; after *yes* and *no*
  - apostrophe: in contractions; in singular and plural possessive nouns
- Recognize and avoid the double negative.

D. VOCABULARY

- Know what prefixes and suffixes are and how the following affect word meaning:
  - Prefixes:
    - *re* meaning "again" (as in reuse, refill)
    - *un* meaning "not" (as in unfriendly, unpleasant)
    - *dis* meaning "not" (as in dishonest, disobey)
    - *un* meaning "opposite of" or "reversing an action" (as in untie, unlock)
    - *dis* meaning "opposite of" or "reversing an action" (as in disappear, dismount)
  - Suffixes:
    - *er* and *or* (as in singer, painter, actor)
    - *less* (as in careless, hopeless)
    - *ly* (as in quickly, calmly)
- Know what homophones are (for example, by, buy; hole, whole) and correct usage of homophones that commonly cause problems:
  - their, there, they're
  - your, you're
  - its, it's
  - here, hear
  - to, too, two
- Recognize common abbreviations (for example, St., Rd., Mr., Mrs., Ms., Dr., U.S.A., ft., in., lb.).

II. Poetry

TEACHERS: The poems listed here constitute a selected core of poetry for this grade. You are encouraged to expose children to more poetry, old and new, and to have children write their own poems. To bring children into the spirit of poetry, read it aloud and encourage them to read it aloud so they can experience the music in the words. At this grade, poetry should be a source of delight; technical analysis should be delayed until later grades.

Adventures of Isabel (Ogden Nash)
The Bee (Isaac Watts; see also below, "The Crocodile")
By Myself (Eloise Greenfield)
Catch a Little Rhyme (Eve Merriam)
The Crocodile (Lewis Carroll)
Dream Variation (Langston Hughes)
Eletelephony (Laura Richards)
Father William (Lewis Carroll)
First Thanksgiving of All (Nancy Byrd Turner)
For want of a nail, the shoe was lost . . . (traditional)
Jimmy Jet and His TV Set (Shel Silverstein)
Knoxville, Tennessee (Nikki Giovanni)
Trees (Sergeant Joyce Kilmer)

III. Fiction

TEACHERS: The titles here constitute a selected core of stories for this grade. Expose children to many more stories, and encourage children to write their own stories. Children should also be exposed to non-fiction prose: biographies, books about science and history, books on art and music, etc. Also, engage children in dramatic activities, possibly with one of the stories below in the form of a play. Some of the following works, such as *Alice in Wonderland* and *The Wind in the Willows*, lend themselves to reading aloud to children.

A. STORIES

Alice in Wonderland (Lewis Carroll)
from *The Arabian Nights*:
    Aladdin and the Wonderful Lamp
    Ali Baba and the Forty Thieves
The Hunting of the Great Bear (an Iroquois legend about the origin of the Big Dipper)
The Husband Who Was to Mind the House (a Norse/English folk tale, also known
    as "Gone is Gone")
The Little Match Girl (Hans Christian Andersen)
The People Who Could Fly (an African American folk tale)
Three Words of Wisdom (a folk tale from Mexico)
William Tell
selections from *The Wind in the Willows*: "The River Bank" and
    "The Open Road" (Kenneth Grahame)

See also American History 3, Slavery in the Colonies, *re* "The People Who Could Fly."

B. MYTHS AND MYTHICAL CHARACTERS

• Norse Mythology
    Asgard (home of the gods)
    Valhalla
    Hel (underworld)
    Odin
    Thor
    trolls
    Norse gods and English names for days of the week: Tyr, Odin [Wodin], Thor, Freya

See also World History 3, Vikings.

See also World History 3,
Ancient Rome.

• More Myths and Legends of Ancient Greece and Rome ·
   Jason and the Golden Fleece
   Perseus and Medusa
   Cupid and Psyche
   The Sword of Damocles
   Damon and Pythias
   Androcles and the Lion
   Horatius at the Bridge

C.   LITERARY TERMS
   biography and autobiography
   fiction and nonfiction

IV. Sayings and Phrases

TEACHERS: Every culture has phrases and proverbs that make no sense when carried over literally into another culture. For many children, this section may not be needed; they will have picked up these sayings by hearing them at home and among friends. But the sayings have been one of the categories most appreciated by teachers who work with children from home cultures that differ from the standard culture of literate American English.

Actions speak louder than words.
His bark is worse than his bite.
Beat around the bush
Beggars can't be choosers.
Clean bill of health
Cold shoulder
A feather in your cap
Last straw
Let bygones be bygones.
One rotten apple spoils the whole barrel.
On its last legs
Rule the roost
The show must go on.
Touch and go
When in Rome do as the Romans do.

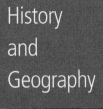

History and Geography: Grade 3

WORLD HISTORY AND GEOGRAPHY

I. World Geography

<u>TEACHERS:</u> The study of geography embraces many topics throughout the Core Knowledge Sequence, including topics in history and science. Geographic knowledge includes a spatial sense of the world, an awareness of the physical processes that shape life, a sense of the interactions between humans and their environment, an understanding of the relations between place and culture, and an awareness of the characteristics of specific regions and cultures.

A. SPATIAL SENSE (Working with Maps, Globes, and Other Geographic Tools)
<u>TEACHERS:</u> Review and reinforce earlier topics, and add new topics as follows:

- Name your continent, country, state, and community.
- Understand that maps have keys or legends with symbols and their uses.
- Find directions on a map: east, west, north, south.
- Identify major oceans: Pacific, Atlantic, Indian, Arctic.
- The seven continents: Asia, Europe, Africa, North America, South America, Antarctica, Australia
- Locate: Canada, United States, Mexico, Central America.
- Locate: the Equator, Northern Hemisphere and Southern Hemisphere, North and South Poles.
- Measure straight-line distances using a bar scale.
- Use an atlas and, if available, on-line sources to find geographic information.

B. GEOGRAPHICAL TERMS AND FEATURES
<u>TEACHERS:</u> Review terms from grade 1 (peninsula, harbor, bay, island) and grade 2 (coast, valley, desert, oasis, prairie), and add:

- boundary, channel, delta, isthmus, plateau, reservoir, strait

See also American History
and Geography 3, Search for
the Northwest Passage.

C. CANADA
- Locate in relation to United States
- French and British heritage, French-speaking Quebec
- Rocky Mountains
- Hudson Bay, St. Lawrence River, Yukon River
- Divided into provinces
- Major cities, including Montreal, Quebec, Toronto

D. IMPORTANT RIVERS OF THE WORLD
- Terms: source, mouth, tributary, drainage basin
- Asia: Ob, Yellow (Huang He), Yangtze (Chang Jiang), Ganges, Indus
- Africa: Nile, Niger, Congo
- South America: Amazon, Parana, Orinoco
- North America: Mississippi and major tributaries, Mackenzie, Yukon
- Australia: Murray-Darling
- Europe: Volga, Danube, Rhine

II. Ancient Rome

TEACHERS: Students will study Rome again in grade 6, with a focus on the legacy of ideas from ancient Greece and Rome.

A. GEOGRAPHY OF THE MEDITERRANEAN REGION
- Mediterranean Sea, Aegean Sea, Adriatic Sea
- Greece, Italy (peninsula), France, Spain
- Strait of Gibraltar, Atlantic Ocean
- North Africa, Asia Minor (peninsula), Turkey
- Bosporus (strait), Black Sea, Istanbul (Constantinople)
- Red Sea, Persian Gulf, Indian Ocean

B. BACKGROUND
- Define B.C. / A.D. and B.C.E. / C.E.
- The legend of Romulus and Remus
- Latin as the language of Rome
- Worship of gods and goddesses, largely based on Greek religion
- The Republic: Senate, Patricians, Plebeians
- Punic Wars: Carthage, Hannibal

See also Language Arts 3, More Myths and Legends of Ancient Greece and Rome.

C. THE EMPIRE
- Julius Caesar
  Defeats Pompey in civil war, becomes dictator
  "Veni, vidi, vici" ("I came, I saw, I conquered")
  Cleopatra of Egypt
  Caesar assassinated in the Senate, Brutus
- Augustus Caesar
- Life in the Roman Empire
  The Forum: temples, marketplaces, etc.
  The Colosseum: circuses, gladiator combat, chariot races
  Roads, bridges, and aqueducts
- Eruption of Mt. Vesuvius, destruction of Pompeii
- Persecution of Christians

D. THE "DECLINE AND FALL" OF ROME
- Weak and corrupt emperors, legend of Nero fiddling as Rome burns
- Civil wars
- City of Rome sacked

See also Visual Arts 3, Art of Ancient Rome and Byzantine Civilization.

E. THE EASTERN ROMAN EMPIRE: BYZANTINE CIVILIZATION
- The rise of the Eastern Roman Empire, known as the Byzantine Empire
- Constantine, first Christian emperor
- Constantinople (now called Istanbul) merges diverse influences and cultures.
- Justinian, Justinian's Code

III. The Vikings

See also Language Arts 3, Norse Myths.

- From area now called Scandinavia (Sweden, Denmark, Norway)
- Also called Norsemen, they were skilled sailors and shipbuilders.
- Traders, and sometimes raiders of the European coast
- Eric the Red and Leif Ericson (Leif "the Lucky")
- Earliest Europeans (long before Columbus) we know of to come to North America
  Locate: Greenland, Canada, Newfoundland

American History and Geography

AMERICAN HISTORY AND GEOGRAPHY

TEACHERS: In third grade, students begin a more detailed and in-depth chronological investigation of topics, some of which have been introduced in grades K-2. Specific topics include: the early exploration of North America; ways of life of specific Native American peoples; life in colonial America before the Revolution. Use of timelines is encouraged. The following guidelines are meant to complement any locally required studies of the family, community, or region. Note that in fifth grade the American Geography requirements include "fifty states and capitals"; teachers in grades two through four may want to introduce these incrementally to prepare for the fifth grade requirement.

I. The Earliest Americans

A. CROSSING THE LAND BRIDGE
- During the Ice Age, nomadic hunters cross what was a land bridge from Asia to North America (now the Bering Strait). Different peoples, with different languages and ways of life, eventually spread out over the North and South American continents. These early peoples include:
  Inuits (Eskimos)
  Anasazi, pueblo builders and cliff dwellers
  Mound builders

B. NATIVE AMERICANS
- In the Southwest
  Pueblos (Hopi, Zuni)
  Dine (Navajo)
  Apaches
- Eastern "Woodland" Indians
  Woodland culture: wigwams, longhouses, farming, peace pipe, Shaman and Sachem
  Major tribes and nations (such as Cherokee Confederacy, Seminole, Powhatan, Delaware, Susquehanna, Mohican, Massachusett, Iroquois Confederacy)

See also Language Arts 3, "The Hunting of the Great Bear" (an Iroquois legend).

II. Early Exploration of North America

TEACHERS: In fifth grade, students will examine European exploration in a more global context. Third grade teachers should look ahead to the fifth grade World History guidelines (under "European Exploration, Trade, and the Clash of Cultures") to see how the topics introduced here will be developed and extended later. It is recommended that third grade teachers keep their focus on the explorers and events specified here, and leave for fifth grade the figures and ideas specified for that grade.

A. EARLY SPANISH EXPLORATION AND SETTLEMENT
- Settlement of Florida
- Ponce de Leon, legend of the Fountain of Youth
- Hernando de Soto
- Founding of St. Augustine (oldest continuous European settlement in what is now the U.S.)
- Geography: Caribbean Sea, West Indies, Puerto Rico, Cuba, Gulf of Mexico, Mississippi River

B. EXPLORATION AND SETTLEMENT OF THE AMERICAN SOUTHWEST
- Early Spanish explorers in the lands that are now the states of Texas, New Mexico, Arizona, and California; missionary settlements (missions), especially in Texas and California
- Coronado and the legend of the "Seven Cities of Cibola" (of Gold)
- Geography: Grand Canyon and Rio Grande
- Conflicts with Pueblo Indians (1680 revolt led by Popé)

NOTE: Students may also be
interested to learn about
Amerigo Vespucci, the unlikely
source of our country's name.

C.   THE SEARCH FOR THE NORTHWEST PASSAGE
- Many explorers undertook the perilous, sometimes fatal, voyage to find a short cut across North America to Asia, including:
    - John Cabot: Newfoundland
    - Champlain: "New France" and Quebec
    - Henry Hudson: the Hudson River
- Geography
    - "New France" and Quebec
    - Canada, St. Lawrence River
    - The Great Lakes: Superior, Michigan, Huron, Erie, Ontario

III. The Thirteen Colonies: Life and Times Before the Revolution

TEACHERS: Discuss with children the definition of "colony" and why countries establish colonies. Help children see that the thirteen English colonies were not alike. Different groups of people came to America with different motivations (hoping to get rich, looking for religious freedom, etc.), and the thirteen colonies developed in different ways.

A.   GEOGRAPHY
- The thirteen colonies by region: New England, Middle Atlantic, Southern
- Differences in climate from north to south: corresponding differences in agriculture (subsistence farming in New England, gradual development of large plantations in the South)
- Important cities in the development of trade and government: Philadelphia, Boston, New York, Charleston

B.   SOUTHERN COLONIES
- Southern colonies: Virginia, Maryland, North Carolina, South Carolina, Georgia
- Virginia
    - Chesapeake Bay, James River
    - 1607: three ships of the London Company (later called the Virginia Company) arrive in Virginia, seeking gold and other riches
    - Establishment of Jamestown, first continuous English colony in the New World
    - Trade with Powhatan Indians (see also Eastern "Woodland" Indians, above)
    - John Smith
    - Pocahontas, marriage to John Rolfe
    - Diseases kill many people, both colonists and Indians
    - The Starving Time
    - Clashes between American Indians and English colonists
    - Development of tobacco as a cash crop, development of plantations
    - 1619: slaves brought to Virginia
- Maryland
    - A colony established mainly for Catholics
    - Lord Baltimore
- South Carolina
    - Charleston
    - Plantations (rice, indigo) and slave labor
- Georgia
    - James Oglethorpe's plan to establish a colony for English debtors
- Slavery in the Southern colonies
    - Economic reasons that the Southern colonies came to rely on slavery (for example, slave labor on large plantations)
    - The difference between indentured servant and slaves: slaves as property
    - The Middle Passage

NOTE: The question of fact
vs. legend regarding the
rescue of John Smith by
Pocahontas presents a good
opportunity to explore what
historians know, and how.

See also Language Arts 3,
"The People Who Could Fly"
re slavery in the colonies.

C. NEW ENGLAND COLONIES

- New England colonies: Massachusetts, New Hampshire, Connecticut, Rhode Island
- Gradual development of maritime economy: fishing and shipbuilding
- Massachusetts

    Colonists seeking religious freedom: in England, an official "established" church (the Church of England), which did not allow people to worship as they chose

    The Pilgrims

    From England to Holland to Massachusetts

    1620: Voyage of the Mayflower

    Significance of the Mayflower Compact

    Plymouth, William Bradford

    Helped by Wampanoag Indians: Massasoit, Tisquantum (Squanto)

    The Puritans

    Massachusetts Bay Colony, Governor John Winthrop: "We shall be as a city upon a hill."

    Emphasis on reading and education, the *New England Primer*

- Rhode Island

    Roger Williams: belief in religious toleration

    Anne Hutchinson

Note: In fifth grade students will explore the social changes that led to the Protestant Reformation.

D. MIDDLE ATLANTIC COLONIES

- Middle Atlantic colonies: New York, New Jersey, Delaware, Pennsylvania
- New York

    Dutch settlements and trading posts in "New Netherland"

    Dutch West India Company acquires Manhattan Island and Long Island through a (probably misunderstood) purchase from the Indians; Dutch establish New Amsterdam (today, New York City)

    English take over from the Dutch, and rename the colony New York

- Pennsylvania

    William Penn

    Society of Friends, "Quakers"

    Philadelphia

History and Geography

Visual Arts: Grade 3

SEE PAGE 3, "The Arts in the Curriculum."

TEACHERS: In schools, lessons on the visual arts should illustrate important elements of making and appreciating art, and emphasize important artists, works of art, and artistic concepts. When appropriate, topics in the visual arts may be linked to topics in other disciplines. While the following guidelines specify a variety of artworks in different media and from various cultures, they are not intended to be comprehensive. Teachers are encouraged to build upon the core content and expose children to a wide range of art and artists.

I.   Elements of Art

TEACHERS: The generally recognized elements of art include line, shape, form, space, light, texture, and color. In third grade, build on what the children have learned in earlier grades as you introduce concepts of light, space, and design.

A.   LIGHT
- Observe how artists use light and shadow (to focus our attention, affect our emotions, etc.) in
  James Chapin, *Ruby Green Singing*
  Jan Vermeer, *Milkmaid*

B.   SPACE IN ARTWORKS
- Understand the following terms: two-dimensional (height, width) and three-dimensional (height, width, depth)
- Observe relationship between two-dimensional and three-dimensional shapes: square to cube, triangle to pyramid, circle to sphere and cylinder
- Observe how artists can make two-dimensional look three-dimensional by creating an illusion of depth, and examine the foreground, middle ground, and background in paintings, including
  Jean Millet, *The Gleaners*
  Pieter Bruegel, *Peasant Wedding*

NOTE: Students will take a more detailed look at perspective in grade 5.

C.   DESIGN: HOW THE ELEMENTS OF ART WORK TOGETHER
- Become familiar with how these terms are used in discussing works of art:
  Figure and ground
  Pattern
  Balance and symmetry
- Examine design—how the elements of art work together—in
  Rosa Bonheur, *The Horse Fair*
  Mary Cassatt, *The Bath*
  Early American quilts
  Edward Hicks, *The Peaceable Kingdom*
  Henri Matisse, cut-outs: *Icarus*
  Edvard Munch, *The Scream*
  Horace Pippin, *Victorian Interior*
  Faith Ringgold, *Tar Beach*

See also American History 3, Colonial America, *re* Early American quilts and *The Peaceable Kingdom*.

II. American Indian Art

Teachers: The works of art specified below are associated with the Southwest and Eastern "Woodland" Indians studied in third grade, thus other works of art, such as totem poles, are not listed here because they would be more appropriately examined when students are introduced to the Pacific Northwest Indians. Students should be made aware of the spiritual purposes and significance of many American Indian works of art.

- Become familiar with American Indian works, including
  - Kachina dolls (Hopi, Zuni)
  - Navajo (Dine) blankets and rugs, sand paintings
  - Masks

III. Art of Ancient Rome and Byzantine Civilization

Teachers: The works of art listed here may be introduced as part of your study of ancient Roman civilization; see World History Grade 3.

- Become familiar with artworks of ancient Roman and Byzantine civilization, including
  - Le Pont du Gard
  - The Pantheon
  - Byzantine mosaics
  - Hagia Sophia

Visual Arts

Music: Grade 3

SEE PAGE 3, "The Arts in the Curriculum."

TEACHERS: In schools, lessons on music should feature activities and works that illustrate important musical concepts and terms, and should introduce important composers and works. When appropriate, topics in music may be linked to topics in other disciplines.

The following guidelines focus on content, not performance skills, though many concepts are best learned through active practice (singing, clapping rhythms, playing instruments, etc.).

I. Elements of Music

- Through participation, become familiar with basic elements of music (rhythm, melody, harmony, form, timbre, etc.).
  - Recognize a steady beat, accents, and the downbeat; play a steady beat.
  - Move responsively to music.
  - Recognize short and long sounds.
  - Discriminate between fast and slow; gradually slowing down and getting faster.
  - Discriminate between differences in pitch: high and low.
  - Discriminate between loud and quiet; gradually increasing and decreasing volume.
  - Understand that melody can move up and down.
  - Hum the melody while listening to music.
  - Echo short rhythms and melodic patterns.
  - Play simple rhythms and melodies.
  - Sing unaccompanied, accompanied, and in unison.
  - Recognize harmony; sing rounds.
  - Recognize verse and refrain.
  - Continue work with timbre and phrasing.
  - Review names of musical notes; scale as a series of notes; singing the C major scale using "do re mi" etc.
- Understand the following notation

  names of lines and spaces in the treble clef

  𝄞 treble clef, ☰ staff, bar line, double bar line, measure, repeat signs

  𝅝 whole note   𝅗𝅥 half note   𝅘𝅥 quarter note   𝅘𝅥𝅮 eighth note

  whole rest, half rest, quarter rest

  meter signature: $\frac{4}{4}$ $\frac{2}{4}$ $\frac{3}{4}$

  quiet *p* *pp*   loud *f* *ff*

II. Listening and Understanding

TEACHERS: Expose children to a wide range of music, including children's music, popular instrumental music, and music from various cultures.

See also below, *re* brass instruments, Composers and Their Music: Aaron Copland's *Fanfare for the Common Man,* and John Philip Sousa, *Stars and Stripes Forever.* See also Language Arts 3, William Tell.

A. THE ORCHESTRA
- Review families of instruments: strings, brass, woodwinds, percussion.
- Become familiar with brass instruments—trumpet, French horn, trombone, tuba—and listen to
  - Gioacchino Rossini, *William Tell Overture*, finale (trumpet)
  - Wolfgang Amadeus Mozart, selections from the *Horn Concertos* (French horn)

NOTE: When you explore woodwinds with children, you may also want to recall Prokofiev's *Peter and the Wolf*: the duck's theme (oboe), cat's theme (clarinet), bird's theme (flute), and Grandfather's theme (bassoon).

- Become familiar with woodwind instruments—flute and piccolo (no reeds); clarinet, oboe, bassoon (with reeds)—and listen to
    Claude Debussy, *Prelude to the Afternoon of a Faun* (flute)
    Opening of George Gershwin's *Rhapsody in Blue* (clarinet)

B. COMPOSERS AND THEIR MUSIC

TEACHERS: Provide brief, child-friendly biographical profiles of the following composers, and listen to representative works:

See below, Songs, "Simple Gifts."

- Peter Ilich Tchaikovsky, *Suite from Swan Lake*
- John Philip Sousa, *Stars and Stripes Forever*
- Aaron Copland, *Fanfare for the Common Man*; "Hoedown" from *Rodeo*, "Simple Gifts" from *Appalachian Spring*

C. MUSICAL CONNECTIONS

TEACHERS: Introduce children to the following in connection with topics in other disciplines:

See also Language Arts 3, Tales from "The Arabian Nights" *re Scheherazade*. Also, *re* Norse mythology, you may want to introduce Wagner's "The Ride of the Valkyries."

- Nikolai Rimsky-Korsakov, *Scheherazade,* part one: "The Sea and Sinbad's Ship"

III. Songs

NOTE: Review from earlier grades "America the Beautiful" and "The Star-Spangled Banner."

Alouette
America ("My country, 'tis of thee")
A Bicycle Built for Two (chorus only)
Down in the Valley
He's Got the Whole World in His Hands
Hey, Ho, Nobody Home (round)
In the Good Old Summertime (chorus only)
Li'l Liza Jane
My Bonnie Lies Over the Ocean
Polly Wolly Doodle
The Man on the Flying Trapeze (chorus only)
The Sidewalks of New York (chorus only)
Simple Gifts ("Tis a gift to be simple")
This Little Light of Mine
You're a Grand Old Flag

Music

Mathematics: Grade 3

TEACHERS: Mathematics has its own vocabulary and patterns of thinking. It is a discipline with its own language and conventions. Thus, while some lessons may offer occasional opportunities for linking mathematics to other disciplines, it is critically important to attend to math as math. From the earliest years, mathematics requires incremental review and steady practice: not only the diligent effort required to master basic facts and operations, but also thoughtful and varied practice that approaches problems from a variety of angles, and gives children a variety of opportunities to apply the same concept or operation in different types of situations. While it is important to work toward the development of "higher-order problem-solving skills," it is equally important—indeed, it is prerequisite to achieving "higher order" skills—to have a sound grasp of basic facts, and an automatic fluency with fundamental operations.

I. Numbers and Number Sense

- Read and write numbers (in digits and words) up to six digits.
- Recognize place value up to hundred-thousands.
- Order and compare numbers to 999,999, using the signs <, >, and = .
- Count by twos, threes, fives, and tens; count by tens from any given number.
- Write numbers in expanded form.
- Use a number line.
- Identify ordinal position, 1st to 100th.
- Review: even and odd numbers; dozen; half-dozen; pair.
- Round to the nearest ten; to the nearest hundred.
- Identify perfect squares (and square roots) to 100, and recognize the square root sign: $\sqrt{}$
- Identify Roman numerals from 1 to 20 (I - XX).
- Understand what negative numbers are in relation to familiar uses (such as temperatures below zero).
- Locate positive and negative whole numbers on a number line.
- Create and interpret bar graphs and line graphs.
- Record outcomes for a simple event (for example, tossing a die) and display the results graphically.

II. Fractions and Decimals

- Recognize fractions to $\frac{1}{10}$.
- Identify numerator and denominator.
- Write mixed numbers.
- Recognize equivalent fractions (for example, $\frac{1}{2} = \frac{3}{6}$).
- Compare fractions with like denominators, using the signs <, >, and = .
- Know and write decimal equivalents to $\frac{1}{4}, \frac{1}{2}, \frac{3}{4}$.
- Read and write decimals to the hundredths.

III. Money

- Write amounts of money using $ and ¢ signs, and the decimal point.
- Make change, using as few coins as possible.
- Add and subtract amounts of money.
- Multiply and divide amounts of money by small whole numbers.

IV. Computation

TEACHERS: Children should know their basic addition and subtraction facts; review and reinforce as necessary to ensure mastery.

A. ADDITION
- Review and practice basic addition facts.
- Mentally estimate a sum.
- Use mental computation strategies.
- Addition with and without regrouping: find the sum (up to 10,000) of any two whole numbers.

B. SUBTRACTION
- Understand addition and subtraction as inverse operations; use addition to check subtraction.
- Review and practice basic subtraction facts.
- Mentally estimate the difference.
- Use mental computation strategies.
- Subtraction with and without regrouping: given two whole numbers of 10,000 or less, find the difference.

C. MULTIPLICATION
- Master basic multiplication facts to 10 x 10.
- Mentally multiply, by 10, 100, and 1,000.
- Multiply two whole numbers, with and without regrouping, in which one factor is 9 or less and the other is a multi-digit number up to three digits.
- Write numbers in expanded form using multiplication, for example: 9,278 = (9 x 1,000) + (2 x 100) + (7 x 10) + 8.
- Estimate a product.
- Solve word problems involving multiplication.

D. DIVISION
- Understand multiplication and division as inverse operations.
- Know the meaning of dividend, divisor, and quotient.
- Know basic division facts to 100 ÷ 10.
- Know that you cannot divide by 0.
- Know that any number divided by 1 = that number.
- Divide two- and three-digit dividends by one-digit divisors.
- Solve division problems with remainders.
- Check division by multiplying (and adding remainder).

E. SOLVING PROBLEMS AND EQUATIONS
- Solve two-step word problems.
- Solve equations in the form of ___ x 9 = 63; 81 ÷ ___ = 9.
- Solve problems with more than one operation, as in (43 - 32) x (5 + 3) = ___.
- Read and write expressions that use parentheses to indicate order of multiple operations.

V. Measurement

A. LINEAR MEASURE
- Make linear measurements in yards, feet, and inches; and, in centimeters and meters.
- Know that one foot = 12 inches; one yard = 36 inches; 3 feet = 1 yard; 1 meter = 100 centimeters; 1 meter is a little more than one yard.
- Measure and draw line segments in inches (to 1/4 inch), and in centimeters.
- Estimate linear measurements, then measure to check estimates.

B. WEIGHT (MASS)
- Compare weights of objects using a balance scale.
- Estimate and measure weight in pounds and ounces; grams and kilograms.
- Know abbreviations: lb., oz., g, kg

C. CAPACITY (VOLUME)
- Estimate and measure liquid capacity in cups, pints, quarts, gallons, and liters.
- Know that 1 quart = 2 pints; 1 gallon = 4 quarts.
- Compare U.S. and metric liquid volumes: quart and liter (one liter is a little more than one quart).

D. TEMPERATURE
- Measure and record temperature in degrees Fahrenheit and Celsius.
- Know the degree sign: °
- Identify freezing point of water as 32° F = 0° C.

E. TIME
- Read a clock face and tell time to the minute as either A.M. or P.M.; tell time in terms of both "minutes before" and "minutes after" the hour.
- Solve problems on elapsed time (how much time has passed?).
- Using a calendar, identify the date, day of the week, month, and year.
- Write the date using words (for name of month) and numbers, and only numbers.

VI. Geometry

- Identify lines as horizontal, vertical, perpendicular, or parallel.
- Name lines and line segments (for example, line AB; segment CD).
- Polygons: recognize vertex (plural: vertices); identify sides as line segments (for example, side CD); identify pentagon, hexagon, and octagon (regular).
- Identify angles by letter names (for example, ∠ ABC); identify a right angle; know that there are four right angles in a square or rectangle.
- Compute area in square inches (in²) and square centimeters (cm²).
- Recognize and draw congruent figures; identify a line of symmetry, and create symmetric figures.
- Identify solid figures: sphere, cube, rectangular solid, pyramid, cone, cylinder.

Science: Grade 3

TEACHERS: Effective instruction in science requires hands-on experience and observation. In the words of the 1993 report from the American Association for the Advancement of Science, *Benchmarks for Science Literacy*, "From their very first day in school, students should be actively engaged in learning to view the world scientifically. That means encouraging them to ask questions about nature and to seek answers, collect things, count and measure things, make qualitative observations, organize collections and observations, discuss findings, etc."

While experience counts for much, book learning is also important, for it helps bring coherence and order to a child's scientific knowledge. Only when topics are presented systematically and clearly can children make steady and secure progress in their scientific learning. The child's development of scientific knowledge and understanding is in some ways a very disorderly and complex process, different for each child. But a systematic approach to the exploration of science, one that combines experience with book learning, can help provide essential building blocks for deeper understanding at a later time.

I. Introduction to Classification of Animals

- Scientists classify animals according to the characteristics they share, for example:
  Cold-blooded or warm-blooded
  Vertebrates (have backbones and internal skeletons) or invertebrates (do not have backbones or internal skeletons)
- Different classes of vertebrates

TEACHERS: Children should become familiar with examples of animals in each class and some basic characteristics of each class, such as:

Fish: aquatic animals, breathe through gills, cold-blooded, most have scales, most develop from eggs that the female lays outside her body

Amphibians: live part of their lives in water and part on land, have gills when young, later develop lungs, cold-blooded, usually have moist skin

Reptiles: hatch from eggs, cold-blooded, have dry, thick, scaly skin

Birds: warm-blooded, most can fly, have feathers and wings, most build nests, hatch from eggs, most baby birds must be fed by parents and cared for until they can survive on their own (though some, like baby chickens and quail, can search for food a few hours after hatching)

Mammals: warm-blooded, have hair on their bodies, parents care for the young, females produce milk for their babies, breathe through lungs, most are terrestrial (live on land) though some are aquatic

II. The Human Body

A. THE MUSCULAR SYSTEM
- Muscles
  Involuntary and voluntary muscles

B. THE SKELETAL SYSTEM
- Skeleton, bones, marrow
- Musculo-skeletal connections
  Ligaments
  Tendons, Achilles tendon
  Cartilage
- Skull, cranium
- Spinal column, vertebrae
- Joints
- Ribs, rib cage, sternum
- Scapula (shoulder blades), pelvis, tibia, fibula
- Broken bones, x-rays

C. THE NERVOUS SYSTEM
- Brain: medulla, cerebellum, cerebrum, cerebral cortex
- Spinal cord
- Nerves
- Reflexes

D. VISION: HOW THE EYE WORKS
- Parts of the eye: cornea, iris and pupil, lens, retina
- Optic nerve
- Farsighted and nearsighted

E. HEARING: HOW THE EAR WORKS
- Sound as vibration
- Outer ear, ear canal
- Eardrum
- Three tiny bones (hammer, anvil, and stirrup) pass vibrations to the cochlea
- Auditory nerve

III. Light and Optics

TEACHERS: Through experimentation and observation, introduce children to some of the basic physical phenomena of light, with associated vocabulary.

NOTE: Students will study light in more detail in grade 8.

- The speed of light: light travels at an amazingly high speed.
- Light travels in straight lines (as can be demonstrated by forming shadows).
- Transparent and opaque objects
- Reflection
  Mirrors: plane, concave, convex
  Uses of mirrors in telescopes and some microscopes
- The spectrum: use a prism to demonstrate that white light is made up of a spectrum of colors.
- Lenses can be used for magnifying and bending light (as in magnifying glass, microscope, camera, telescope, binoculars).

IV. Sound

TEACHERS: Through experimentation and observation, introduce children to some of the basic physical phenomena of sound, with associated vocabulary.

NOTE: Students will study sound in more detail in grade 8.

- Sound is caused by an object vibrating rapidly.
- Sounds travel through solids, liquids, and gases.
- Sound waves are much slower than light waves.
- Qualities of sound
  Pitch: high or low, faster vibrations = higher pitch, slower vibrations = lower pitch
  Intensity: loudness and quietness
- Human voice
  Larynx (voice box)
  Vibrating vocal cords: longer, thicker vocal cords create lower, deeper voices
- Sound and how the human ear works
- Protecting your hearing

See above, II.E. Hearing.

V. Ecology

TEACHERS: Some topics here, such as habitats, were introduced in first grade. In this grade, develop in more detail, and explore new topics.

- Habitats, interdependence of organisms and their environment
- The concept of a "balance of nature" (constantly changing, not a static condition)
- The food chain: producers, consumers, decomposers
- Ecosystems: how they can be affected by changes in environment (for example, rainfall, food supply, etc.), and by man-made changes
- Man-made threats to the environment
    Air pollution: emissions, smog
    Water pollution: industrial waste, run-off from farming
- Measures we can take to protect the environment (for example, conservation, recycling)

VI. Astronomy

- The "Big Bang"
- The universe: an extent almost beyond imagining
- Galaxies: Milky Way and Andromeda
- Our solar system
    Sun: source of energy (heat and light)
    The nine planets: Mercury, Venus, Earth, Mars, Jupiter, Saturn, Uranus, Neptune, Pluto
- Planetary motion: orbit and rotation
    How day and night on earth are caused by the earth's rotation
    Sunrise in the east and sunset in the west
    How the seasons are caused by the earth's orbit around the sun, tilt of the earth's axis
- Gravity, gravitational pull
    Gravitational pull of the moon (and to a lesser degree, the sun) causes
        ocean tides on earth
    Gravitational pull of "black holes" prevents even light from escaping
- Asteroids, meteors ("shooting stars"), comets, Halley's Comet
- How an eclipse happens
- Stars and constellations
- Orienteering (finding your way) by using North Star, Big Dipper
- Exploration of space
    Observation through telescopes
    Rockets and satellites: from unmanned to manned flights
    Apollo 11, first landing on the moon: "One small step for a man, one giant leap
        for mankind."
    Space shuttle

VII. Science Biographies

See above, Sound, *re* Alexander Graham Bell; Astronomy, *re* Copernicus; Exploration of Space, *re* Mae Jemison; Ecology, *re* John Muir.

Alexander Graham Bell
Copernicus
Mae Jemison
John Muir

Grade 4

Language Arts

I. Writing, Grammar, and Usage
  A. Writing and Research
  B. Grammar and Usage
II. Poetry
  A. Poems
  B. Terms
III. Fiction
  A. Stories
  B. Myths and Mythical Characters
  C. Literary Terms
IV. Speeches
V. Sayings and Phrases

History and Geography

World:
I. World Geography
  A. Spatial Sense
  B. Mountains and Mountain Ranges
II. Europe in the Middle Ages
  A. Background
  B. Geography Related to the Development of Western
     Europe
  C. Developments in History of the Christian Church
  D. Feudalism
  E. The Norman Conquest
  F. Growth of Towns
  G. England in the Middle Ages
III. The Spread of Islam and the "Holy Wars"
  A. Islam
  B. Development of Islamic Civilization
  C. Wars Between Muslims and Christians
IV. Early and Medieval African Kingdoms
  A. Early African Kingdoms
  B. Medieval Kingdoms of the Sudan
  C. Geography of Africa
V. China: Dynasties and Conquerors

American:
I. The American Revolution
  A. Background: The French and Indian War
  B. Causes and Provocations
  C. The Revolution
II. Making a Constitutional Government
  A. Main Ideas Behind the Declaration of Independence
  B. Making a New Government: From the Declaration
     to the Constitution
  C. The Constitution of the United States
  D. Levels and Functions of Government (National, State, Local)

III. Early Presidents and Politics
IV. Reformers
V. Symbols and Figures

Visual Arts

I. Art of the Middle Ages in Europe
II. Islamic Art and Architecture
III. The Art of Africa
IV. The Art of China
V. The Art of a New Nation: The United States

Music

I. Elements of Music
II. Listening and Understanding
  A. The Orchestra
  B. Vocal Ranges
  C. Composers and Their Music
  D. Musical Connections
III. Songs

Mathematics

I. Numbers and Number Sense
II. Fractions and Decimals
  A. Fractions
  B. Decimals
III. Money
IV. Computation
  A. Multiplication
  B. Division
  C. Solving Problems and Equations
V. Measurement
VI. Geometry

Science

I. The Human Body
  A. The Circulatory System
  B. The Respiratory System
II. Chemistry: Basic Terms and Concepts
  A. Atoms
  B. Properties of Matter
  C. Elements
  D. Solutions
III. Electricity
IV. Geology: The Earth and Its Changes
  A. The Earth's Layers
  B. How Mountains Are Formed
  C. Rocks
  D. Weathering and Erosion
V. Meteorology
VI. Science Biographies

Language Arts: Grade 4

I. Writing, Grammar, and Usage

Teachers: Children should be given many opportunities for writing, both imaginative and expository, but place a stronger emphasis than in previous grades on expository writing, including, for example, summaries, book reports, and descriptive essays. Provide guidance that strikes a balance between encouraging creativity and requiring correct use of conventions. Children should be given more responsibility for (and guidance in) editing for organization and development of ideas, and proofreading to correct errors in spelling, usage, and mechanics. In fourth grade, children should be able to spell most words or provide a highly probable spelling, and know how to use a dictionary to check and correct words that present difficulty. They should receive regular practice in vocabulary enrichment.

Note: Introduce fourth graders to the purpose of a bibliography, and have them prepare one that identifies basic publication information about the sources used, such as author, title, and date of publication.

A. WRITING AND RESEARCH
- Produce a variety of types of writing—including stories, reports, summaries, descriptions, poems, letters—with a coherent structure or story line.
- Know how to gather information from different sources (such as an encyclopedia, magazines, interviews, observations, atlas, on-line), and write short reports presenting the information in his or her own words, with attention to the following:
  understanding the purpose and audience of the writing
  defining a main idea and sticking to it
  providing an introduction and conclusion
  organizing material in coherent paragraphs
  documenting sources in a rudimentary bibliography
- Organize material in paragraphs and understand
  how to use a topic sentence
  how to develop a paragraph with examples and details
  that each new paragraph is indented

B. GRAMMAR AND USAGE
- Understand what a complete sentence is, and
  identify subject and predicate in single-clause sentences
  distinguish complete sentences from fragments
  identify and correct run-on sentences
- Identify subject and verb in a sentence and understand that they must agree.
- Identify and use different sentence types: declarative, interrogative, imperative, exclamatory.
- Know the following parts of speech and how they are used: nouns, pronouns, verbs (action verbs and auxiliary verbs), adjectives (including articles), adverbs, conjunctions (*and, but, or*), interjections.
- Know how to use the following punctuation:
  end punctuation: period, question mark, or exclamation point
  comma: between day and year when writing a date, between city and state in an address, in a series, after *yes* and *no*, before conjunctions that combine sentences, inside quotation marks in dialogue
  apostrophe: in contractions, in singular and plural possessive nouns
  quotation marks: in dialogue, for titles of poems, songs, short stories, magazine articles
- Understand what synonyms and antonyms are, and provide synonyms or antonyms for given words.

NOTE: A brief review of prefixes and suffixes introduced in third grade is recommended. Prefixes: *re, un, dis.* Suffixes: *er* and *or, less, ly.*

- Use underlining or italics for titles of books.
- Know how the following prefixes and suffixes affect word meaning:
    Prefixes:
        im, in (as in impossible, incorrect)
        non (as in nonfiction, nonviolent)
        mis (as in misbehave, misspell)
        en (as in enable, endanger)
        pre (as in prehistoric, pregame)
    Suffixes:
        ily, y (as in easily, speedily, tricky)
        ful (as in thoughtful, wonderful)
        able, ible (as in washable, flexible)
        ment (as in agreement, amazement)
- Review correct usage of problematic homophones:
    their, there, they're
    your, you're
    its, it's
    here, hear
    to, too, two

II. Poetry

TEACHERS: The poems listed here constitute a selected core of poetry for this grade. You are encouraged to expose children to more poetry, old and new, and to have children write their own poems. To bring children into the spirit of poetry, read it aloud and encourage them to read it aloud so they can experience the music in the words. At this grade, poetry should be a source of delight; technical analysis should be delayed until later grades.

A. POEMS
Afternoon on a Hill (Edna St. Vincent Millay)
Clarence (Shel Silverstein)
Clouds (Christina Rossetti)
Concord Hymn (Ralph Waldo Emerson)
Dreams (Langston Hughes)
the drum (Nikki Giovanni)
The Fog (Carl Sandburg)
George Washington (Rosemary and Stephen Vincent Benet)
Humanity (Elma Stuckey)
Life Doesn't Frighten Me (Maya Angelou)
Monday's Child Is Fair of Face (traditional)
Paul Revere's Ride (Henry Wadsworth Longfellow)
The Pobble Who Has No Toes (Edward Lear)
The Rhinoceros (Ogden Nash)
Things (Eloise Greenfield)
A Tragic Story (William Makepeace Thackeray)

B. TERMS
stanza and line

III. Fiction

TEACHERS: In fourth grade, children should be fluent, competent readers of appropriate materials. Decoding skills should be automatic, allowing the children to focus on meaning. Regular practice in reading aloud and independent silent reading should continue. Children should read outside of school at least 20 minutes daily.

The titles below constitute a selected core of stories for this grade. Teachers and parents are encouraged to expose children to many more stories, and to encourage children to write their own stories. Children should also be exposed to non-fiction prose: biographies, books about science and history, books on art and music, etc. Also, engage children in dramatic activities, possibly with one of the stories below in the form of a play. Some of the stories below, such as *Gulliver's Travels, Robinson Crusoe*, and the stories by Washington Irving are available in editions adapted for young readers.

See also American History 4, American Revolution, *re* stories by Washington Irving.

NOTE: "The Magic Brocade" is also known as "The Chuang Brocade," "The Enchanged Tapestry," "The Magic Tapestry," and "The Weaving of a Dream."

See also World History 4, The Middle Ages, *re* "Robin Hood" and "St. George and the Dragon."

See also World History 4, Middle Ages: Feudalism and chivalry, *re* Lengends of King Arthur.

A. STORIES

The Fire on the Mountain (an Ethiopian folktale)
from *Gulliver's Travels*: Gulliver in Lilliput and Brobdingnag (Jonathan Swift)
The Legend of Sleepy Hollow and *Rip Van Winkle* (Washington Irving)
The Magic Brocade (a Chinese folktale)
Pollyanna (Eleanor Porter)
Robinson Crusoe (Daniel Defoe)
Robin Hood
St. George and the Dragon
Treasure Island (Robert Louis Stevenson)

B. MYTHS AND MYTHICAL CHARACTERS

Legends of King Arthur and the Knights of the Round Table
 How Arthur Became King
 The Sword in the Stone
 The Sword Excalibur
 Guinevere
 Merlin and the Lady of the Lake
 Sir Lancelot

C. LITERARY TERMS

novel
plot
setting

IV. Speeches

TEACHERS: Famous passages from the following speeches should be taught in connection with topics in American History 4.

Patrick Henry: "Give me liberty or give me death"
Sojourner Truth: "Ain't I a Woman"

V. Sayings and Phrases

TEACHERS: Every culture has phrases and proverbs that make no sense when carried over literally into another culture. For many children, this section may not be needed; they will have picked up these sayings by hearing them at home and among friends. But the sayings have been one of the categories most appreciated by teachers who work with children from home cultures that differ from the standard culture of literate American English.

As the crow flies
Beauty is only skin deep.
The bigger they are, the harder they fall.
Birds of a feather flock together.
Blow hot and cold
Break the ice
Bull in a china shop
Bury the hatchet
Can't hold a candle to
Don't count your chickens before they hatch.
Don't put all your eggs in one basket.
Etc.
Go to pot
Half a loaf is better than none.
Haste makes waste.
Laugh and the world laughs with you.
Lightning never strikes twice in the same place.
Live and let live.
Make ends meet.
Make hay while the sun shines.
Money burning a hole in your pocket
An ounce of prevention is worth a pound of cure.
Once in a blue moon
One picture is worth a thousand words.
On the warpath
RSVP
Run-of-the-mill
Seeing is believing.
Shipshape
Through thick and thin
Timbuktu
Two wrongs don't make a right.
When it rains, it pours.
You can lead a horse to water, but you can't make it drink.

History and Geography: Grade 4

WORLD HISTORY AND GEOGRAPHY

I. World Geography

TEACHERS: The study of geography embraces many topics throughout the Core Knowledge Sequence, including topics in history and science. Geographic knowledge includes a spatial sense of the world, an awareness of the physical processes that shape life, a sense of the interactions between humans and their environment, an understanding of the relations between place and culture, and an awareness of the characteristics of specific regions and cultures. Many geographic topics are listed below in connection with historical topics.

A. SPATIAL SENSE (Working with Maps, Globes, and Other Geographic Tools)

TEACHERS: Review as necessary map-reading skills and concepts, as well as geographic terms, from previous grades (see Geography guidelines for grade 3).

- Measure distances using map scales.
- Read maps and globes using longitude and latitude, coordinates, degrees.
- Prime Meridian (0 degrees); Greenwich, England; 180° Line (International Date Line)
- Relief maps: elevations and depressions

See also Science 4, How Mountains Are Formed.

B. MOUNTAINS AND MOUNTAIN RANGES
- Major mountain ranges
  South America: Andes
  North America: Rockies and Appalachians
  Asia: Himalayas and Urals
  Africa: Atlas Mountains
  Europe: Alps
- High mountains of the world
  Asia: Everest
  North America: McKinley
  South America: Aconcagua
  Europe: Mont Blanc
  Africa: Kilimanjaro

II. Europe in the Middle Ages

A. BACKGROUND

NOTE: The term "Dark Ages" applies primarily to the Western Roman Empire, which was then suffering troubles and setbacks.

- Beginning about A.D. 200, nomadic, warlike tribes began moving into western Europe, attacking the western Roman Empire; city of Rome sacked by Visigoths in A.D. 410
  The Huns: Attila the Hun
- Peoples settling in old Roman Empire included Vandals (cf. English word "vandalism"), Franks in Gaul (now France), Angles (in England: cf. "Angle-land") and Saxons.
- The "Middle Ages" are generally dated from about A.D. 450 to 1400. Approximately the first three centuries after the fall of Rome (A.D. 476) are sometimes called the "Dark Ages."

B. GEOGRAPHY RELATED TO THE DEVELOPMENT OF WESTERN EUROPE
- Rivers: Danube, Rhine, Rhone, and Oder
- Mountains: Alps, Pyrenees
- Iberian Peninsula: Spain and Portugal, proximity to North Africa
- France: the region known as Normandy
- Mediterranean Sea, North Sea, Baltic Sea
- British Isles: England, Ireland, Scotland, Wales; the English Channel

See also Visual Arts 4, Art of the Middle Ages in Europe: Medieval Madonnas and Gothic architecture. And see Music 4, Gregorian chant.

C. DEVELOPMENTS IN HISTORY OF THE CHRISTIAN CHURCH
- Growing power of the pope (Bishop of Rome)
- Arguments among Christians: split into Roman Catholic Church and Eastern Orthodox Church
- Conversion of many Germanic peoples to Christianity
- Rise of monasteries, preservation of classical learning
- Charlemagne
    Temporarily unites the western Roman Empire
    Crowned Emperor by the pope in A.D. 800, the idea of a united "Holy Roman Empire"
    Charlemagne's love and encouragement of learning

D. FEUDALISM
- Life on a manor, castles
- Lords, vassals, knights, freedmen, serfs
- Code of chivalry
- Knight, squire, page

See also Language Arts 4, Legends of King Arthur.

E. THE NORMAN CONQUEST
- Locate the region called Normandy.
- William the Conqueror: Battle of Hastings, 1066

F. GROWTH OF TOWNS
- Towns as centers of commerce, guilds and apprentices
- Weakening of feudal ties

G. ENGLAND IN THE MIDDLE AGES
- Henry II
    Beginnings of trial by jury
    Murder of Thomas Becket in Canterbury Cathedral
    Eleanor of Aquitaine
- Significance of the Magna Carta, King John, 1215
- Parliament: beginnings of representative government
- The Hundred Years' War
    Joan of Arc
- The Black Death sweeps across Europe

III. The Spread of Islam and the "Holy Wars"

A. ISLAM
- Muhammad: the last prophet
- Allah, Qur'an, *jihad*
- Sacred city of Makkah, mosques
- "Five pillars" of Islam:
    Declaration of faith
    Prayer (five times daily), facing toward Makkah
    Fasting during Ramadan
    Help the needy
    Pilgrimage to Makkah
- Arab peoples unite to spread Islam in northern Africa, through the eastern Roman empire, and as far west as Spain.
- Islamic Turks conquer region around the Mediterranean; in 1453, Constantinople becomes Istanbul.
- The first Muslims were Arabs, but today diverse people around the world are Muslims.

NOTE: In older sources you may find these formerly used spellings: Mohammed, Mecca, Koran.

B. DEVELOPMENT OF ISLAMIC CIVILIZATION

See also Visual Arts 4, Islamic Art and Architecture.

- Contributions to science and mathematics: Avicenna (Ibn Sina), Arabic numerals
- Muslim scholars translate and preserve writings of Greeks and Romans
- Thriving cities as centers of Islamic art and learning, such as Cordoba (Spain)

C. WARS BETWEEN MUSLIMS AND CHRISTIANS

- The Holy Land, Jerusalem
- The Crusades
- Saladin and Richard the Lion-Hearted
- Growing trade and cultural exchange between east and west

IV. Early and Medieval African Kingdoms

A. EARLY AFRICAN KINGDOMS

See also Language Arts 4, "The Fire on the Mountain."

- Kush (in a region also called Nubia): once ruled by Egypt, then became rulers of Egypt
- Axum (also spelled Aksum): a trading kingdom in what is now Ethiopia

B. MEDIEVAL KINGDOMS OF THE SUDAN

See also Visual Arts 4: The Art of Africa.

- Trans-Sahara trade led to a succession of flourishing kingdoms: Ghana, Mali, and Songhai
  Camel caravans
  Trade in gold, iron, salt, ivory, and slaves
  The city of Timbuktu: center of trade and learning
  Spread of Islam into West Africa through merchants and travelers
  Ibn Batuta (also spelled Battutah, Batuta), world traveler and geographer
- Mali: Sundiata Keita, Mansa Musa
  - Songhai: Askia Muhammad

C. GEOGRAPHY OF AFRICA

- Mediterranean Sea and Red Sea, Atlantic and Indian Oceans
- Cape of Good Hope
- Madagascar
- Major rivers: Nile, Niger, Congo
- Atlas Mountains, Mt. Kilimanjaro
- Contrasting climate in different regions:
  Deserts: Sahara, Kalahari
  Tropical rain forests (along lower West African coast and Congo River)
  Savanna (grasslands)
  The Sahel (the fertile region below the Sahara)

V. China: Dynasties and Conquerors

- Qin Shihuangdi, first emperor, begins construction of Great Wall
- Han dynasty: trade in silk and spices, the Silk Road, invention of paper
- Tang and Song dynasties: highly developed civilization, extensive trade, important inventions (including compass, gunpowder, paper money)
- Mongol invasions and rule
  Chinggis Khan and the "Golden Horde"
  Khubilai Khan: establishes capital at what is now Beijing
  Marco Polo
- Ming dynasty
  The "Forbidden City"
  Explorations of Zheng He

NOTE: In older sources you are likely to find Chinggis Khan spelled as Genghis Khan, and Khubilai Khan spelled as Kublai Khan.

See also Visual Arts 4, The Art of China; and Language Arts 4, "The Magic Brocade."

AMERICAN HISTORY AND GEOGRAPHY

<u>TEACHERS</u>: The following guidelines are meant to complement any locally required studies of the family, community, state, or region. Note that in fifth grade the American Geography requirements include "fifty states and capitals"; teachers in grades two through four may want to introduce these incrementally to prepare for the fifth grade requirement.

I.   The American Revolution

<u>TEACHERS</u>:   In fourth grade students should undertake a detailed study of the causes, major figures, and consequences of the American Revolution, with a focus on main events and figures, as well as these questions: What caused the colonists to break away and become an independent nation? What significant ideas and values are at the heart of the American Revolution?

A.   BACKGROUND: THE FRENCH AND INDIAN WAR
- Also known as the Seven Years' War, part of an ongoing struggle between Britain and France for control of colonies in various regions around the world (in this case, in North America)
- Alliances with Native Americans
- The Battle of Quebec
- British victory gains territory but leaves Britain financially weakened.

B.   CAUSES AND PROVOCATIONS
- British taxes, "No taxation without representation"
- Boston Massacre, Crispus Attucks
- Boston Tea Party
- The Intolerable Acts close the port of Boston and require Americans to provide quarters for British troops
- First Continental Congress protests to King George III

C.   THE REVOLUTION
- Paul Revere's ride, "One if by land, two if by sea"
- Concord and Lexington
  The "shot heard 'round the world"
  Redcoats and Minute Men
- Bunker Hill
- Second Continental Congress: George Washington appointed commander in chief of Continental Army
- Thomas Paine's *Common Sense*
- Declaration of Independence
  Primarily written by Thomas Jefferson
  Adopted July 4, 1776
  "We hold these truths to be self-evident, that all men are created equal, that they are endowed by their Creator with certain unalienable Rights, that among these are Life, Liberty, and the pursuit of Happiness."
- Women in the Revolution: Elizabeth Freeman, Deborah Sampson, Phillis Wheatley, Molly Pitcher
- Loyalists (Tories)
- Victory at Saratoga, alliance with France
- European helpers (Lafayette, the French fleet, Bernardo de Galvez, Kosciusko, von Steuben)
- Valley Forge

See also Language Arts 4, stories by Washington Irving, and speech by Patrick Henry, "Give me liberty. . ."

- Benedict Arnold
- John Paul Jones: "I have not yet begun to fight."
- Nathan Hale: "I only regret that I have but one life to lose for my country."
- Cornwallis: surrender at Yorktown

II. Making a Constitutional Government

<u>Teachers:</u> Examine some of the basic values and principles of American democracy, in both theory and practice, as defined in the Declaration of Independence and the U. S. Constitution, both in historical context and in terms of present-day practice. In examining the significance of the U. S. Constitution, introduce students to the unique nature of the American experiment, the difficult task of establishing a democratic government, the compromises the framers of the Constitution were willing to make, and the persistent threats to success. In order to appreciate the boldness and fragility of the American attempt to establish a republican government based on a constitution, students should know that republican governments were rare at this time. Discuss with students basic questions and issues about government, such as: Why do societies need government? Why does a society need laws? Who makes the laws in the United States? What might happen in the absence of government and laws?

History and Geography

A. MAIN IDEAS BEHIND THE DECLARATION OF INDEPENDENCE
- The proposition that "All men are created equal"
- The responsibility of government to protect the "unalienable rights" of the people
- Natural rights: "Life, liberty, and the pursuit of happiness"
- The "right of the people ... to institute new government"

B. MAKING A NEW GOVERNMENT: FROM THE DECLARATION TO THE CONSTITUTION
- Definition of "republican" government: republican = government by elected representatives of the people
- Articles of Confederation: weak central government
- "Founding Fathers": James Madison as "Father of the Constitution"
- Constitutional Convention
    Arguments between small and large states
    The divisive issue of slavery, "three-fifths" compromise

C. THE CONSTITUTION OF THE UNITED STATES
- Preamble to the Constitution: "We the people of the United States, in order to form a more perfect union, establish justice, insure domestic tranquility, provide for the common defense, promote the general welfare, and secure the blessings of liberty to ourselves and our posterity, do ordain and establish this Constitution for the United States of America."
- The separation and sharing of powers in American government: three branches of government
    Legislative branch: Congress = House of Representatives and Senate, makes laws
    Executive branch: headed by the president, carries out laws
    Judicial branch: a court system headed by the Supreme Court (itself headed by the Chief Justice), deals with those who break laws and with disagreements about laws
- Checks and balances, limits on government power, veto
- The Bill of Rights: first ten amendments to the Constitution, including:
    Freedom of religion, speech, and the press (First Amendment)
    Protection against "unreasonable searches and seizures"
    The right to "due process of law"
    The right to trial by jury
    Protection against "cruel and unusual punishments"

<u>Note:</u> The National Standards for Civics and Government recommend that students address the issue of power vs. authority: "Where do people in government get the authority to make, apply, and enforce rules and laws and manage disputes about them?" "Identify examples of authority, e.g., the authority of teachers and administrators to make rules for schools, the authority of a crossing guard to direct traffic, the authority of the president to represent the United States in dealing with other nations." "Identify examples of power without authority, e.g., a neighborhood bully forcing younger children to give up their lunch money, a robber holding up a bank, a gang leader ordering members to injure others." Available from the Center for Civic Education, 5146 Douglas Fir Road, Calabasas, CA 91302-1467; tel. (818) 591-9321.

D. LEVELS AND FUNCTIONS OF GOVERNMENT (NATIONAL, STATE, LOCAL)
- Identify current government officials, including
    President and vice-president of the U.S.
    State governor
- State governments: established by state constitutions (which are subordinate to the U.S. Constitution, the highest law in the land), like the national government, each state government has its legislative, executive, and judicial branches
- Local governments: purposes, functions, and officials
- How government services are paid for (taxes on individuals and businesses, fees, tolls, etc.)
- How people can participate in government

III. Early Presidents and Politics

- Define: cabinet and administration
- George Washington as first President, Vice-President John Adams
- John Adams, second president, Abigail Adams
- National capitol established at Washington, D.C.
- Growth of political parties
    Arguments between Thomas Jefferson and Alexander Hamilton: two opposed visions of America, as an agricultural or industrial society
    Modern-day system: two main parties (Democrats and Republicans), and independents

See also Visual Arts 4, The Art of a New Nation, Architecture of Monticello; and Science Biographies 4, Benjamin Banneker.

- Thomas Jefferson, third president
    Correspondence between Jefferson and Benjamin Banneker
    Jefferson as multifaceted leader (architect, inventor, musician, etc.)
    The Louisiana Purchase (review from grade 1) doubles the nation's size and gains control of Mississippi River.
- James Madison, fourth president
    War of 1812 (briefly review from grade 2)
- James Monroe, fifth president, the Monroe Doctrine
- John Quincy Adams, sixth president
- Andrew Jackson, seventh president
    Popular military hero, Battle of New Orleans in War of 1812
    Presidency of "the common man"
    Indian removal policies

IV. Reformers

TEACHERS: Introduce children to some prominent people and movements in the ferment of social change in America prior to the Civil War:

- Abolitionists
- Dorothea Dix and the treatment of the insane
- Horace Mann and public schools
- Women's rights
    Seneca Falls convention
    Elizabeth Cady Stanton
    Lucretia Mott
    Amelia Bloomer
    Sojourner Truth

See also Language Arts 4, Speeches, Sojourner Truth's "Ain't I a Woman."

V. Symbols and Figures

- Recognize and become familiar with the significance of
    Spirit of '76 (painting)
    White House and Capitol Building
    Great Seal of the United States

Visual Arts: Grade 4

SEE PAGE 3, "The Arts in the Curriculum."

TEACHERS: In schools, lessons on the visual arts should illustrate important elements of making and appreciating art, and emphasize important artists, works of art, and artistic concepts. When appropriate, topics in the visual arts may be linked to topics in other disciplines. While the following guidelines specify a variety of artworks in different media and from various cultures, they are not intended to be comprehensive. Teachers are encouraged to build upon the core content and expose children to a wide range of art and artists.

In studying the works of art specified below, and in creating their own art, students should review, develop, and apply concepts introduced in previous grades, such as line, shape, form, space, texture, color, light, design, symmetry, etc.

I.   Art of the Middle Ages in Europe

TEACHERS: Study of the following works of art may be integrated with study of related topics in fourth grade World History: Europe in the Middle Ages.

- Note the generally religious nature of European art in the Middle Ages, including
  Examples of medieval Madonnas (such as *Madonna and Child on a Curved Throne*—13th century Byzantine)
  Illuminated manuscripts (such as *The Book of Kells*)
  Tapestries (such as the Unicorn tapestries)
- Become familiar with features of Gothic architecture (spires, pointed arches, flying buttresses, rose windows, gargoyles and statues) and famous cathedrals, including Notre Dame (Paris).

II. Islamic Art and Architecture

TEACHERS: Study of the following works of art may be integrated with study of related topics in fourth grade World History: The Spread of Islam.

- Become familiar with examples of Islamic art, including illuminated manuscript and illumination of the Qur'an (Koran).
- Note characteristic features of Islamic architecture, such as domes and minarets, in Dome of the Rock (Mosque of Omar), Jerusalem
  Alhambra Palace, Spain
  Taj Mahal, India

III. The Art of Africa

TEACHERS: Study of the following works of art may be integrated with study of related topics in fourth grade World History: Early and Medieval African Kingdoms.

- Note the spiritual purposes and significance of many African works of art, such as masks used in ceremonies for planting, harvesting, or hunting.
- Become familiar with examples of art from specific regions and peoples in Africa, such as
  Antelope headdresses of Mali
  Sculptures by Yoruba artists in the city of Ife
  Ivory carvings and bronze sculptures of Benin

IV. The Art of China

TEACHERS: Study of the following works of art may be integrated with study of related topics in fourth grade World History, China: Dynasties and Conquerors.

- Become familiar with examples of Chinese art, including
  Silk scrolls
  Calligraphy (the art of brush writing and painting)
  Porcelain

V. The Art of a New Nation: The United States

TEACHERS: Study of the following works of art may be integrated with study of related topics in fourth grade American History.

- Become familiar with famous portraits and paintings, including
  John Singleton Copley, *Paul Revere*
  Gilbert Stuart, *George Washington*
  Washington Crossing the Delaware
- Become familiar with the architecture of Thomas Jefferson's Monticello.

NOTE: While *Washington Crossing the Delaware* is not in origin an American work of art—it was painted by Emanuel Leutze, a German, some seventy-five years after the event it depicts—it has become widely recognized and embraced as a symbol of the American Revolution.

Music: Grade 4

SEE PAGE 3, "The Arts in the Curriculum."

TEACHERS: In schools, lessons on music should feature activities and works that illustrate important musical concepts and terms, and should introduce important composers and works. When appropriate, topics in music may be linked to topics in other disciplines.

The following guidelines focus on content, not performance skills, though many concepts are best learned through active practice (singing, clapping rhythms, playing instruments, etc.).

I. Elements of Music

- Through participation, become familiar with basic elements of music (rhythm, melody, harmony, form, timbre, etc.).

  Recognize a steady beat, accents, and the downbeat; play a steady beat and a simple rhythm pattern.

  Discriminate between fast and slow; gradually slowing down and getting faster.

  Discriminate between differences in pitch: high and low.

  Discriminate between loud and quiet; gradually increasing and decreasing volume.

  Understand *legato* (smoothly flowing progression of notes) and *staccato* (crisp, distinct notes).

  Sing unaccompanied, accompanied, and in unison.

  Recognize harmony; sing simple rounds and canons.

  Recognize verse and refrain; also, introduction and coda.

  Continue work with timbre and phrasing.

  Recognize theme and variations, and listen to Mozart, *Variations on "Ah! vous dirai-je Maman"* (familiarly known as "Twinkle Twinkle Little Star").

  Sing or play simple melodies.

- Understanding the following notation:

  names of lines and spaces in the treble clef; middle C

  𝄞 treble clef, ≡ staff, bar line, double bar line, measure, repeat signs

  ○ whole note   ♩ half note   ♩ quarter note   ♪ eighth note

  whole rest, half rest, quarter rest

  tied notes and dotted notes

  ♯ sharps   ♭ flats

  Da capo [D.C.] *al fine*

  meter signature: $\frac{4}{4}$ $\frac{2}{4}$ $\frac{3}{4}$

  quiet *pp* *mp* *p*   loud *mf* *f* *ff*

II. Listening and Understanding

TEACHERS: Expose children to a wide range of music, including children's music, popular instrumental music, and music from various cultures.

A. THE ORCHESTRA

- Review the orchestra, including families of instruments and specific instruments, by listening to Benjamin Britten, *The Young Person's Guide to the Orchestra.*

B. VOCAL RANGES

See below, Composers and Their Music: Mozart, *Magic Flute*.

TEACHERS: Students should learn to recognize and name the different vocal ranges, and apply their knowledge by beginning part singing.

Recognize vocal ranges of the female voice:
    high = soprano
    middle = mezzo soprano
    low = alto
Recognize vocal ranges of the male voice:
    high = tenor
    middle = baritone
    low = bass

C. COMPOSERS AND THEIR MUSIC

TEACHERS: Provide brief, child-friendly biographical profiles of the following composers, and listen to representative works.

NOTE: Children were introduced to Mozart and the first movement of *A Little Night Music* in first grade.

- George Frederick Handel, "Hallelujah Chorus" from *The Messiah*
- Franz Joseph Haydn, *Symphony No. 94* ("*Surprise*")
- Wolfgang Amadeus Mozart, *The Magic Flute*, selections, including:
    Overture; Introduction, "Zu Hilfe! Zu Hilfe!" (Tamino, Three Ladies); Aria, "Der Vogelfänger bin ich ja" (Papageno); Recitative and Aria, "O zittre nicht, mein lieber Sohn!" (Queen of the Night); Aria, "Ein Mädchen oder Weibchen" (Papageno); Duet, "Pa-pa-gena! Pa-pa-geno!" (Papageno and Papagena); Finale, Recitative and Chorus, "Die Strahlen der Sonne" (Sarastro and Chorus)

D. MUSICAL CONNECTIONS

See also World History 4, The Middle Ages, *re* Gregorian Chant.

TEACHERS: Introduce children to the following in connection with topics in other disciplines:

- Gregorian chant

III. Songs

Auld Lang Syne
Blow the Man Down
Cockles and Mussels
Comin' Through the Rye
I Love the Mountains (round)
Loch Lomond
My Grandfather's Clock
Taps
The Yellow Rose of Texas
Waltzing Matilda

Songs of the U.S. Armed Forces:
    Air Force Song
    Anchors Aweigh
    The Army Goes [Caissons Go] Rolling Along
    The Marine's Hymn

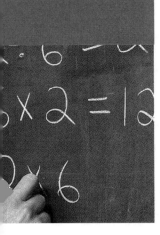

Mathematics

Mathematics: Grade 4

TEACHERS: Mathematics has its own vocabulary and patterns of thinking. It is a discipline with its own language and conventions. Thus, while some lessons may offer occasional opportunities for linking mathematics to other disciplines, it is critically important to attend to math as math. From the earliest years, mathematics requires incremental review and steady practice: not only the diligent effort required to master basic facts and operations, but also thoughtful and varied practice that approaches problems from a variety of angles, and gives children a variety of opportunities to apply the same concept or operation in different types of situations. While it is important to work toward the development of "higher-order problem-solving skills," it is equally important—indeed, it is prerequisite to achieving "higher order" skills—to have a sound grasp of basic facts, and an automatic fluency with fundamental operations.

I. Numbers and Number Sense

- Read and write numbers (in digits and words) up to nine digits.
- Recognize place value up to hundred-millions.
- Order and compare numbers to 999,999,999 using the signs <, >, and = .
- Write numbers in expanded form.
- Use a number line; locate positive and negative whole numbers on a number line.
- Round to the nearest ten; to the nearest hundred; to the nearest thousand.
- Identify perfect squares (and square roots) to 144; recognize the square root sign: $\sqrt{}$
- Identify Roman numerals from 1 to 1,000 (I - M), and identify years as written in Roman numerals.
- Create and interpret bar graphs and line graphs.
- Plot points on a coordinate plane (grid), using ordered pairs of positive whole numbers.
- Know the meanings of multiple, factor, prime number, and composite number.

II. Fractions and Decimals

A. FRACTIONS

- Recognize fractions to one-twelfth.
- Identify numerator and denominator.
- Write mixed numbers; change improper fractions to mixed numbers and vice versa.
- Recognize equivalent fractions (for example, $\frac{1}{2} = \frac{3}{6}$).
- Put fractions in lowest terms.
- Rename fractions with unlike denominators to fractions with common denominators.
- Compare fractions with like and unlike denominators, using the signs <, >, and = .
- Solve problems in the form of $\frac{2}{3} = \frac{?}{12}$.
- Add and subtract fractions with like denominators.
- Express simple outcomes as fractions (for example, 3 out of 4 as $\frac{3}{4}$).

B. DECIMALS

- Read and write decimals to the nearest thousandth.
- Read and write decimals as fractions (for example, 0.39 = 39/100).
- Write decimal equivalents for halves, quarters, eighths, and tenths.
- Compare fractions to decimals using the signs <, >, and =.
- Write decimals in expanded form.
- Round decimals to the nearest tenth; to the nearest hundredth.
- Compare decimals, using the signs <, >, and = .
- Read and write decimals on a number line.
- Add and subtract with decimal numbers to two places.

III. Money

- Solve problems involving making change in amounts up to $100.00.
- Solve multiplication and division problems with money.

IV. Computation

TEACHERS: By this grade level, children should have mastered all basic whole number operations for addition and subtraction. Review and reinforce topics from previous grades as necessary.

A. MULTIPLICATION

- Review and reinforce basic multiplication facts to 10 x 10.
- Mentally multiply by 10, 100, and 1,000.
- Identify multiples of a given number; common multiples of two given numbers.
- Multiply by two-digit and three-digit numbers.
- Write numbers in expanded form using multiplication.
- Estimate a product.
- Use mental computation strategies for multiplication, such as breaking a problem into partial products, for example: 3 x 27 = (3 x 20) + (3 x 7) = 60 + 21 = 81.
- Check multiplication by changing the order of the factors.
- Multiply three factors in any given order.
- Solve word problems involving multiplication.

B. DIVISION

- Understand multiplication and division as inverse operations.
- Review the meaning of dividend, divisor, and quotient.
- Review and reinforce basic division facts to 100 ÷ 10.
- Identify different ways of writing division problems: 28 ÷ 7   7)28   28/7
- Identify factors of a given number; common factors of two given numbers.
- Review: you cannot divide by 0; any number divided by 1 = that number.
- Estimate the quotient.
- Divide dividends up to four-digits by one-digit and two-digit divisors.
- Solve division problems with remainders.
- Check division by multiplying (and adding remainder).

C. SOLVING PROBLEMS AND EQUATIONS

- Solve two-step word problems.
- Solve equations in the form of ___ x 9 = 63; 81 ÷ ___ = 9.
- Solve problems with more than one operation, as in (72 ÷ 9) x (36 ÷ 4) = ___
- Equality properties
   Know that equals added to equals are equal.
   Know that equals multiplied by equals are equal.
- Use letters to stand for any number, as in working with a formula (for example, area of rectangle: A = L x W).

V. Measurement

- Linear measure: estimate and make linear measurements in yards, feet, and inches (to 1/8 in.); and in meters, centimeters, and millimeters.
- Weight (mass): estimate and measure weight in pounds and ounces; grams and kilograms.
- Capacity (volume): estimate and measure liquid capacity in teaspoons, tablespoons, cups, pints, quarts, gallons; and in milliliters and liters.
- Know the following equivalences among U. S. customary units of measurement, and solve problems involving changing units of measurement:

4

<u>Linear measure</u>
1 ft. = 12 in.
1 yd. = 3 ft. = 36 in.
1 mi. = 5,280 ft.
1 mi. = 1,760 yd.
<u>Weight</u>
1 lb. = 16 oz.
1 ton = 2,000 lb.
<u>Capacity (volume)</u>
1 cup = 8 fl. oz. (fluid ounces)
1 pt. = 2 c.
1 qt. = 2 pt.
1 gal. = 4 qt.
- Know the following equivalences among metric units of measurement, and solve problems involving changing units of measurement:
  <u>Linear measure</u>
  1 cm = 10 mm (millimeters)
  1 m = 1,000 mm
  1 m = 100 cm
  1 km = 1,000 m
  <u>Mass</u>
  1 cg (centigram) = 10 mg (milligrams)
  1 g = 1,000 mg
  1 g = 100 cg
  1 kg = 1,000 g
  <u>Capacity (volume)</u>
  1 cl (centiliter) = 10 ml (milliliters)
  1 liter = 1,000 ml
  1 liter = 100 cl
- Time: solve problems on elapsed time.

VI. Geometry

- Identify and draw points, segments, rays, lines.
- Identify and draw lines: horizontal; vertical; perpendicular; parallel; intersecting.
- Identify angles; identify angles as right, acute, or obtuse.
- Identify polygons:
  Triangle, quadrilateral, pentagon, hexagon, and octagon (regular)
  Parallelogram, trapezoid, rectangle, square
- Identify and draw diagonals of quadrilaterals.
- Circles: Identify radius (plural: radii) and diameter; radius = $\frac{1}{2}$ diameter
- Recognize similar and congruent figures.
- Know the formula for the area of a rectangle (Area = length x width) and solve problems involving finding area in a variety of square units (such as mi^2; yd^2; ft^2; in^2; km^2; m^2; cm^2; mm^2)
- Compute volume of rectangular prisms in cubic units (cm^3, in^3).

Science: Grade 4

TEACHERS: Effective instruction in science requires hands-on experience and observation. In the words of the 1993 report from the American Association for the Advancement of Science, Benchmarks for Science Literacy, "From their very first day in school, students should be actively engaged in learning to view the world scientifically. That means encouraging them to ask questions about nature and to seek answers, collect things, count and measure things, make qualitative observations, organize collections and observations, discuss findings, etc."

While experience counts for much, book learning is also important, for it helps bring coherence and order to a child's scientific knowledge. Only when topics are presented systematically and clearly can children make steady and secure progress in their scientific learning. The child's development of scientific knowledge and understanding is in some ways a very disorderly and complex process, different for each child. But a systematic approach to the exploration of science, one that combines experience with book learning, can help provide essential building blocks for deeper understanding at a later time.

I. The Human Body

A. THE CIRCULATORY SYSTEM
- Pioneering work of William Harvey
- Heart: four chambers (auricles and ventricles), aorta
- Blood
    Red blood cells (corpuscles), white blood cells (corpuscles), platelets, hemoglobin, plasma, antibodies
    Blood vessels: arteries, veins, capillaries
    Blood pressure, pulse
    Coagulation (clotting)
- Filtering function of liver and spleen
- Fatty deposits can clog blood vessels and cause a heart attack.
- Blood types (four basic types: A, B, AB, O) and transfusions

NOTE: The lymphatic system will be studied in grade 6.

See below, Science Biographies, Charles Drew.

B. THE RESPIRATORY SYSTEM
- Process of taking in oxygen and getting rid of carbon dioxide
- Nose, throat, voice box, trachea (windpipe)
- Lungs, bronchi, bronchial tubes, diaphragm, ribs, alveoli (air sacs)
- Smoking: damage to lung tissue, lung cancer

II. Chemistry: Basic Terms and Concepts

A. ATOMS
- All matter is made up of particles too small for the eye to see, called atoms.
- Scientists have developed models of atoms; while these models have changed over time as scientists make new discoveries, the models help us imagine what we cannot see.
- Atoms are made up of even tinier particles: protons, neutrons, electrons.
- The concept of electrical charge
    Positive charge (+): proton
    Negative charge (-): electron
    Neutral (neither positive nor negative): neutron
    "Unlike charges attract, like charges repel" (relate to magnetic attraction and repulsion)

NOTE: Children are likely to have a notion of atoms that, in absolute scientific terms, is inaccurate. There is no need to be concerned with this inaccuracy at this grade level, since the goal here is to introduce concepts and terms that, over time, will be more precisely defined and understood in greater depth.

B. PROPERTIES OF MATTER
- Mass: the amount of matter in an object, similar to weight
- Volume: the amount of space a thing fills
- Density: how much matter is packed into the space an object fills
- Vacuum: the absence of matter

C. ELEMENTS
- Elements are the basic kinds of matter, of which there are a little more than one-hundred. There are many different kinds of atoms, but an element has only one kind of atom. Familiar elements, such as gold, copper, aluminum, oxygen, iron
  Most things are made up of a combination of elements.

D. SOLUTIONS
- A solution is formed when a substance (the solute) is dissolved in another substance (the solvent), such as when sugar or salt is dissolved in water; the dissolved substance is present in the solution even though you cannot see it.
- Concentration and saturation (as demonstrated through simple experiments with crystallization)

III. Electricity

TEACHERS: Through reading, observation, and experiment, examine the following:

See above, Chemistry, *re* electrons.

NOTE: Students will study electricity in more detail in grade 8.

- Electricity as the flow of electrons
- Static electricity
- Electric current
- Electric circuits, and experiments with simple circuits (battery, wire, light bulb, filament, switch, fuse)
  Closed circuit, open circuit, short circuit
- Conductors and insulators
- Electromagnets: how they work and common uses
- Using electricity safely

IV. Geology: The Earth and Its Changes
A. THE EARTH'S LAYERS
- Crust, mantle, core (outer core and inner core)
- Movement of crustal plates
- Earthquakes
  Faults, San Andreas fault
  Measuring intensity: seismograph and Richter Scale
  Tsunamis (also called tidal waves)
- Volcanoes
  Magma
  Lava and lava flow
  Active, dormant, or extinct
  Famous volcanoes: Vesuvius, Krakatoa, Mount St. Helens
- Hot springs and geysers: Old Faithful (in Yellowstone National Park)
- Theories of how the continents and oceans were formed: Pangaea and continental drift

See also Geography 4, Major Mountain Ranges.

B. HOW MOUNTAINS ARE FORMED
- Volcanic mountains, folded mountains, fault-block mountains, dome-shaped mountains
- Undersea mountain peaks and trenches (Mariana Trench)

C. ROCKS
- Formation and characteristics of metamorphic, igneous, and sedimentary rock

D. WEATHERING AND EROSION
- Physical and chemical weathering
- Weathering and erosion by water, wind, and glaciers
- The formation of soil: topsoil, subsoil, bedrock

Science

V. Meteorology

- The water cycle (review from grade 2): evaporation, condensation, precipitation
- Clouds: cirrus, stratus, cumulus (review from grade 2)
- The atmosphere
  Troposphere, stratosphere, mesosphere, ionosphere
  How the sun and the earth heat the atmosphere
- Air movement: wind direction and speed, prevailing winds, air pressure, low and high pressure, air masses
- Cold and warm fronts: thunderheads, lightning and electric charge, thunder, tornadoes, hurricanes
- Forecasting the weather: barometers (relation between changes in atmospheric pressure and weather), weather maps, weather satellites
- Weather and climate: "weather" refers to daily changes in temperature, rainfall, sunshine, etc., while "climate" refers to weather trends that are longer than the cycle of the seasons.

VI. Science Biographies

See also American History 4, Early Presidents *re* Benjamin Banneker. See above, Circulatory System, *re* Charles Drew; and Electricity, *re* Michael Faraday.

Benjamin Banneker
Elizabeth Blackwell
Charles Drew
Michael Faraday

Grade5

Overview of Topics   Grade 5

5

Language
Arts

Language Arts: Grade 5

I. Writing, Grammar, and Usage

TEACHERS: Students should be given many opportunities for writing with teacher guidance that strikes a balance between encouraging creativity and requiring correct use of conventions. Continue imaginative writing but place a stronger emphasis than in previous grades on expository writing, including, for example, summaries, book reports, essays that explain a process, and descriptive essays. In fifth grade, it is appropriate to place a greater emphasis on revision, with the expectation that students will revise and edit to produce (in some cases) a finished product that is thoughtful, well-organized, and reasonably correct in grammar, mechanics, and spelling. In fifth grade, students should be reasonably competent spellers, and in the habit of using a dictionary to check and correct words that present difficulty. They should receive regular practice in vocabulary enrichment.

A. WRITING AND RESEARCH

- Produce a variety of types of writing—including reports, summaries, letters, descriptions, research essays, essays that explain a process, stories, poems—with a coherent structure or story line.
- Know how to gather information from different sources (such as an encyclopedia, magazines, interviews, observations, atlas, on-line), and write short reports synthesizing information from at least three different sources, presenting the information in his or her own words, with attention to the following:
    understanding the purpose and audience of the writing
    defining a main idea and sticking to it
    providing an introduction and conclusion
    organizing material in coherent paragraphs
    illustrating points with relevant examples
    documenting sources in a rudimentary bibliography

NOTE: Review from grade 4: how to use a topic sentence; how to develop a paragraph with examples and details.

B. GRAMMAR AND USAGE

- Understand what a complete sentence is, and
    identify subject and predicate
    correct fragments and run-ons
- Identify subject and verb in a sentence and understand that they must agree.
- Know the following parts of speech and how they are used: nouns, verbs (action verbs and auxiliary verbs), adjectives (including articles), adverbs, conjunctions, interjections.
- Understand that pronouns must agree with their antecedents in case (nominative, objective, possessive), number, and gender.
- Correctly use punctuation studied in earlier grades, as well as
    the colon before a list
    commas with an appositive
- Use underlining or italics for titles of books.

NOTE: Punctuation studied in earlier grades includes: end punctuation (period, question mark, or exclamation point); comma (between day and year when writing a date; between city and state in an address; in a series; after yes and no; before conjunctions that combine sentences; inside quotation marks in dialogue); apostrophe (in contractions; in singular and plural possessive nouns); and, quotation marks (in dialogue; for titles of poems, songs, short stories, magazine articles).

C. VOCABULARY

- Know how the following prefixes and suffixes affect word meaning:
    Prefixes:
        anti (as in antisocial, antibacterial)   *inter* (as in interstate)
        co (as in coeducation, co-captain)   *mid* (as in midnight, Midwest)
        fore (as in forefather, foresee)   *post* (as in postseason, postwar)
        il, ir (as in illegal, irregular)   *semi* (as in semicircle, semiprecious)
    Suffixes:
        ist (as in artist, pianist)
        ish (as in stylish, foolish)
        ness (as in forgiveness, happiness)
        tion, sion (as in relation, extension)

NOTE: A brief review of prefixes and suffixes introduced in earlier grades is recommended. Prefixes: *re, un, dis, im (in), non, mis, en, pre.* Suffixes: *er* and *or, less, ly, ily, y, ful, able, ible, ment.*

II. Poetry

TEACHERS: The poems listed here constitute a selected core of poetry for this grade. Expose children to more poetry, old and new, and have children write their own poems. To bring children into the spirit of poetry, read it aloud and encourage them to read it aloud so they can experience the music in the words. At this grade, poetry should be primarily a source of delight. This is also an appropriate grade at which to begin looking at poems in more detail, asking questions about the poet's use of language, noting the use of devices such as simile, metaphor, alliteration, etc.

A. POEMS

The Arrow And The Song (Henry Wadsworth Longfellow)
Barbara Frietchie (John Greenleaf Whittier)
Battle Hymn of the Republic (Julia Ward Howe)
A bird came down the walk (Emily Dickinson)
Casey at the Bat (Ernest Lawrence Thayer)
The Eagle (Alfred Lord Tennyson)
I Hear America Singing (Walt Whitman)
I like to see it lap the miles (Emily Dickinson)
I, too, sing America (Langston Hughes)
Incident (Countee Cullen)
Jabberwocky (Lewis Carroll)
Narcissa (Gwendolyn Brooks)
O Captain! My Captain! (Walt Whitman)
A Poison Tree (William Blake)
The Road Not Taken (Robert Frost)
The Snowstorm (Ralph Waldo Emerson)
Some Opposites (Richard Wilbur)
The Tiger (William Blake)
A Wise Old Owl (Edward Hersey Richards)

NOTE: See also below, III.D, Literary Terms: Literal and Figurative Language.

B. TERMS

onomatopoeia
alliteration

III. Fiction and Drama

TEACHERS: In fifth grade, students should be fluent, competent readers of appropriate materials. Regular independent silent reading should continue. Students should read outside of school at least 25 minutes daily.

The titles below constitute a selected core of stories for this grade. Expose children to many more stories, and encourage children to write their own stories. Children should also be exposed to non-fiction prose: biographies, books about science and history, books on art and music, etc.

Some of the works below, such as *Don Quixote, Narrative of the Life of Frederick Douglass*, or *A Midsummer Night's Dream* are available in editions adapted for young readers.

See also World History 5, The Renaissance, *re Don Quixote*.

A. STORIES

The Adventures of Tom Sawyer (Mark Twain)
episodes from *Don Quixote* (Miguel de Cervantes)
Little Women (Part First) (Louisa May Alcott)
Narrative of the Life of Frederick Douglass (Frederick Douglass)
The Secret Garden (Frances Hodgson Burnett)
Tales of Sherlock Holmes, including "The Red-Headed League" (Arthur Conan Doyle)

See also World History 5, The Renaissance, *re A Midsummer Night's Dream.*

B. DRAMA

- *A Midsummer Night's Dream* (William Shakespeare)
- Terms:
    tragedy and comedy
    act, scene
    Globe Theater

See also World History 5, Feudal Japan, *re* "A Tale of the Oki Islands."

C. MYTHS AND LEGENDS

- A Tale of the Oki Islands (a legend from Japan, also known as "The Samurai's Daughter")
- Morning Star and Scarface: the Sun Dance (a Plains Indian legend, also known as "The Legend of Scarface")
- American Indian trickster stories (for example, tales of Coyote, Raven, or Grandmother Spider)

See also American History 5, Native American Cultures, *re* "Morning Star and Scarface" and American Indian trickster stories.

D. LITERARY TERMS

- Pen name (pseudonym)
- Literal and figurative language
    imagery
    metaphor and simile
    symbol
    personification

IV. Speeches

See also American History 5, Civil War; and, Native Americans: Cultures and Conflicts.

- Abraham Lincoln: The Gettysburg Address
- Chief Joseph (Highh'moot Tooyalakekt): "I will fight no more forever"

V. Sayings and Phrases

TEACHERS: Every culture has phrases and proverbs that make no sense when carried over literally into another culture. For many children, this section may not be needed; they will have picked up these sayings by hearing them at home and among friends. But the sayings have been one of the categories most appreciated by teachers who work with children from home cultures that differ from the standard culture of literate American English.

Birthday suit
Bite the hand that feeds you.
Chip on your shoulder
Count your blessings.
Eat crow
Eleventh hour
Eureka!
Every cloud has a silver lining.
Few and far between
Forty winks
The grass is always greener on the other side of the hill.
To kill two birds with one stone
Lock, stock and barrel
Make a mountain out of a molehill
A miss is as good as a mile.

It's never too late to mend.
Out of the frying pan and into the fire.
A penny saved is a penny earned.
Read between the lines.
Sit on the fence
Steal his/her thunder
Take the bull by the horns.
Till the cows come home
Time heals all wounds.
Tom, Dick and Harry
Vice versa
A watched pot never boils.
Well begun is half done.
What will be will be.

History and Geography: Grade 5

WORLD HISTORY AND GEOGRAPHY

I. World Geography

TEACHERS: The study of geography embraces many topics throughout the Core Knowledge Sequence, including topics in history and science. Geographic knowledge includes a spatial sense of the world, an awareness of the physical processes that shape life, a sense of the interactions between humans and their environment, an understanding of the relations between place and culture, and an awareness of the characteristics of specific regions and cultures. Many geographic topics are listed below in connection with historical topics.

A. SPATIAL SENSE (Working with Maps, Globes, and Other Geographic Tools)

TEACHERS: Review as necessary map-reading skills and concepts, as well as geographic terms, from previous grades.
- Read maps and globes using longitude and latitude, coordinates, degrees.
- Tropic of Cancer and Tropic of Capricorn: relation to seasons and temperature
- Climate zones: Arctic, Tropic, Temperate
- Time zones (review from Grade 4): Prime Meridian (O degrees); Greenwich, England; 180° Line (International Date Line)
- Arctic Circle (imaginary lines and boundaries) and Antarctic Circle
- From a round globe to a flat map: Mercator projection, conic and plane projections

B. GREAT LAKES OF THE WORLD
- Eurasia: Caspian Sea
- Asia: Aral Sea
- Africa: Victoria, Tanganyika, Chad
- North America: Superior, Huron, Michigan
- South America: Maracaibo, Titicaca

See also below, II.A:
Geography of Meso-
American Civilizations; III.C:
Trade and Slavery; VI.B:
Geography of Russia; VII.B:
Geography of Japan.

II. Meso-American Civilizations

TEACHERS: Discuss with students: How do we know about these ancient civilizations? (Through archaeological findings; ancient artifacts and writings; writings by European missionaries and conquerors, etc.).

A. GEOGRAPHY
- Identify and locate Central America and South America on maps and globes.
    Largest countries in South America: Brazil and Argentina
- Amazon River
- Andes Mountains

B. MAYA, INCA, AND AZTEC CIVILIZATIONS
- The Mayas
    Ancient Mayas lived in what is now southern Mexico and parts of Central America; their descendants still live there today.
    Accomplishments as architects and artisans: pyramids and temples
    Development of a system of hieroglyphic writing
    Knowledge of astronomy and mathematics; development of a 365-day calendar; early use of concept of zero

- The Aztecs
  - A warrior culture, at its height in the 1400s and early 1500s, the Aztec empire covered much of what is now central Mexico.
  - The island city of Tenochtitlan: aqueducts, massive temples, etc.
  - Moctezuma (also spelled Montezuma)
  - Ruler-priests; practice of human sacrifice

- The Inca
  - Ruled an empire stretching along the Pacific coast of South America
  - Built great cities (Machu Picchu, Cuzco) high in the Andes, connected by a system of roads

C. SPANISH CONQUERORS
- Conquistadors: Cortés and Pizzaro
  - Advantage of Spanish weapons (guns, cannons)
  - Diseases devastate native peoples

III. European Exploration, Trade, and the Clash of Cultures

TEACHERS: It is recommended that you use timelines to place these people and events in the context of the students' previous studies (especially in grade 3) of the early exploration and settlement of North America. Fifth grade teachers should examine the third grade guidelines for American History in order to use the familiar topics as a foundation upon which to build knowledge of the new topics.

A. BACKGROUND

NOTE: Place the great wave of exploration by Europeans in the context of various peoples exploring beyond their own borders, including Islamic traders and (recall from Grade 4) Zheng He of China.

- Beginning in the 1400s Europeans set forth in a great wave of exploration and trade.
- European motivations
  - Muslims controlled many trade routes.
  - Profit through trade in goods such as gold, silver, silks, sugar, and spices
  - Spread of Christianity: missionaries, Bartolomé de las Casas speaks out against enslavement and mistreatment of native peoples
- Geography of the spice trade
  - The Moluccas, also called the "Spice Islands": part of present-day Indonesia
  - Locate: the region known as Indochina, the Malay Peninsula, the Philippines
  - Definition of "archipelago"
  - "Ring of Fire": earthquakes and volcanic activity

B. EUROPEAN EXPLORATION, TRADE, AND COLONIZATION

NOTE: Briefly review from American History 3, "Early Spanish Exploration and Settlement." Also, see above, II.C, Spanish Conquerors.

NOTE: Briefly review from American History 3, search for Northwest Passage. You may also want to introduce other explorers, such as Verrazano and Cartier.

- Portugal
  - Prince Henry the Navigator, exploration of the West African coast
  - Bartolomeu Dias rounds the Cape of Good Hope
  - Vasco da Gama: spice trade with India, exploration of East Africa
  - Portuguese conquer East African Swahili city-states
  - Cabral claims Brazil
- Spain
  - Two worlds meet: Christopher Columbus and the Tainos
  - Treaty of Tordesillas between Portugal and Spain
  - Magellan crosses the Pacific, one of his ships returns to Spain, making the first round-the-world voyage
  - Balboa reaches the Pacific
- England and France
  - Search for Northwest Passage (review from grade 3)
  - Colonies in North America and West Indies
  - Trading posts in India

- Holland (The Netherlands)
  The Dutch take over Portuguese trade routes and colonies in Africa and the East Indies
  The Dutch in South Africa, Cape Town
  The Dutch in North America: New Netherland (review from grade 3), later lost to
  England

C. TRADE AND SLAVERY
- The sugar trade
  African slaves on Portuguese sugar plantations on islands off West African coast,
  such as São Tomé
  Sugar plantations on Caribbean islands
  West Indies: Cuba, Puerto Rico, Bahamas, Dominican Republic, Haiti, Jamaica
- Transatlantic slave trade: the "triangular trade" from Europe to Africa to colonies
  in the Caribbean and the Americas
  The "Slave Coast" in West Africa
  The Middle Passage

IV. The Renaissance and the Reformation

A. THE RENAISSANCE
- Islamic scholars translate Greek works and so help preserve classical civilization.
- A "rebirth" of ideas from ancient Greece and Rome
- New trade and new wealth
- Italian city states: Venice, Florence, Rome
- Patrons of the arts and learning
  The Medici Family and Florence
  The Popes and Rome
- Leonardo da Vinci, Michelangelo
- Renaissance ideals and values as embodied in
  The Courtier by Castiglione: the "Renaissance man"
  The Prince by Machiavelli: real-world politics

See also Visual Arts 5, The Art of the Renaissance; and Language Arts 5, Shakespeare, *A Midsummer Night's Dream*; Cervantes, *Don Quixote*.

B. THE REFORMATION
- Gutenberg's printing press: the Bible made widely available
- The Protestant Reformation
  Martin Luther and the 95 Theses
  John Calvin
- The Counter-Reformation
- Copernicus and Galileo: Conflicts between science and the church
  Ptolemaic (earth-centered) vs. sun-centered models of the universe

V. England from the Golden Age to the Glorious Revolution

A. ENGLAND IN THE GOLDEN AGE
- Henry VIII and the Church of England
- Elizabeth I
- British naval dominance
  Defeat of the Spanish Armada
  Sir Francis Drake
  British exploration and North American settlements

See also Language Arts 5, Shakespeare.

B. FROM THE ENGLISH REVOLUTION TO THE GLORIOUS REVOLUTION
- The English Revolution
  - King Charles I, Puritans and Parliament
  - Civil War: Cavaliers and Roundheads
  - Execution of Charles I
  - Oliver Cromwell and the Puritan regime
  - The Restoration (1660): Charles II restored to the English throne, many Puritans leave England for America
- The "Glorious Revolution" (also called the Bloodless Revolution)
  - King James II replaced by William and Mary
  - Bill of Rights: Parliament limits the power of the monarchy

VI. Russia: Early Growth and Expansion

A. HISTORY AND CULTURE
- Russia as successor to Byzantine Empire: Moscow as new center of Eastern Orthodox Church and of Byzantine culture (after the fall of Constantinople in 1453)
- Ivan III (the Great), czar (from the Latin "Caesar")
- Ivan IV (the Terrible)
- Peter the Great: modernizing and "Westernizing" Russia
- Catherine the Great
  - Reforms of Peter and Catherine make life even harder for peasants

B. GEOGRAPHY
- Moscow and St. Petersburg
- Ural Mountains, Siberia, steppes
- Volga and Don Rivers
- Black, Caspian, and Baltic Seas
- Search for a warm-water port

VII. Feudal Japan

See also Language Arts 5, "A Tale of the Oki Islands."

NOTE: Review from grade 2: Buddhism's origins in India, spread throughout Asia.

A. HISTORY AND CULTURE
- Emperor as nominal leader, but real power in the hands of shoguns
- Samurai, code of Bushido
- Rigid class system in feudal Japanese society
- Japan closed to outsiders
- Religion
  - Buddhism: the four Noble Truths and the Eightfold Path, Nirvana
  - Shintoism: reverence for ancestors, reverence for nature, *kami*

B. GEOGRAPHY
- Pacific Ocean, Sea of Japan
- Four main islands: Hokkaido, Honshu (largest), Shikoku, Kyushu
- Tokyo
- Typhoons, earthquakes
- The Pacific Rim

AMERICAN HISTORY AND GEOGRAPHY

I. Westward Expansion

TEACHERS: Guidelines for the study of Westward Expansion are divided into two parts, with part A focusing on the decades before the Civil War, and part B focusing on the years after the Civil War. You may wish to plan a single unit on Westward Expansion, or divide your studies with a unit on the Civil War (see II below).

A. WESTWARD EXPANSION BEFORE THE CIVIL WAR
- Early exploration of the west
  - Daniel Boone, Cumberland Gap, Wilderness Trail
  - Lewis and Clark, Sacagawea
  - "Mountain men," fur trade
  - Zebulon Pike, Pike's Peak
- Pioneers
  - Getting there in wagon trains, flatboats, steamboats
  - Many pioneers set out from St. Louis (where the Missouri and Mississippi Rivers meet).
  - Land routes: Santa Fe Trail and Oregon Trail
  - Mormons (Latter-day Saints) settle in Utah, Brigham Young, Great Salt Lake
  - Gold Rush, '49ers
- Geography
  - Erie Canal connecting the Hudson River and Lake Erie
  - Rivers: James, Hudson, St. Lawrence, Mississippi, Missouri, Ohio, Columbia, Rio Grande
  - Appalachian and Rocky Mountains
  - Great Plains stretching from Canada to Mexico
  - Continental Divide and the flow of rivers: east of Rockies to the Arctic or Atlantic Oceans, west of Rockies to the Pacific Ocean
- Indian resistance
  - More and more settlers move onto Indian lands, treaties made and broken
  - Tecumseh (Shawnee): attempted to unite tribes in defending their land
  - Battle of Tippecanoe
  - Osceola, Seminole leader
- "Manifest Destiny" and conflict with Mexico
  - The meaning of "manifest destiny"
  - Early settlement of Texas: Stephen Austin
  - General Antonio Lopez de Santa Anna
  - Battle of the Alamo ("Remember the Alamo"), Davy Crockett, Jim Bowie
- The Mexican War
  - General Zachary Taylor ("Old Rough and Ready")
  - Some Americans strongly oppose the war, Henry David Thoreau's "Civil Disobedience"
  - Mexican lands ceded to the United States (California, Nevada, Utah, parts of Colorado, New Mexico, Arizona)

B. WESTWARD EXPANSION AFTER THE CIVIL WAR
- Homestead Act (1862), many thousands of Americans and immigrants start farms in the West
- "Go west, young man" (Horace Greeley's advice)
- Railroads, Transcontinental Railroad links east and west, immigrant labor
- Cowboys, cattle drives
- The "wild west," reality versus legend: Billy the Kid, Jesse James, Annie Oakley, Buffalo Bill
- "Buffalo Soldiers," African American troops in the West
- U. S. purchases Alaska from Russia, "Seward's folly"
- 1890: the closing of the American frontier (as acknowledged in the U. S. Census), the symbolic significance of the frontier

II. The Civil War: Causes, Conflicts, Consequences

A. TOWARD THE CIVIL WAR

See also Language Arts 5, *Narrative of the Life of Frederick Douglass*.

- Abolitionists: William Lloyd Garrison and *The Liberator*, Frederick Douglass
- Slave life and rebellions
- Industrial North versus agricultural South
- Mason-Dixon Line
- Controversy over whether to allow slavery in territories and new states
  Missouri Compromise of 1820
  Dred Scott decision allows slavery in the territories
- Importance of Harriet Beecher Stowe's *Uncle Tom's Cabin*
- John Brown, Harper's Ferry
- Lincoln: "A house divided against itself cannot stand."
  Lincoln-Douglas debates
  Lincoln elected president, Southern states secede

B. THE CIVIL WAR

See also Language Arts / Music 5, "The Battle Hymn of the Republic"; and Language Arts 5, Gettysburg Address.

NOTE: Those who wish to examine other battles may want to include Vicksburg (and Lincoln's famous words, "The Father of Waters again goes unvexed to the sea") and the Battle of Mobile Bay (with Admiral David Farragut's famous words, "Damn the torpedoes, full speed ahead!").

See also Language Arts 5, Walt Whitman's poem "O Captain! My Captain!" *re* the assassination of Lincoln.

- Fort Sumter
- Confederacy, Jefferson Davis
- Yankees and Rebels, Blue and Gray
- First Battle of Bull Run
- Robert E. Lee and Ulysses S. Grant
- General Stonewall Jackson
- Ironclad ships, battle of the USS *Monitor* and the CSS *Virginia* (formerly the USS *Merrimack*)
- Battle of Antietam Creek
- The Emancipation Proclamation
- Gettysburg and the Gettysburg Address
- African-American troops, Massachusetts Regiment led by Colonel Shaw
- Sherman's march to the sea, burning of Atlanta
- Lincoln re-elected, concluding words of the Second Inaugural Address ("With malice toward none, with charity for all. . . .")
- Richmond (Confederate capital) falls to Union forces
- Surrender at Appomattox
- Assassination of Lincoln by John Wilkes Booth

C. RECONSTRUCTION

- The South in ruins
- Struggle for control of the South, Radical Republicans vs. Andrew Johnson, impeachment
- Carpetbaggers and scalawags
- Freedmen's Bureau, "40 acres and a mule"
- 13th, 14th, and 15th Amendments to the Constitution
- Black Codes, the Ku Klux Klan and "vigilante justice"
- End of Reconstruction, Compromise of 1877, all federal troops removed from the South

III. Native Americans: Cultures and Conflicts

A. CULTURE AND LIFE

See also Language Arts 5, American Indian trickster myths; and, Chief Joseph, "I will fight no more forever."

- Great Basin and Plateau (for example, Shoshone, Ute, Nez Perce)
- Northern and Southern Plains (for example, Arapaho, Cheyenne, Lakota [Sioux], Shoshone, Blackfoot, Crow)
  Extermination of buffalo (review from grade 2)
- Pacific Northwest (for example, Chinook, Kwakiutl, Yakima)

B. AMERICAN GOVERNMENT POLICIES
- Bureau of Indian Affairs
- Forced removal to reservations
- Attempts to break down tribal life, assimilation policies, Carlisle School

C. CONFLICTS
- Sand Creek Massacre
- Little Big Horn: Crazy Horse, Sitting Bull, Custer's Last Stand
- Wounded Knee
  Ghost Dance

IV. U. S. Geography

- Locate: Western Hemisphere, North America, Caribbean Sea, Gulf of Mexico
- The Gulf Stream, how it affects climate
- Regions and their characteristics: New England, Mid-Atlantic, South, Midwest, Great Plains, Southwest, West, Pacific Northwest
- Fifty states and capitals

Visual Arts: Grade 5

SEE PAGE 3, "The Arts in the Curriculum."

TEACHERS: In schools, lessons on the visual arts should illustrate important elements of making and appreciating art, and emphasize important artists, works of art, and artistic concepts. When appropriate, topics in the visual arts may be linked to topics in other disciplines. While the following guidelines specify a variety of artworks in different media and from various cultures, they are not intended to be comprehensive. Teachers are encouraged to build upon the core content and expose children to a wide range of art and artists.

In studying the works of art specified below, and in creating their own art, students should review, develop, and apply concepts introduced in previous grades, such as line, shape, form, space, texture, color, light, design, and symmetry.

I. Art of the Renaissance

TEACHERS: Study of the following artists and works of art may be integrated with study of related topics in World History 5: The Renaissance.

NOTE: When you study perspective, review from grade 3 foreground, middle ground, and background; and, for contrast, examine paintings that do not attempt to create an illusion of depth, for example, *Madonna and Child on a Curved Throne* (see Visual Arts 4, Art of the Middle Ages).

- The shift in world view from medieval to Renaissance art, a new emphasis on humanity and the natural world
- The influence of Greek and Roman art on Renaissance artists (classical subject matter, idealization of human form, balance and proportion)
- The development of linear perspective during the Italian Renaissance
  The vantage point or point-of-view of the viewer
  Convergence of parallel lines toward a vanishing point, the horizon line
- Observe and discuss works in different genres—such as portrait, fresco, Madonna—by Italian Renaissance artists, including
  Sandro Botticelli, *The Birth of Venus*
  Leonardo da Vinci: *The Proportions of Man, Mona Lisa, The Last Supper*
  Michelangelo, Ceiling of the Sistine Chapel, especially the detail known as *The Creation of Adam*
  Raphael: *The Marriage of the Virgin*, examples of his Madonnas (such as *Madonna and Child with the Infant St. John, The Alba Madonna,* or *The Small Cowper Madonna*)
- Become familiar with Renaissance sculpture, including
  Donatello, *Saint George*
  Michelangelo, *David*
- Become familiar with Renaissance architecture, including
  The Florence Cathedral, dome designed by Filippo Brunelleschi
  St. Peter's in Rome
- Observe and discuss paintings of the Northern Renaissance, including
  Pieter Bruegel, *Peasant Wedding*
  Albrecht Dürer, *Self-Portrait* (such as from 1498 or 1500)
  Jan van Eyck, *Giovanni Arnolfini and His Wife* (also known as *Arnolfini Wedding*)

II. American Art: Nineteenth-Century United States

- Become familiar with the Hudson River School of landscape painting, including
  Thomas Cole, *The Oxbow* (*The Connecticut River Near Northampton*) (also known as *View from Mount Holyoke, Northampton, Massachusetts, after a Thunderstorm*)
  Albert Bierstadt, *Rocky Mountains, Lander's Peak*
- Become familiar with genre paintings, including
  George Caleb Bingham, *Fur Traders Descending the Missouri*
  William Sidney Mount, *Eel Spearing at Setauket*

See also American History 5, Civil War, *re* photographs by Brady; and African American troops in the Civil War: Shaw and the Massachusetts 54th, *re* Saint-Gaudens's *Shaw Memorial*.

See also World History 5, Feudal Japan.

- Become familiar with art related to the Civil War, including
    Civil War photography of Matthew Brady and his colleagues
    The Shaw Memorial sculpture of Augustus Saint-Gaudens
- Become familiar with popular prints by Currier and Ives.

III. Art of Japan

- Become familiar with
    The Great Buddha (also known as the Kamakura Buddha)
    Landscape gardens

Music: Grade 5

SEE PAGE 3, "The Arts in the Curriculum."

<u>TEACHERS:</u> In schools, lessons on music should feature activities and works that illustrate important musical concepts and terms, and should introduce important composers and works. When appropriate, topics in music may be linked to topics in other disciplines.

The following guidelines focus on content, not performance skills, though many concepts are best learned through active practice (singing, clapping rhythms, playing instruments, etc.).

I. Elements of Music

- Through participation, become familiar with basic elements of music (rhythm, melody, harmony, form, timbre, etc.).

  Recognize a steady beat, accents, and the downbeat; play a steady beat, a simple rhythm pattern, simultaneous rhythm patterns, and syncopation patterns.

  Discriminate between fast and slow; gradually slowing down and getting faster; *accelerando* and *ritardando*.

  Discriminate between differences in pitch: high and low.

  Discriminate between loud and quiet; gradually increasing and decreasing volume; *crescendo* and *decrescendo*.

  Understand *legato* (smoothly flowing progression of notes) and *staccato* (crisp, distinct notes).

  Sing unaccompanied, accompanied, and in unison.

  Recognize harmony; sing rounds and canons; two- and three-part singing.

  Recognize introduction, interlude, and coda in musical selections.

  Recognize verse and refrain.

  Continue work with timbre and phrasing.

  Recognize theme and variations.

  Sing or play simple melodies while reading scores.

- Understand the following notation and terms:

  names of lines and spaces in the treble clef; middle C

  𝄞 treble clef, ≡ staff, bar line, double bar line, measure, repeat signs

  ○ whole note, ♩ half note, ♩ quarter note, ♪ eighth note

  whole rest, half rest, quarter rest, eighth rest

  ♬ grouped sixteenth notes

  tied notes and dotted notes

  ♯ sharps ♭ flats

  Da capo [*D.C.*] *al fine*

  meter signature: $\frac{4}{4}$ or common time $\frac{2}{4}$ $\frac{3}{4}$ $\frac{6}{8}$

  quiet *pp* *p* *mp* loud *ff* *f* *mf*

II. Listening and Understanding

TEACHERS: Expose children to a wide range of music, including children's music, popular instrumental music, and music from various cultures.

A. COMPOSERS AND THEIR MUSIC

TEACHERS: Provide brief, child-friendly biographical profiles of the following composers, and listen to representative works:

NOTE: Children were introduced to Beethoven in grade 2.

See also below, Songs, "Greensleeves"; and see World History 5, The Renaissance.

See also Language Arts 5, Shakespeare's *A Midsummer Night's Dream.*

- Ludwig van Beethoven, *Symphony No. 5*
- Modest Mussorgsky, *Pictures at an Exhibition* (as orchestrated by Ravel)

B. MUSICAL CONNECTIONS

TEACHERS: Introduce children to the following works in connection with topics in other disciplines:

- Music from the Renaissance (such as choral works of Josquin Desprez; lute songs by John Dowland)
- Felix Mendelssohn, Overture, Scherzo, and Wedding March from *A Midsummer Night's Dream*

III. American Musical Traditions

NOTE: Spirituals introduced in earlier grades include "Swing Low Sweet Chariot," "He's Got the Whole World in His Hands," and "This Little Light of Mine."

- Spirituals
   Originated by African-Americans, many spirituals go back to the days of slavery. Familiar spirituals, such as:
   Down by the Riverside
   Sometimes I Feel Like a Motherless Child
   Wayfaring Stranger
   We Shall Overcome

IV. Songs

See also above, III. American Musical Traditions, Spirituals.

See also American History 5, Civil War, *re* "Battle Hymn of the Republic." Also, you may wish to recall songs from grade 2: "Dixie," "Follow the Drinking Gourd," and "When Johnny Comes Marching Home."

Battle Hymn of the Republic
Danny Boy
Dona Nobis Pacem (round)
Git Along Little Dogies
God Bless America
Greensleeves
The Happy Wanderer
Havah Nagilah
If I Had a Hammer
Red River Valley
Sakura
Shenandoah
Sweet Betsy from Pike

Mathematics: Grade 5

TEACHERS: Mathematics has its own vocabulary and patterns of thinking. It is a discipline with its own language and conventions. Thus, while some lessons may offer occasional opportunities for linking mathematics to other disciplines, it is critically important to attend to math as math. From the earliest years, mathematics requires incremental review and steady practice: not only the diligent effort required to master basic facts and operations, but also thoughtful and varied practice that approaches problems from a variety of angles, and gives children a variety of opportunities to apply the same concept or operation in different types of situations. While it is important to work toward the development of "higher-order problem-solving skills," it is equally important—indeed, it is prerequisite to achieving "higher order" skills—to have a sound grasp of basic facts, and an automatic fluency with fundamental operations.

I. Numbers and Number Sense

- Read and write numbers (in digits and words) up to the billions.
- Recognize place value up to billions.
- Order and compare numbers to 999,999,999 using the signs <, >, and = .
- Write numbers in expanded form.
- Integers
  Locate positive and negative integers on a number line.
  Compare integers using the symbols <, >, = .
  Know that the sum of an integer and its opposite is 0.
  Add and subtract positive and negative integers.
- Using a number line, locate positive and negative whole numbers.
- Round to the nearest ten; to the nearest hundred; to the nearest thousand; to the nearest hundred-thousand.
- Exponents
  Review perfect squares and square roots to 144; recognize the square root sign, $\sqrt{}$.
  Using the terms *squared* and *cubed* and *to the nth power*, read and evaluate numerical expressions with exponents.
  Identify the powers of ten up to 10^6.
- Identify a set and the members of a set, as indicated by { }.
- Identify numbers under 100 as prime or composite.
- Identify prime factors of numbers to 100 and write using exponential notation for multiple primes.
- Determine the greatest common factor (GCF) of given numbers.
- Determine the least common multiple (LCM) of given numbers.

II. Ratio and Percent

A. RATIO
- Determine and express simple ratios.
- Use ratio to create a simple scale drawing.
- Ratio and rate: solve problems on speed as a ratio, using the formula
  $S = D/T$ (or $D = R \times T$).

B. PERCENT
- Recognize the percent sign (%) and understand percent as "per hundred."
- Express equivalences between fractions, decimals, and percents, and know common equivalences:
  $\frac{1}{10}$ = 10%
  $\frac{1}{4}$ = 25%
  $\frac{1}{2}$ = 50%
  $\frac{3}{4}$ = 75%
- Find the given percent of a number.

III. Fractions and Decimals

A. FRACTIONS
- Determine the least common denominator (LCD) of fractions with unlike denominators.
- Recognize equivalent fractions (for example, $\frac{1}{2} = \frac{3}{6}$).
- Put fractions in lowest terms.
- Compare fractions with like and unlike denominators, using the signs <, >, and =.
- Identify the reciprocal of a given fraction; know that the product of a given number and its reciprocal = 1.
- Add and subtract mixed numbers and fractions with like and unlike denominators.
- Multiply and divide fractions.
- Add and subtract fractions with like and unlike denominators.
- Add and subtract mixed numbers and fractions; multiply mixed numbers and fractions.
- Round fractions to the nearest whole number.
- Write fractions as decimals (e.g., $\frac{1}{4} = 0.25$; $\frac{17}{25} = 0.68$; $\frac{1}{3} = 0.3333\ldots$ or 0.33, rounded to the nearest hundredth).

B. DECIMALS
- Read, write, and order decimals to the nearest ten-thousandth.
- Write decimals in expanded form.
- Read and write decimals on a number line.
- Round decimals (and decimal quotients) to the nearest tenth; to the nearest hundredth; to the nearest thousandth.
- Estimate decimal sums, differences, and products by rounding.
- Add and subtract decimals through ten-thousandths.
- Multiply decimals: by 10, 100, and 1,000; by another decimal.
- Divide decimals by whole numbers and decimals.

IV. Computation

A. ADDITION
- Commutative and associative properties: know the names and understand the properties.

B. MULTIPLICATION
- Commutative, associative, and distributive properties: know the names and understand the properties.
- Multiply two factors of up to four digits each.
- Write numbers in expanded form using multiplication.
- Estimate a product.
- Use mental computation strategies for multiplication, such as breaking a problem into partial products, for example: $3 \times 27 = (3 \times 20) + (3 \times 7) = 60 + 21 = 81$.
- Solve word problems involving multiplication.

C. DIVISION
- Understand multiplication and division as inverse operations.
- Know what it means for one number to be "divisible" by another number.
- Know that you cannot divide by 0; that any number divided by 1 = that number.
- Estimate the quotient.
- Know how to move the decimal point when dividing by 10, 100, or 1,000.
- Divide dividends up to four digits by one-digit, two-digit, and three-digit divisors.
- Solve division problems with remainders; round a repeating decimal quotient.
- Check division by multiplying (and adding remainder).

D. SOLVING PROBLEMS AND EQUATIONS
- Solve word problems with multiple steps.
- Solve problems with more than one operation.

V. Measurement

TEACHERS: Review and reinforce as necessary from grade 4 topics on linear measure, weight (mass), and capacity (volume). Also review various equivalences, which students should be able to recall from memory.

- Convert to common units in problems involving addition and subtraction of different units.
- Time: Solve problems on elapsed time; regroup when multiplying and dividing amounts of time.

VI. Geometry

- Identify and draw points, segments, rays, lines.
- Identify and draw lines: horizontal; vertical; perpendicular; parallel; intersecting.
- Measure the degrees in angles, and know that
  right angle = 90°   acute angle: less than 90°
  obtuse angle: greater than 90°   straight angle = 180°
- Identify and construct different kinds of triangles: equilateral, right, and isosceles.
- Know what it means for triangles to be congruent.
- Identify polygons:
  triangle, quadrilateral, pentagon, hexagon, and octagon
  parallelogram, trapezoid, rhombus, rectangle, square
- Know that regular polygons have sides of equal length and angles of equal measure.
- Identify and draw diagonals of polygons.
- Circles
  Identify arc, chord, radius (plural: radii), and diameter (radius = $\frac{1}{2}$ diameter).
  Using a compass, draw circles with a given diameter or radius.
  Find the circumference of a circle using the formulas C = πd, and C = 2 πr,
      using 3.14 as the value of *pi*.
- Area
  Review the formula for the area of a rectangle (Area = length x width) and solve
      problems involving finding area in a variety of square units (such as mi²; yd²;
      ft²; in²; km²; m²; cm²; mm²).
  Find the area of triangles, using the formula A = $\frac{1}{2}$(b x h).
  Find the area of a parallelogram using the formula A = b x h.
  Find the area of an irregular figure (such as a trapezoid) by dividing into regular figures
      for which you know how to find the area.
  Find the surface area of a rectangular prism.
- Compute volume of rectangular prisms in cubic units (cm³, in³), using the formula
  V = l x w x h.

VII. Probability and Statistics

- Understand probability as a measure of the likelihood that an event will happen; using
    simple models, express probability of a given event as a fraction, as a percent, and as a
    decimal between 0 and 1.
- Collect and organize data in graphic form (bar, line, and circle graphs).
- Solve problems requiring interpretation and application of graphically displayed data.
- Find the average (mean) of a given set of numbers.
- Plot points on a coordinate plane, using ordered pairs of positive and
    negative whole numbers.
- Graph simple functions.

VIII. Pre-Algebra

- Recognize variables and solve basic equations using variables.
- Write and solve equations for word problems.
- Find the value of an expression given the replacement values for the variables,
    for example: What is *7 - c* if *c* is 3.5?

125

Science: Grade 5

TEACHERS: Effective instruction in science requires hands-on experience and observation. In the words of the 1993 report from the American Association for the Advancement of Science, Benchmarks for Science Literacy, "From their very first day in school, students should be actively engaged in learning to view the world scientifically. That means encouraging them to ask questions about nature and to seek answers, collect things, count and measure things, make qualitative observations, organize collections and observations, discuss findings, etc."

While experience counts for much, book learning is also important, for it helps bring coherence and order to a child's scientific knowledge. Only when topics are presented systematically and clearly can children make steady and secure progress in their scientific learning. The child's development of scientific knowledge and understanding is in some ways a very disorderly and complex process, different for each child. But a systematic approach to the exploration of science, one that combines experience with book learning, can help provide essential building blocks for deeper understanding at a later time.

I. Classifying Living Things

TEACHERS: As the children study animal classification, discuss: Why do we classify? How does classification help us understand the natural world?

NOTE: A useful mnemonic device is "King Philip Came Over For Good Spaghetti."

- Scientists have divided living things into five large groups called kingdoms, as follows:
  Plant
  Animal
  Fungus (mushrooms, yeast, mold, mildew)
  Protist (algae, protozoans, amoeba, euglena)
  Moneran (bacteria, blue-green algae)
- Each kingdom is divided into smaller groupings as follows:
  Kingdom
    Phylum
      Class
        Order
          Family
            Genus
              Species
                (Variety)
- When classifying living things, scientists use special names made up of Latin words (or words made to sound like Latin words), which help scientists around the world understand each other and ensure that they are using the same names for the same living things.
  Homo sapiens: the scientific name for the species to which human beings belong (genus *Homo*, species *sapiens*)
  Taxonomists: biologists who specialize in classification
- Different classes of vertebrates and major characteristics: fish, amphibians, reptiles, birds, mammals (review from grade 3)

TEACHERS: Introduce an example of how an animal is classified, in order for students to become familiar with the system of classification, not to memorize specific names. For example, a collie dog is classified as follows:
Kingdom: Animalia
Phylum: Chordata (Subphylum: Vertebrata)
Class: Mammalia (mammal)
Order: Carnivora (eats meat)
Family: Canidae (a group with doglike characteristics)
Genus: Canis (a coyote, wolf, or dog)
Species: familiaris (a domestic dog)
Variety: Collie

II. Cells: Structures and Processes

NOTE: Students will study cell division in more detail, including the processes of mitosis and meiosis, in grade 7.

See below, III. B, Photosynthesis *re* plant cells.

- All living things are made up of cells.
- Structure of cells (both plant and animal)
  - Cell membrane: selectively allows substances in and out
  - Nucleus: surrounded by nuclear membrane, contains genetic material, divides for reproduction
  - Cytoplasm contains organelles, small structures that carry out the chemical activities of the cell, including mitochondria (which produce the cell's energy) and vacuoles (which store food, water, or wastes).
- Plant cells, unlike animal cells, have cell walls and chloroplasts.
- Cells without nuclei: monerans (bacteria)
- Some organisms consist of only a single cell: for example, amoeba, protozoans, some algae.
- Cells are shaped differently in order to perform different functions.
- Organization of cells into tissues, organs, and systems:
  - In complex organisms, groups of cells form tissues (for example, in animals, skin tissue or muscle tissue; in plants, the skin of an onion or the bark of a tree).
  - Tissues with similar functions form organs (for example, in some animals, the heart, stomach, or brain; in some plants, the root or flower).
  - In complex organisms, organs work together in a system (recall, for example, from earlier studies of the human body, the digestive, circulatory, and respiratory systems).

III. Plant Structures and Processes

A. STRUCTURE: NON-VASCULAR AND VASCULAR PLANTS
- Non-vascular plants (for example, algae)
- Vascular plants
  - Vascular plants have tubelike structures that allow water and dissolved nutrients to move through the plant.
  - Parts and functions of vascular plants: roots, stems and buds, leaves

B. PHOTOSYNTHESIS
- Photosynthesis is an important life process that occurs in plant cells, but not animal cells (photo = light; synthesis = putting together). Unlike animals, plants make their own food, through the process of photosynthesis.
- Role in photosynthesis of: energy from sunlight, chlorophyll, carbon dioxide and water, xylem and phloem, stomata, oxygen, sugar (glucose)

C. REPRODUCTION
- Asexual reproduction
  - Example of algae
  - Vegetative reproduction: runners (for example, strawberries) and bulbs (for example, onions), growing plants from eyes, buds, leaves, roots, and stems
- Sexual reproduction by spore-bearing plants (for example, mosses and ferns)
- Sexual reproduction of non-flowering seed plants: conifers (for example, pines), male and female cones, wind pollination
- Sexual reproduction of flowering plants (for example, peas)
  - Functions of sepals and petals, stamen (male), anther, pistil (female), ovary (or ovule)
  - Process of seed and fruit production: pollen, wind, insect and bird pollination, fertilization, growth of ovary, mature fruit
  - Seed germination and plant growth: seed coat, embryo and endosperm, germination (sprouting of new plant), monocots (for example, corn) and dicots (for example, beans)

See below, IV. Life Cycles and Reproduction: asexual and sexual reproduction.

Science

IV. Life Cycles and Reproduction

A. THE LIFE CYCLE AND REPRODUCTION

- Life cycle: development of an organism from birth to growth, reproduction, death
    Example: Growth stages of a human: embryo, fetus, newborn, infancy, childhood, adolescence, adulthood, old age
- All living things reproduce themselves. Reproduction may be asexual or sexual.
    Examples of asexual reproduction: fission (splitting) of bacteria, spores from mildews, molds, and mushrooms, budding of yeast cells, regeneration and cloning
    Sexual reproduction requires the joining of special male and female cells, called gametes, to form a fertilized egg.

B. SEXUAL REPRODUCTION IN ANIMALS

- Reproductive organs: testes (sperm) and ovaries (eggs)
- External fertilization: spawning
- Internal fertilization: birds, mammals
- Development of the embryo: egg, zygote, embryo, growth in uterus, fetus, newborn

V. The Human Body

A. CHANGES IN HUMAN ADOLESCENCE

- Puberty
    Glands and hormones (see below, Endocrine System), growth spurt, hair growth, breasts, voice change

B. THE ENDOCRINE SYSTEM

- The human body has two types of glands: duct glands (such as the salivary glands), and ductless glands, also known as endocrine glands.
- Endocrine glands secrete (give off) chemicals called hormones. Different hormones control different body processes.
- Pituitary gland: located at the bottom of the brain, secretes hormones that control other glands, and hormones that regulate growth
- Thyroid gland: located below the voice box, secretes a hormone that controls the rate at which the body burns and uses food
- Pancreas: both a duct and ductless gland, secretes a hormone called insulin that regulates how the body uses and stores sugar, when the pancreas does not produce enough insulin, a person has a sickness called diabetes (which can be controlled)
- Adrenal glands: secrete a hormone called adrenaline, especially when a person is frightened or angry, causing rapid heartbeat and breathing

C. THE REPRODUCTIVE SYSTEM

- Females: ovaries, fallopian tubes, uterus, vagina, menstruation
- Males: testes, scrotum, penis, urethra, semen
- Sexual reproduction: intercourse, fertilization, zygote, implantation of zygote in the uterus, pregnancy, embryo, fetus, newborn

NOTE: There is some flexibility in the grade-level placement of the study of topics relating to human reproduction, as different schools and districts have differing local requirements, typically introducing these topics in either fifth or sixth grade.

VI. Chemistry: Matter and Change

A. ATOMS, MOLECULES, AND COMPOUNDS

- Basics of atomic structure: nucleus, protons (positive charge), neutrons (neutral), electrons (negative charge)
- Atoms are constantly in motion, electrons move around the nucleus in paths called shells (or energy levels).
- Atoms may join together to form molecules and compounds.
- Common compounds and their formulas:
  water H_2O
  salt NaCl
  carbon dioxide CO_2

B. ELEMENTS

NOTE: Students will examine the relation between the periodic table and atomic structure in more detail in grade 7.

- Elements have atoms of only one kind, having the same number of protons. There are a little more than 100 different elements.
- The Periodic Table: organizes elements with common properties
  Atomic symbol and atomic number
- Some well-known elements and their symbols:

Hydrogen	H
Helium	He
Carbon	C
Nitrogen	N
Oxygen	O
Sodium	Na
Aluminum	Al
Silicon	Si
Chlorine	Cl
Iron	Fe
Copper	Cu
Silver	Ag
Gold	Au

- Two important categories of elements: metals and non-metals
  Metals comprise about $\frac{2}{3}$ of the known elements.
  Properties of metals: most are shiny, ductile, malleable, conductive

C. CHEMICAL AND PHYSICAL CHANGE

NOTE: Qualitative description and investigation of chemical change is sufficient at this grade level.

- Chemical change changes what a molecule is made up of and results in a new substance with a new molecular structure. Examples of chemical change: rusting of iron, burning of wood, milk turning sour
- Physical change changes only the properties or appearance of the substance, but does not change what the substance is made up of. Examples of physical change: cutting wood or paper, breaking glass, freezing water

VII. Science Biographies

See also World History 5, The Renaissance, *re* Galileo. See above, Classifying Living Things, *re* Linnaeus; Cells, *re* Ernest Just; Human Body—Endocrine System (Hormones), *re* Percy Lavon Julian.

Galileo
Percy Lavon Julian
Ernest Just
Carl Linnaeus

Science

Grade6

Overview of Topics   Grade 6

English
I. Writing, Grammar, and Usage
   A. Writing and Research
   · B. Speaking and Listening
   C. Grammar and Usage
   D. Spelling
   E. Vocabulary
II. Poetry
   A. Poems
   B. Terms
III. Fiction and Drama
   A. Stories
   B. Drama
   C. Classical Mythology
   D. Literary Terms
IV. Sayings and Phrases

History and Geography
World:
I. World Geography
   A. Spatial Sense
   B. Great Deserts of the World
II. Lasting Ideas from Ancient Civilizations
   A. Judaism and Christianity
   B. Ancient Greece
   C. Ancient Rome
III. The Enlightenment
IV. The French Revolution
V. Romanticism
VI. Industrialism, Capitalism, and Socialism
   A. The Industrial Revolution
   B. Capitalism
   C. Socialism
VII. Latin American Independence Movements
   A. History
   B. Geography of Latin America

American:
I. Immigration, Industrialization, and Urbanization
   A. Immigration
   B. Industrialization and Urbanization
II. Reform

Visual Arts
I. Art History: Periods and Schools
   A. Classical Art: The Art of Ancient Greece and Rome
   B. Gothic Art
   C. The Renaissance
   D. Baroque
   E. Rococo
   F. Neoclassical
   G. Romantic
   H. Realism

Music
I. Elements of Music
II. Classical Music: From Baroque to Romantic
   A. Baroque
   B. Classical
   C. Romantic

Mathematics
I. Numbers and Number Sense
II. Ratio, Percent, and Proportion
   A. Ratio and Proportion
   B. Percent
III. Computation
   A. Addition
   B. Multiplication
   C. Division
   D. Solving Problems and Equations
IV. Measurement
V. Geometry
VI. Probability and Statistics
VII. Pre-Algebra

Science
I. Plate Tectonics
II. Oceans
III. Astronomy: Gravity, Stars, and Galaxies
IV. Energy, Heat, and Energy Transfer
   A. Energy
   B. Heat
   C. Physical Change: Energy Transfer
V. The Human Body: Lymphatic and Immune Systems
VI. Science Biographies

English: Grade 6

I. Writing, Grammar, and Usage

<u>TEACHERS:</u> Students should be given many opportunities for writing, both imaginative and expository, with teacher guidance that strikes a balance between encouraging creativity and requiring correct use of conventions. In sixth grade, it is appropriate to emphasize revision, with the expectation that students will revise and edit to produce (in some cases) a finished product that is thoughtful, well-organized, and reasonably correct in grammar, mechanics, and spelling. Continue imaginative writing but place a stronger emphasis than in previous grades on expository writing, including, for example, summaries, book reports, essays that explain a process, and descriptive essays. Note also the requirement below for writing persuasive essays, a research essay, and a standard business letter.

A. WRITING AND RESEARCH
- Learn strategies and conventions for writing a persuasive essay, with attention to
  - defining a thesis (that is, a central proposition, a main idea)
  - supporting the thesis with evidence, examples, and reasoning
  - distinguishing evidence from opinion
  - anticipating and answering counter-arguments
  - maintaining a reasonable tone
- Write a research essay, with attention to
  - asking open-ended questions
  - gathering relevant data through library and field research
  - summarizing, paraphrasing, and quoting accurately when taking notes
  - defining a thesis
  - organizing with an outline
  - integrating quotations from sources
  - acknowledging sources and avoiding plagiarism
  - preparing a bibliography
- Write a standard business letter.

B. SPEAKING AND LISTENING
- Participate civilly and productively in group discussions.
- Give a short speech to the class that is well-organized and well-supported.
- Demonstrate an ability to use standard pronunciation when speaking to large groups and in formal circumstances, such as a job interview.

C. GRAMMAR AND USAGE
- Understand what a complete sentence is, and
  - identify subject and predicate
  - identify independent and dependent clauses
  - correct fragments and run-ons
- Identify different sentence types, and write for variety by using
  - simple sentences
  - compound sentences
  - complex sentences
  - compound-complex sentences
- Correctly use punctuation introduced in earlier grades, and learn how to use a semi-colon or comma with *and, but,* or *or* to separate the sentences that form a compound sentence.
- Recognize verbs in active voice and passive voice, and avoid unnecessary use of passive voice.

- Recognize the following troublesome verbs and how to use them correctly:
  - sit, set
  - rise, raise
  - lie, lay
- Correctly use the following:
  - good / well
  - between / among
  - bring / take
  - accept / except
  - fewer / less
  - like / as
  - affect / effect
  - who / whom
  - imply / infer
  - principle / principal
  - their / there / they're

D. SPELLING

NOTE: More commonly misspelled words listed in grades 7 and 8.

- Review spelling rules for use of *ie* and *ei;* for adding prefixes and suffixes
- Continue work with spelling, with special attention to commonly misspelled words, including:

acquaintance	develop	naturally	separate
amateur	embarrassed	occurrence	similar
analyze	exaggerate	parallel	sophomore
answer	exercise	peasant	substitute
athlete	fulfill	philosopher	success
Britain	gymnasium	possess	suspicion
characteristic	hypocrite	privilege	tragedy
committee	innocence	receipt	woman
conscious	interrupt	recommendation	writing
cooperate	license	repetition	
criticize	marriage	restaurant	
dependent	minimum	rhythm	

E. VOCABULARY

TEACHERS: **Students should know the meaning of these Latin and Greek words that form common word roots and be able to give examples of English words that are based on them.**

NOTE: More Latin and Greek words and roots are listed in grades 7 and 8. In the listings here, L = Latin, G = Greek. No single form of the Latin or Greek words is consistently used here, but rather the form most similar to related English words.

Latin/Greek Word	Meaning	Examples
annus [L]	year	annual, anniversary
ante [L]	before	antebellum, antecedent
aqua [L]	water	aquarium
astron [G]	star	astronaut, astronomy
bi [L]	two	bisect, bipartisan
bios [G]	life	biology, biography
centum [L]	hundred	cent, percent
decem [L]	ten	decade, decimal
dico, dictum [L]	say, thing said	dictation, dictionary
duo [G, L]	two	duplicate
ge [G]	earth	geology, geography
hydor [G]	water	hydrant, hydroelecrtric
magnus [L]	large, great	magnificent, magnify
mega [G]	large, great	megaphone, megalomania
mikros [G]	small	microscope, microfilm
minus [L]	smaller	diminish, minor
monos [G]	single	monologue, monarch, monopoly

omnis [L]	all	omnipotent, omniscient
phileo [G]	to love	philosophy, philanthropist
phone [G]	sound, voice	phonograph, telephone
photo [from G *phos*]	light	photograph, photocopy
poly [G]	many	polygon
post [L]	after	posthumous, posterity
pre [L]	before	predict, prepare
primus [L]	first	primary, primitive
protos [G]	first	prototype, protozoa
psyche[G]	soul, mind	psychology
quartus [L]	fourth	quadrant, quarter
tele [G]	at a distance	telephone, television, telepathy
thermos [G]	heat	thermometer, thermostat
tri [G, L]	three	trilogy, triangle
unus [L]	one	unanimous, unilateral
video, visum [L]	see, seen	evident, visual
vita [L]	life	vitality, vitamin

II. Poetry

A. POEMS

TEACHERS: The poems listed here constitute a selected core of poetry for this grade. You are encouraged to expose students to more poetry, old and new, and to have students write their own poems. To bring students into the spirit of poetry, read it aloud and encourage them to read it aloud so they can experience the music in the words. At this grade, poetry should be a source of delight, and, upon occasion, the subject of close attention. Students should examine some poems in detail, discussing what the poems mean as well as asking questions about the poet's use of language.

See also World History 6, Romanticism, *re* "Apostrophe to the Ocean" and "I Wandered Lonely as a Cloud."

All the world's a stage [from *As You Like It*]   (William Shakespeare)
Apostrophe to the Ocean [from *Childe Harold's Pilgrimage*, Canto 4,
     Nos. 178-184]   (George Gordon Byron)
I Wandered Lonely as a Cloud (William Wordsworth)
If (Rudyard Kipling)
Mother to Son (Langston Hughes)
Lift Ev'ry Voice and Sing (James Weldon Johnson)
A narrow fellow in the grass (Emily Dickinson)
A Psalm of Life (Henry Wadsworth Longfellow)
The Raven (Edgar Allan Poe)
A Song of Greatness (a Chippewa song, trans. Mary Austin)
Stopping by Woods on a Snowy Evening (Robert Frost)
Sympathy (Paul Laurence Dunbar)
There is no frigate like a book (Emily Dickinson)
The Walloping Window-blind (Charles E. Carryl)
Woman Work (Maya Angelou)

B. TERMS

meter
iamb
couplet
rhyme scheme
free verse

III. Fiction and Drama

TEACHERS: *The Iliad, The Odyssey,* and *Julius Caesar* are available in editions adapted for young readers.

See also World History 6, Ancient Greece, re The Iliad and The Odyssey.

See also World History 6, Ancient Rome, re Julius Caesar.

See also World History 6, Ancient Greece and Rome. Students who are not familiar with classical myths specified in grades 2 and 3 of the Core Knowledge Sequence should read those selections as well.

A. STORIES
The Iliad and *The Odyssey* (Homer)
The Prince and the Pauper (Mark Twain)

B. DRAMA
Julius Caesar (William Shakespeare)

C. CLASSICAL MYTHOLOGY
Apollo and Daphne
Orpheus and Eurydice
Narcissus and Echo
Pygmalion and Galatea

D. LITERARY TERMS
- Epic
- Literal and figurative language (review from grade 5)
    imagery
    metaphor and simile
    symbol
    personification

IV. Sayings and Phrases

TEACHERS: Every culture has phrases and proverbs that make no sense when carried over literally into another culture. For many children, this section may not be needed; they will have picked up these sayings by hearing them at home and among friends. But the sayings have been one of the categories most appreciated by teachers who work with children from home cultures that differ from the standard culture of literate American English.

All for one and one for all.
All's well that ends well.
Bee in your bonnet
The best-laid plans of mice and men oft go awry.
A bird in the hand is worth two in the bush.
Bite the dust
Catch-as-catch-can
Don't cut off your nose to spite your face.
Don't lock the stable door after the horse is stolen.
Don't look a gift horse in the mouth.
Eat humble pie
A fool and his money are soon parted.
A friend in need is a friend indeed.
Give the devil his due.
Good fences make good neighbors.
He who hesitates is lost.
He who laughs last laughs best.
Hitch your wagon to a star.
If wishes were horses, beggars would ride.
The leopard doesn't change his spots.
Little strokes fell great oaks.
Money is the root of all evil.
Necessity is the mother of invention.

It's never over till it's over.
Nose out of joint
Nothing will come of nothing.
Once bitten, twice shy.
On tenterhooks
Pot calling the kettle black
Procrastination is the thief of time.
The proof of the pudding is in the eating.
RIP
The road to hell is paved with good intentions.
Rome wasn't built in a day.
Rule of thumb
A stitch in time saves nine.
Strike while the iron is hot.
Tempest in a teapot
Tenderfoot
There's more than one way to skin a cat.
Touché!
Truth is stranger than fiction.

History and Geography: Grade 6

TEACHERS: The World History guidelines for sixth grade begin with a study of ancient civilizations introduced in earlier grades in the Core Knowledge Sequence. Topics include Judaism, Christianity, and the civilizations of ancient Greece and Rome. The focus in sixth grade should be on the legacy of enduring ideas from these civilizations—ideas about democracy and government, for example, or about right and wrong. After this study of lasting ideas from ancient civilizations, the World History guidelines pick up the chronological thread from earlier grades with a study of the Enlightenment. You are encouraged to use timelines and engage students in a brief review of some major intervening events in order to help students make a smooth transition across the gap in centuries between the ancient civilizations and the Enlightenment.

In sixth grade, the World History guidelines catch up chronologically with the American History guidelines. The World History guidelines take students up to the consequences of industrialization in the mid-nineteenth century, and this is where the American History guidelines begin.

WORLD HISTORY AND GEOGRAPHY

I.   World Geography

TEACHERS: By sixth grade, children should have a good working knowledge of map-reading skills, as well as geographic terms and features introduced in earlier grades. The study of geography embraces many topics throughout the Core Knowledge Sequence, including topics in history and science. Geographic knowledge includes a spatial sense of the world, an awareness of the physical processes that shape life, a sense of the interactions between humans and their environment, an understanding of the relations between place and culture, and an awareness of the characteristics of specific regions and cultures. Many geographic topics are listed below in connection with historical topics.

A.   SPATIAL SENSE (Working with Maps, Globes, and Other Geographic Tools)
TEACHERS: As necessary, review and reinforce topics from earlier grades, including:

- Continents and major oceans
- How to read maps and globes using longitude and latitude, coordinates, degrees
- Tropic of Cancer and Tropic of Capricorn: relation to seasons and temperature
- Climate zones: Arctic, Tropic, Temperate
- Time zones (review from Grade 4): Prime Meridian (O degrees); Greenwich, England; 180° Line (International Date Line)
- Arctic Circle (imaginary lines and boundaries) and Antarctic Circle

B.   GREAT DESERTS OF THE WORLD
- What is a desert? Hot and cold deserts
- Major deserts in
   Africa: Sahara, Kalahari
   Australia: a mostly desert continent
   Asia: Gobi; much of Arabian Peninsula
   North America: Mojave, Chihuahuan, Sonoran
   South America: Patagonia

NOTE: In earlier grades, children were introduced to major rivers (see Geography 3), mountains (see Geography 4), and lakes (see Geography 5) of the world.

II. Lasting Ideas from Ancient Civilizations

A. JUDAISM AND CHRISTIANITY

TEACHERS: Since religion is a shaping force in the story of civilization, the Core Knowledge Sequence introduces children in the early grades to major world religions, beginning with a focus on geography and major symbols and figures. Here in the sixth grade the focus is on history, geography, and ideas. The purpose is not to explore matters of theology but to understand the place of religion and religious ideas in history. The goal is to familiarize, not proselytize; to be descriptive, not prescriptive. The tone should be one of respect and balance: no religion should be disparaged by implying that it is a thing of the past.

A review of major religions introduced in earlier grades in the Core Knowledge Sequence is recommended: Hinduism (grade 2), Islam (grade 4), and Buddhism and Shintoism (grade 5).

NOTE: Students will examine the political and physical geography of the modern-day Middle East in grade 8.

- Basic ideas in common
    - The nature of God and of humanity
    - Hebrew Bible and Old Testament of Christian Bible
- Judaism: central ideas and moral teachings
    - Torah, monotheism
    - The idea of a "covenant" between God and man
    - Concepts of law, justice, and social responsibility: the Ten Commandments
- Christianity: central ideas and moral teachings
    - New Testament
    - The Sermon on the Mount and the two "great commandments" (Matthew 22: 37-40)
- Geography of the Middle East
    - Birthplace of major world religions: Judaism, Christianity, Islam
    - Anatolian Peninsula, Arabian Peninsula
    - Mesopotamia, Tigris and Euphrates Rivers
    - Atlas Mountains, Taurus Mountains
    - Mediterranean Sea, Red Sea, Black Sea, Arabian Sea, Persian Gulf
    - The "silk road"
    - Climate and terrain: vast deserts (Sahara, Arabian)

See also English 6, Homer, *The Iliad* and *The Odyssey* and Classical Mythology.

B. ANCIENT GREECE

TEACHERS: Briefly review from grade 2: religion, art, architecture, daily life of ancient Greece.

- The Greek polis (city-state) and patriotism
- Beginnings of democratic government: Modern American democratic government has its roots in Athenian democracy (despite the obvious limitations on democracy in ancient Greece, for example, slavery, vote denied to women)
    - The Assembly
    - Suffrage, majority vote
- The "classical" ideal of human life and works
    - The ideal of the well-rounded individual and worthy citizen
    - Pericles and the "Golden Age"
    - Architecture: the Parthenon
    - Games: The Olympics
- Greek wars: victory and hubris, defeat and shame
    - Persian Wars: Marathon, Thermopylae, Salamis
    - The Peloponnesian War: Sparta defeats Athens
- Socrates and Plato
    - Socrates was Plato's teacher; we know of him through Plato's writings.
    - For Socrates, wisdom is knowing that you do not know.
    - The trial of Socrates

See also Visual Arts 6, Raphael's *School of Athens*. You may also want to examine David's *Death of Socrates*.

6

- Plato and Aristotle
  Plato was Aristotle's teacher.
  They agreed that reason and philosophy should rule our lives, not emotion
    and rhetoric.
  They disagreed about where true "reality" is: Plato says it is beyond physical things in
    ideas (cf. the "allegory of the cave"); Aristotle says reality is only in physical things.
- Alexander the Great and the spread of Greek ("Hellenistic") culture: the library
    at Alexandria

C. ANCIENT ROME

TEACHERS: Briefly review from grade 3: Romulus and Remus, Roman gods, legends, daily life, etc.

- The Roman Republic
  Builds upon Greek and classical ideals
  Class and status: patricians and plebeians, slaves
  Roman government: consuls, tribunes, and senators
- The Punic Wars: Rome vs. Carthage
- Julius Caesar
- Augustus Caesar
  Pax Romana
  Roman law and the administration of a vast, diverse empire
  Virgil, *The Aeneid*: epic on the legendary origins of Rome
- Christianity under the Roman Empire
  Jesus's instruction to "Render unto Caesar the things which are Caesar's, and unto God
    the things that are God's" [Matthew 22:21]
  Roman persecution of Christians
  Constantine: first Christian Roman emperor
- The "decline and fall" of the Roman Empire
  Causes debated by historians for many hundreds of years (outer forces such as
    shrinking trade, attacks and invasions vs. inner forces such as disease, jobless
    masses, taxes, corruption and violence, rival religions and ethnic groups,
    weak emperors)
  Rome's "decline and fall" perceived as an "object lesson" for later generations
    and societies

*See also English 6,
Shakespeare's Julius Caesar.*

III. The Enlightenment

TEACHERS: You are encouraged to use timelines and engage students in a brief review of some major
intervening events in order to help students make a smooth transition across the gap in centuries
between the ancient civilizations and the Enlightenment. Place the Enlightenment (17th and 18th
centuries) in chronological context, in relation to eras and movements studied in earlier grades (Middle
Ages, Age of Exploration & Renaissance, American Revolution, etc.).

*See also Science 6, Science
Biographies: Isaac Newton.*

- Faith in science and human reason, as exemplified by
  Isaac Newton and the laws of nature
  Descartes: "cogito ergo sum"
- Two ideas of "human nature": Thomas Hobbes and John Locke
  Hobbes: the need for a strong governing authority as a check on "the condition of
    man . . . [which] is a condition of war of everyone against everyone"
  Locke: the idea of man as a "tabula rasa" and the optimistic belief in education;
    argues against doctrine of divine right of kings and for government by consent of
    the governed
- Influence of the Enlightenment on the beginnings of the United States
  Thomas Jefferson: the idea of "natural rights" in the Declaration of Independence
  Montesquieu and the idea of separation of powers in government

IV. The French Revolution

TEACHERS: While the focus here is on the French Revolution, make connections with what students already know about the American Revolution, and place the American and French Revolutions in the larger global context of ideas and movements.

- The influence of Enlightenment ideas and of the English Revolution on revolutionary movements in America and France
- The American Revolution: the French alliance and its effect on both sides
- The Old Regime in France (*L'Ancien Regime*)
    - The social classes: the three Estates
    - Louis XIV, the "Sun King": Versailles
    - Louis XV: *"Apres moi, le deluge"*
    - Louis XVI: the end of the Old Regime
    - Marie Antoinette: the famous legend of "Let them eat cake"
- 1789: from the Three Estates to the National Assembly
    - July 14, Bastille Day
    - Declaration of the Rights of Man
    - October 5, Women's March on Versailles
    - "Liberty, Equality, Fraternity"
- Louis XVI and Marie Antoinette to the guillotine
- Reign of Terror: Robespierre, the Jacobins, and the "Committee of Public Safety"
- Revolutionary arts and the new classicism
- Napoleon Bonaparte and the First French Empire
    - Napoleon as military genius
    - Crowned Emperor Napoleon I: reinventing the Roman Empire
    - The invasion of Russia
    - Exile to Elba
    - Wellington and Waterloo

See also Visual Arts 6: David, *Oath of the Horatii;* Delacroix, *Liberty Leading the People.*

V. Romanticism

See also English 6, Wordsworth, "I Wandered Lonely as a Cloud"; Byron, "Apostrophe to the Ocean" (from *Childe Harold's Pilgrimage*); Visual Arts 6, Romantic Art; and Music 6, Romantic Music.

- Beginning in early nineteenth century Europe, Romanticism refers to the cultural movement characterized by:
    - The rejection of classicism and classical values
    - An emphasis instead on emotion and imagination (instead of reason)
    - An emphasis on nature and the private self (instead of society and man in society)
- The influence of Jean-Jacques Rousseau's celebration of man in a state of nature (as opposed to man in society): "Man is born free and everywhere he is in chains"; the idea of the "noble savage"
- Romanticism in literature, the visual arts, and music

VI. Industrialism, Capitalism, and Socialism

A. THE INDUSTRIAL REVOLUTION

NOTE: In sixth grade, the World History guidelines catch up chronologically with the American History guidelines. The World History guidelines take students up to the consequences of industrialization in the mid-nineteenth century, and this is where the American History guidelines begin. See American History 6, Industrialization and Urbanization.

- Beginnings in Great Britain
    - Revolution in transportation: canals, railroads, new highways
    - Steam power: James Watt
- Revolution in textiles: Eli Whitney and the cotton gin, factory production
- Iron and steel mills
- The early factory system
    - Families move from farm villages to factory towns
    - Unsafe, oppressive working conditions in mills and mines
    - Women and child laborers
    - Low wages, poverty, slums, disease in factory towns
    - Violent resistance: Luddites

B. **CAPITALISM**
- Adam Smith and the idea of laissez faire vs. government intervention in economic and social matters
- Law of supply and demand
- Growing gaps between social classes: Disraeli's image of "two nations" (the rich and the poor)

C. **SOCIALISM**
- An idea that took many forms, all of which had in common their attempt to offer an alternative to capitalism
   - For the public ownership of large industries, transport, banks, etc., and the more equal distribution of wealth
- Marxism: the Communist form of Socialism
   - Karl Marx and Friedrich Engels, The Communist Manifesto: "Workers of the world, unite!"
   - Class struggle: bourgeoisie and proletariat
   - Communists, in contrast to Socialists, opposed all forms of private property.

See also American History 6, Labor, International Workers of the World; Eugene Debs.

VII. Latin American Independence Movements

A. **HISTORY**
- The name "Latin America" comes from the Latin origin of the languages now most widely spoken (Spanish and Portuguese).
- Haitian revolution
   - Toussaint L'Ouverture
   - Abolition of West Indian slavery
- Mexican revolutions
   - Miguel Hidalgo
   - José María Morelos
   - Santa Anna vs. the United States
   - Benito Juárez
   - Pancho Villa, Emiliano Zapata
- Liberators
   - Simon Bolivar
   - José de San Martín
   - Bernardo O'Higgins
- New nations in Central America: Costa Rica, El Salvador, Guatemala, Honduras, Nicaragua
- Brazilian independence from Portugal

B. **GEOGRAPHY OF LATIN AMERICA**
- Mexico: Yucatan Peninsula, Mexico City
- Panama: isthmus, Panama Canal
- Central America and South America: locate major cities and countries including
   - Caracas (Venezuela)
   - Bogota (Colombia)
   - Quito (Ecuador)
   - Lima (Peru)
   - Santiago (Chile)
   - La Paz (Bolivia)
- Andes Mountains
- Brazil: largest country in South America, rain forests, Rio de Janeiro, Amazon River
- Argentina: Rio de la Plata, Buenos Aires, Pampas

See below, Reform: Jane
Addams, settlement houses;
Jacob Riis, ghettos in the
modern city.

See also World History 6,
Industrial Revolution.

See also World History 6,
Capitalism, laissez faire.

AMERICAN HISTORY AND GEOGRAPHY

TEACHERS: The sixth grade American History guidelines pick up chronologically with the World History guidelines on mid-nineteenth century industrialism and its consequences.

I. Immigration, Industrialization, and Urbanization

A. IMMIGRATION

- Waves of new immigrants from about 1830 onward
  - Great migrations from Ireland (potato famine) and Germany
  - From about 1880 on, many immigrants arrive from southern and eastern Europe.
  - Immigrants from Asian countries, especially China
  - Ellis Island, "The New Colossus" (poem on the Statue of Liberty, written by Emma Lazarus)
  - Large populations of immigrants settle in major cities, including New York, Chicago, Philadelphia, Detroit, Cleveland, Boston, San Francisco
- The tension between ideals and realities
  - The metaphor of America as a "melting pot"
  - America perceived as "land of opportunity" vs. resistance, discrimination, and "nativism"
  - Resistance to Catholics and Jews
  - Chinese Exclusion Act

B. INDUSTRIALIZATION AND URBANIZATION

- The post-Civil War industrial boom
  - The "Gilded Age"
  - The growing gap between social classes
  - Horatio Alger and the "rags to riches" story
  - Growth of industrial cities: Chicago, Cleveland, Pittsburgh
  - Many thousands of African-Americans move north.
  - Urban corruption, "machine" politics: "Boss" Tweed in New York City, Tammany Hall
- The condition of labor
  - Factory conditions: "sweat shops," long work hours, low wages, women and child laborers
  - Unions: American Federation of Labor, Samuel Gompers
  - Strikes and retaliation: Haymarket Square; Homestead, Pennsylvania
  - Labor Day
- The growing influence of big business: industrialists and capitalists
  - "Captains of industry" and "robber barons": Andrew Carnegie, J. P. Morgan, Cornelius Vanderbilt
  - John D. Rockefeller and the Standard Oil Company as an example of the growing power of monopolies and trusts
  - Capitalists as philanthropists (funding museums, libraries, universities, etc.)
- "Free enterprise" vs. government regulation of business: Interstate Commerce Act and Sherman Antitrust Act attempt to limit power of monopolies

II. Reform

- Populism
  - Discontent and unrest among farmers
  - The gold standard vs. "free silver"
  - William Jennings Bryan
- The Progressive Era
  - "Muckraking": Ida Tarbell on the Standard Oil Company; Upton Sinclair, *The Jungle*, on the meat packing industry
  - Jane Addams: settlement houses
  - Jacob Riis, *How the Other Half Lives*: tenements and ghettos in the modern city
  - President Theodore (Teddy) Roosevelt: conservation and trust-busting

See also English 6, Poetry, Paul Laurence Dunbar, "Sympathy."

NOTE: Briefly review people and ideas studied in grade 4, American History, Reformers: Women's Rights.

See also World History 6, Socialism and Capitalism.

- Reform for African-Americans
  - Ida B. Wells: campaign against lynching
  - Booker T. Washington: Tuskegee Institute, Atlanta Exposition Address, "Cast down your bucket where you are"
  - W. E. B. DuBois: founding of NAACP, "The problem of the twentieth century is the problem of the color line," *The Souls of Black Folk*
- Women's suffrage
  - Susan B. Anthony
  - Nineteenth Amendment (1920)
- The Socialist critique of America: Eugene V. Debs

History and Geography

Visual Arts: Grade 6

SEE PAGE 3, "The Arts in the Curriculum."

<u>TEACHERS:</u> In schools, lessons on the visual arts should illustrate important elements of making and appreciating art, and emphasize important artists, works of art, and artistic concepts. When appropriate, topics in the visual arts may be linked to topics in other disciplines. While the following guidelines specify a variety of artworks in different media and from various cultures, they are not intended to be comprehensive. Teachers are encouraged to build upon the core content and expose children to a wide range of art and artists.

In studying the works of art specified below, and in creating their own art, students should review, develop, and apply concepts introduced in previous grades, such as line, shape, form, space, texture, color, light, design, and symmetry.

I.   Art History: Periods and Schools

<u>TEACHERS:</u> The focus here is intended to combine art history with analysis of specific illustrative works. Introduce the idea of classifying Western art by periods and schools, with major characteristics of each period and school. Timelines may help students situate the periods and schools. Note that the periods and characteristics are not absolute distinctions but generally helpful categories (to which there are always exceptions) often used in discussions of art. The following topics extend to the mid-nineteenth century. In later grades, students will examine late-nineteenth and twentieth-century art movements.

See also World History 6, Lasting Ideas from Greece and Rome, *re* Classical art.

See Visual Arts 4 for more detailed guidelines on Gothic architecture.

See Visual Arts 5 for more detailed guidelines on Renaissance art. See also World History 6, Lasting Ideas from Greece and Rome, *re* Raphael's *School of Athens*.

A.   CLASSICAL ART: THE ART OF ANCIENT GREECE AND ROME
   - Observe characteristics considered "classic"—emphasis on balance and proportion, idealization of human form—in
      The Parthenon and the Pantheon
      The Discus Thrower and *Apollo Belvedere*

B.   GOTHIC ART (ca. 12th - 15th centuries)
   - Briefly review the religious inspiration and characteristic features of Gothic cathedrals.

C.   THE RENAISSANCE (ca. 1350-1600)
   - Briefly review main features of Renaissance art (revival of classical subjects and techniques, emphasis on humanity, discovery of perspective) and examine representative works, including
      Raphael, *The School of Athens*
      Michelangelo, *David* (review from grade 5)

D.   BAROQUE (ca. 17th century)
   - Note the dramatic use of light and shade, turbulent compositions, and vivid emotional expression in
      El Greco, *View of Toledo* (also known as *Toledo in a Storm*)
      Rembrandt: a self-portrait, such as *Self-Portrait, 1659*

E.   ROCOCO (ca. mid- to late-1700's)
   - Note the decorative and "pretty" nature of Rococo art, the use of soft pastel colors, and the refined, sentimental, or playful subjects in
      Jean Honoré Fragonard, *The Swing*

See also World History 6, French Revolution, *re* David. You may also wish to introduce David's *Death of Socrates* when you study Lasting Ideas from Greece and Rome—see World History 6.

See also World History 6, Romanticism, *re* Romantic art; and French Revolution, *re* Delacroix's *Liberty Leading the People*.

F. NEOCLASSICAL (ca. late 18th - early 19th century)
- Note as characteristic of Neoclassical art the reaction against Baroque and Rococo, the revival of classical forms and subjects, belief in high moral purpose of art, and balanced, clearly articulated forms in
  - Jacques Louis David, *Oath of the Horatii*

G. ROMANTIC (ca. late 18th - 19th century)
- Note how Romantic art is in part a reaction against Neoclassicism, with a bold, expressive, emotional style, and a characteristic interest in the exotic or in powerful forces in nature, in
  - Francisco Goya, *The Bullfight*
  - Eugene Delacroix, *Liberty Leading the People*
  - Caspar David Friedrich, *The Chalk Cliffs of Rugen*

H. REALISM (ca. mid- to late-19th century)
- Note the Realist's characteristic belief that art should represent ordinary people and activities, that art does not have to be uplifting, edifying, or beautiful, in
  - Jean Millet, *The Gleaners*
  - Gustave Courbet, *The Stone Breakers*
- Become familiar with examples of American realism, including
  - Winslow Homer, *Noreaster*
  - Thomas Eakins, *The Gross Clinic*
  - Henry O. Tanner, *The Banjo Lesson*

Visual Arts

145

Music: Grade 6

SEE PAGE 3, "The Arts in the Curriculum."

I. Elements of Music

TEACHERS: The Music guidelines for grades 6-8 share a basic vocabulary of the elements of music that can inform the discussion, appreciation, and study of selected musical works. Following these guidelines are recommendations in each grade for a core of musical content, broadly organized as a history of music from early to modern times, with attention to specific periods, composers, and genres. While these guidelines focus on musical vocabulary, appreciation, and history, musical performance should be encouraged and emphasized as local resources allow.

- Review as necessary from earlier grades:
  - The orchestra and families of instruments (strings, wind, brass, percussion); keyboard instruments
  - Vocal ranges: soprano, mezzo-soprano, alto; tenor, baritone, bass
- Recognize frequently used Italian terms:
  - *grave* (very very slow)
  - *largo* (very slow)
  - *adagio* (slow)
  - *andante* (moderate; "walking")
  - *moderato* (medium)
  - *allegro* (fast)
  - *presto* (very fast)
  - *prestissimo* (as fast as you can go)
  - *ritardando* and *accelerando* (gradually slowing down and getting faster)
  - *crescendo* and *decrescendo* (gradually increasing and decreasing volume)
  - *legato* (smoothly flowing progression of notes), *staccato* (crisp, distinct notes)
- Recognize introduction, interlude, and coda in musical selections.
- Recognize theme and variations.
- Identify chords [such as I (tonic), IV (subdominant), V (dominant); V7]; major and minor chords; chord changes; intervals (third, fourth, fifth).
- Understand what an octave is.
- Understand the following notation and terms:

  names of lines and spaces in the treble clef; middle C

  𝄞 treble clef   𝄢 bass clef   ≣ staff, bar line, double bar line, measure, repeat signs

  ○ whole note   ♩ half note   ♩ quarter note   ♪ eighth notes

  whole rest, half rest, quarter rest, eighth rest

  𝅘𝅥𝅯 grouped sixteenth notes

  tied notes and dotted notes

  ♯ sharps   ♭ flats   ♮ naturals

  Da capo [*D.C.*] *al fine*

  meter signature: $\frac{4}{4}$ or common time $\frac{2}{4}$ $\frac{3}{4}$ $\frac{6}{8}$

  quiet *pp* *p* *mp*   loud *ff* *f* *mf*

II. Classical Music: From Baroque to Romantic

TEACHERS: While these guidelines focus on musical vocabulary, appreciation, and history, musical performance should be encouraged and emphasized as resources allow. The focus here combines music history with appreciation of illustrative works, and introduces the idea of classifying Western music by periods, with examples of specific composers and works, as well as some associated musical terms. Timelines may help students situate the periods. The periods and their characteristics are not absolute distinctions but generally helpful categories often used in discussions of music. A brief review of Medieval (grade 4) and Renaissance (grade 5) music is suggested.

NOTE: *re* Baroque music, recall from grade 2, Antonio Vivaldi, *The Four Seasons.*

A. BAROQUE (ca. 1600-1750)
- Counterpoint, fugue, oratorio
- Johann Sebastian Bach: selections from *Brandenburg Concertos*, selections from *The Well-Tempered Clavier*, selections from the *Cantatas* such as *BWV 80, BWV 140,* or *BWV 147*
- George Frederick Handel: selections from *Water Music*, "Hallelujah Chorus" from *The Messiah*

NOTE: *re* classical symphony, recall from grade 4, Haydn, *Symphony No. 94* (*"Surprise"*); and, from grade 5, Beethoven, *Symphony No. 5.*

B. CLASSICAL (ca. 1750-1825)
- The classical symphony (typically in four movements)
  Wolfgang Amadeus Mozart, *Symphony No. 40*
- The classical concerto: soloist, cadenza
  Wolfgang Amadeus Mozart, *Piano Concerto No. 21*
- Chamber music: string quartet, sonata
  Franz Joseph Haydn, *String Quartet Opus 76 No. 3, "Emperor"*
  Ludwig van Beethoven, *Piano Sonata No. 14 ("Moonlight" Sonata)*

NOTE: Beethoven and Schubert are often considered transitional figures between Classic and Romantic. Students will study other Romantic composers in seventh grade, including Brahams, Berlioz, Liszt, and Wagner.

C. ROMANTIC (ca. 1800-1900)
- Beethoven as a transitional figure: *Symphony No. 9* (fourth movement)
- Romantic composers and works:
  Franz Schubert, lieder (art songs): *Die Forelle* ("The Trout"), *Gretchen am Spinnrade* ("Gretchen at the Spinning Wheel")
  Frederic Chopin: "Funeral March" from *Piano Sonata No. 2 in B flat minor, "Minute" Waltz, "Revolutionary" Etude in C minor*
  Robert Schumann, *Piano Concerto in A Minor*

Music

Mathematics: Grade 6

TEACHERS: Mathematics has its own vocabulary and patterns of thinking. It is a discipline with its own language and conventions. Thus, while some lessons may offer occasional opportunities for linking mathematics to other disciplines, it is critically important to attend to math as math. From the earliest years, mathematics requires incremental review and steady practice: not only the diligent effort required to master basic facts and operations, but also thoughtful and varied practice that approaches problems from a variety of angles, and gives children a variety of opportunities to apply the same concept or operation in different types of situations. While it is important to work toward the development of "higher-order problem-solving skills," it is equally important—indeed, it is prerequisite to achieving "higher order" skills—to have a sound grasp of basic facts, and an automatic fluency with fundamental operations.

I. Numbers and Number Sense

- Read and write numbers (in digits and words) up to the trillions.
- Recognize place value up to hundred-billions.
- Integers (review):
  - Locate positive and negative integers on a number line.
  - Compare integers using <, >, =.
  - Know that the sum of an integer and its opposite is 0.
  - Add and subtract positive and negative integers.
- Determine whether a number is a prime number or composite number.
- Round to the nearest ten; to the nearest hundred; to the nearest thousand; to the nearest hundred-thousand; to the nearest million.
- Compare and order whole numbers, mixed numbers, fractions, and decimals, using the symbols <, >, =.
- Determine the greatest common factor (GCF) of given numbers.
- Determine the least common multiple (LCM) of given numbers.
- Exponents:
  - Review squares and square roots.
  - Using the terms *squared* and *cubed* and *to the nth power*, read and evaluate numerical expressions with exponents.
  - Review powers of ten.
  - Write numbers in expanded notation using exponents.

NOTE: See Math 5, Fractions and Decimals; review these topics as needed.

II. Ratio, Percent, and Proportion

A. RATIO AND PROPORTION
- Solve proportions, including word problems involving proportions with one unknown.
- Use ratios and proportions to interpret map scales and scale drawings.
- Set up and solve proportions from similar triangles.
- Understand the justification for solving proportions by cross-multiplication.

B. PERCENT
- Convert between fractions, decimals, and percents.
- Find the given percent of a number, and find what percent a given number is of another number.
- Solve problems involving percent increase and decrease.
- Find an unknown number when a percent of the number is known.
- Use expressions with percents greater than 100% and less than 1%.

III. Computation

A. ADDITION
- Addition, commutative and associative properties: know the names and understand the properties.
    Understand addition and subtraction as inverse operations.
    Add and subtract with integers, fractions and decimals, both positive and negative.

B. MULTIPLICATION
- Commutative, associative, and distributive properties: know the names and understand the properties.
- Multiply multi-digit factors, with and without a calculator.
- Estimate a product.
- Multiply with integers, fractions, and decimals, both positive and negative.
- Distributive property for multiplication over addition or subtraction, that is, A x (B+C) or A x (B-C): understand its use in procedures such as multi-digit multiplication.

C. DIVISION
- Understand multiplication and division as inverse operations.
- Estimate the quotient.
- Divide multi-digit dividends by up to three-digit divisors, with and without a calculator.
- Divide with integers, fractions, or decimals, both positive and negative.

D. SOLVING PROBLEMS AND EQUATIONS
- Solve word problems with multiple steps.
- Solve problems with more than one operation, according to order of operations (with and without a calculator).

IV. Measurement

TEACHERS: Students should know all information regarding measurement presented in grades 4 and 5; review and reinforce as necessary.

- Solve problems requiring conversion of units within the U. S. Customary System, and within the metric system.
- Associate prefixes used in metric system with quantities:
    kilo = thousand
    hecto = hundred
    deka = ten
    deci = tenth
    centi = hundredth
    milli = thousandth
- Time: solve problems on elapsed time; express parts of an hour in fraction or decimal form.

V. Geometry
- Identify and use signs that mean
    congruent ≅
    similar ~
    parallel ||
    perpendicular ⊥
- Construct parallel lines and a parallelogram.
- Construct a perpendicular bisector.
- Know that if two lines are parallel, any line perpendicular to one is also perpendicular to the other; and, that two lines perpendicular to the same line are parallel.

- Angles:
    Identify and measure the degrees in angles (review terms: right, acute, obtuse, straight).
    Bisect an angle.
    Construct an angle congruent to a given angle.
    Construct a figure congruent to a given figure, using reflection over a line of symmetry, and identify corresponding parts.
    Show how congruent plane figures can be made to correspond through reflection, rotation, and translation.
- Triangles:
    Know that the sum of the measures of the angles of a triangle is 180°.
    Construct different kinds of triangles.
    Know terms by which we classify kinds of triangles:
        by length of sides: equilateral, isosceles, scalene
        by angles: right, acute, obtuse
- Identify congruent angles and sides, and axes of symmetry, in parallelograms, rhombuses, rectangles, and squares.
- Find the area (A) and perimeter (P) of plane figures, or given the area or perimeter find the missing dimension, using the following formulas:
    rectangle
        $A = lw$
        $P = 2(l + w)$
    square
        $A = s^2$
        $P = 4s$
    triangle
        $A = \frac{1}{2}bh$
        $P = s1 + s2 + s3$
    parallelogram
        $A = bh$
        $P = 2(b + s)$
- Circles:
    Identify arc, chord, radius (plural: radii), and diameter; know that radius = $\frac{1}{2}$ diameter.
    Using a compass, draw circles with a given diameter or radius.
    Solve problems involving application of the formulas for finding the circumference of a circle: $C = \pi d$, and $C = 2\pi r$, using 3.14 as the value of *pi*.
    Find the area of a circle using the formula $A = \pi r^2$
- Find volume of rectangular solids, or given the volume find a missing dimension, using the formulas $V = lwh$, or $V = bh$ (in which b = area of base).

VI. Probability and Statistics

- Find the range and measures of central tendency (mean, median, and mode) of a given set of numbers.
- Understand the differences among the measures of central tendency and when each might be used.
- Understand the use of a sample to estimate a population parameter (such as the mean), and that larger samples provide more stable estimates.
- Represent all possible outcomes of independent compound events in an organized way and determine the theoretical probability of each outcome.
- Compute the probability of any one of a set of disjoint events as the sum of their individual probabilities.
- Solve problems requiring interpretation and application of graphically displayed data.
- Given a set of data, find the mean, median, range, and mode.
- Construct a histogram; a tree diagram.

- Coordinate plane:
    Plot points on a coordinate plane, using ordered pairs of positive and negative
        whole numbers.
    Use the terms *origin* (0,0), *x-axis*, and, *y-axis*.
    Graph simple functions and solve problems involving use of a coordinate plane.

VII. Pre-Algebra

- Recognize uses of variables and solve linear equations in one variable.
- Solve word problems by assigning variables to unknown quantities, writing appropriate
    equations, and solving them.
- Find the value for an expression, given replacement values for the variables; for example,
    what is $7/x - y$ when x is 2 and y is 10?
- Simplify expressions with variables by combining like terms.
- Understand the use of the distributive property in variable expressions such as $2x(2y +3)$.

Mathematics

Science: Grade 6

<u>Teachers:</u> Effective instruction in science requires not only hands-on experience and observation but also book learning, which helps bring coherence and order to a student's scientific knowledge. Only when topics are presented systematically and clearly can students make steady and secure progress in their scientific learning. The Science sequence for the middle school grades aims for more intensive and selective study of topics, a number of which were introduced in earlier grades. It also continues the practice of studying topics from each of the major realms of science (physical, life, and earth science). Students are expected to do experiments and write reports on their findings.

I. Plate Tectonics

- The surface of the earth

  The surface of the earth is in constant movement.

  The present features of earth come from its ongoing history. After the sun was formed, matter cooled creating the planets. The continents were once joined (Pangaea).
- Layered structure of the earth

  Crust: surface layer of mainly basalt or granite, 5 to 25 miles thick

  Mantle: 1,800 miles thick, rock of intermediate density, moves very slowly

  Outer core: liquid iron and nickel

  Inner core: solid iron and nickel, 800 miles thick, about 7,000 degrees C
- Crust movements

  The surface of earth is made up of rigid plates that are in constant motion.

  Plates move because molten rock rises and falls under the crust causing slowly flowing currents under the plates.

  Plates move at speeds ranging from 1 to 4 inches (5-10 centimeters) per year.

  Earthquakes usually occur where stress has been built up by plates moving in opposite directions against each other. Earthquakes cause waves (vibrations) which have:

  focus, the point below the surface where the quake begins

  epicenter, the point on the surface above the focus

  Severity of ground shaking is measured on the Richter scale; each unit on the scale represents a tenfold severity increase (approximately 31-fold increase in energy released).
- Volcanoes usually occur where plates are pulling apart or coming together, but some occur at holes (hot spots) in the crust away from plate boundaries. As plates move over these hot spots, they cause chains of volcanoes and island chains like the Hawaiian Islands.
- Evidence for long-term movement of plates includes fit of continents and matches of rock types, fossils, and structures; ocean floor age and topography; ancient climate zones; locations of earthquakes, volcanoes, and mountain ranges; magnetic directions in ancient rocks.

II. Oceans

- Surface

  The world ocean covers most of the earth's surface (71 per cent).

  Three major subdivisions of the world ocean: Atlantic, Pacific,and Indian Oceans

  Islands consist of high parts of submerged continents, volcanic peaks, coral atolls.
- Subsurface land features

  Continental shelf, continental slope, continental rise, abyssal plains

  Mid-ocean ridges and trenches, plate tectonics

  Mid-Atlantic Ridge, Mariana Trench
- Ocean bottom: average depth of sediment .3 mile, consists of rock particles and organic remains
- Composition of seawater: dilute solution of salts which come from weathering and erosion of continental rocks.

  Sodium chloride is the main salt.

  Elements needed for life, such as carbon and phosphorus, exist in relatively weak concentration and limit the amount of ocean life.

- Currents, tides, and waves
    - Surface currents: large circular streams kept in motion by prevailing winds and rotation of the earth; Gulf Stream (North Atlantic), Kuroshio (North Pacific)
    - Subsurface currents are caused by upwelling from prevailing offshore winds (Peru, Chile) and density differences (Antarctica); the upwelling pushes up nutrients from the ocean floor.
    - Tides are caused by gravitational forces of the sun and moon; there are two tides daily.
    - Waves are caused by wind on the ocean's surface.
        - Water molecules tend to move up and down in place and not move with the wave.
        - Crest and trough, wave height and wavelength, shoreline friction
        - Tsunamis: destructive, fast-moving large waves caused mainly by earthquakes
- Marine life
    - Life zones are determined by the depth to which light can penetrate making photosynthesis possible, and by the availability of nutrients.
        - The bottom (benthic zone) extends from sunlit continental shelf to dark sparsely populated depths. Shallow lighted water extending over continental shelf contains 90% of marine species.
        - Pelagic zone: water in open oceans
    - Classification of marine life
        - Bottom-living (benthic) such as kelp and mollusks
        - Free-swimming (nekton) such as fish and whales
        - Small drifting plants and animals (plankton), which are the dominant life and food source of the ocean
    - The basis for most marine life is phytoplankton (plant-plankton), which carry on photosynthesis near surface; contrast zooplankton (animal plankton).
    - Most deepwater life depends on rain of organic matter from above. The densest concentration of marine life is found in surface waters, such as those off Chile, where nutrient-rich water wells up to the bright surface.

III. Astronomy: Gravity, Stars, and Galaxies

- Gravity: an attractive force between objects
    - Newton's law of universal gravitation: Between any two objects in the universe there is an attractive force, gravity, which grows greater as the objects move closer to each other.
    - How gravity keeps the planets in orbit

See below, Energy: Nuclear energy, *re* Stars.

- Stars
    - The sun is a star.
    - Kinds of stars (by size): giants, dwarfs, pulsars
    - Supernova; black holes
    - Apparent movement of stars caused by rotation of the earth
    - Constellations: visual groupings of stars, for example, Big Dipper, Orion
    - Astronomical distance measured in light years
- Galaxies
    - The Milky Way is our galaxy; the Andromeda Galaxy is closest to the Milky Way.
    - Quasars are the most distant visible objects (because the brightest).

IV. Energy, Heat, and Energy Transfer

A. ENERGY

- Six forms of energy: mechanical, heat, electrical, wave, chemical, nuclear
- The many forms of energy are interchangeable, for example, gasoline in a car, windmills, hydroelectric plants.
- Sources of energy: for example, heat (coal, natural gas, solar, atomic, geothermal, and thermonuclear), mechanical motion (such as falling water, wind)
- Fossil fuels: a finite resource

Science

Carbon, coal, oil, natural gas
Environmental impact of fossil fuels: carbon dioxide and global warming theory, greenhouse effect, oil spills, acid rain
- Nuclear energy
Uranium, fission, nuclear reactor, radioactive waste
Nuclear power plants: safety and accidents (for example, Three Mile Island, Chernobyl)

B. HEAT
- Heat and temperature: how vigorously atoms are moving and colliding
- Three ways that heat energy can be transferred: conduction, convection, radiation
The direction of heat transfer

C. PHYSICAL CHANGE: ENERGY TRANSFER
- States of matter (solid, liquid, gas) in terms of molecular motion
In gases, loosely packed atoms and molecules move independently and collide often. Volume and shape change readily.
In liquids, atoms and molecules are more loosely packed than in solids and can move past each other. Liquids change shape readily but resist change in volume.
In solids, atoms and molecules are more tightly packed and can only vibrate. Solids resist change in shape and volume.
- Most substances are solid at low temperatures, liquid at medium temperatures, and gaseous at high temperatures.
- A change of phase is a physical change (no new substance is produced).
- Matter can be made to change phases by adding or removing energy.
- Expansion and contraction
Expansion is adding heat energy to a substance, which causes the molecules to move more quickly and the substance to expand.
Contraction is when a substance loses heat energy, the molecules slow down, and the substance contracts.
Water as a special case: water expands when it changes from a liquid to a solid.
- Changing phases: condensation; freezing; melting; boiling
Different amounts of energy are required to change the phase of different substances.
Each substance has its own melting and boiling point.
The freezing point and boiling point of water (in degrees Celsius and Fahrenheit)
- Distillation: separation of mixtures of liquids with different boiling points.

V. The Human Body

NOTE: See Science 5 for the human reproductive system. There is some flexibility in the grade-level placement of the study of topics relating to human reproduction, as different schools and districts have differing local requirements, typically introducing these topics in either fifth or sixth grade.

- The circulatory and lymphatic systems
Briefly review from grade 4: circulatory system
Lymph, lymph nodes, white cells, tonsils, blood pressure, hardening and clogging of arteries
- The immune system fights infections from bacteria, viruses, fungi.
White cells, antibodies, antigens
Vaccines, communicable and non-communicable diseases, epidemics
Bacterial diseases: tetanus, typhoid, tuberculosis; antibiotics like penicillin, discovered by Alexander Fleming
Viral diseases: common cold, chicken pox, mononucleosis, rabies, polio, AIDS

VI. Science Biographies

Marie Curie
Lewis Howard Latimer
Isaac Newton
Alfred Wegner

See above, Plate Tectonics re Wegner; Energy re Curie; Astronomy, Gravity, re Newton. See also World History 6, The Enlightenment, re Newton.

Grade7

Overview of Topics — Grade 7

English
I. Writing, Grammar, and Usage
  A. Writing and Research
  B. Speaking and Listening
  C. Grammar
  D. Spelling
  E. Vocabulary
II. Poetry
  A. Poems
  B. Elements of Poetry
III. Fiction, Nonfiction, and Drama
  A. Short Stories
  B. Novels
  C. Elements of Fiction
  D. Essays and Speeches
  E. Autobiography
  F. Drama
  G. Literary Terms
IV. Foreign Phrases Commonly Used in English

History and Geography
I. America Becomes a World Power
II. World War I: "The Great War," 1914-1918
  A. History
  B. Geography of Western and Central Europe
III. The Russian Revolution
  A. History
  B. Geography
IV. America from the Twenties to the New Deal
  A. America in the Twenties
  B. The Great Depression
  C. Roosevelt and the New Deal
V. World War II
  A. The Rise of Totalitarianism in Europe
  B. World War II in Europe and at Home, 1939-45
  C. World War II in the Pacific, and the End of the War
VI. Geography of the United States

Visual Arts
I. Art History: Periods and Schools
  A. Impressionism
  B. Post-Impressionism
  C. Expressionism and Abstraction
  D. Modern American Painting

Music
I. Elements of Music
II. Classical Music: Romantics and Nationalists
  A. Romantic Composers and Works
  B. Music and National Identity
III. American Musical Traditions (Blues and Jazz)

Mathematics
I. Pre-Algebra
  A. Properties of the Real Numbers
  B. Linear Applications and Proportionality
  C. Polynomial Arithmetic
  D. Equivalent Equations and Inequalities
  E. Integer Exponents
II. Geometry
  A. Three-Dimensional Objects
  B. Angle Pairs
  C. Triangles
  D. Measurement
III. Probability and Statistics

Science
I. Atomic Structure
II. Chemical Bonds and Reactions
III. Cell Division and Genetics
IV. History of the Earth and Life Forms
  A. Paleontology
  B. Geologic Time
V. Evolution
  A. Evolution
  B. Natural Selection
  C. Extinction and Speciation
VI. Science Biographies

English: Grade 7

I.   Writing, Grammar, and Usage

A.   WRITING AND RESEARCH

TEACHERS: Students should be given opportunities to write fiction, poetry, or drama, but instruction should emphasize repeated expository writing. Students should examine their work with attention to unity, coherence, and emphasis. Expository essays should have a main point and stick to it, and have a coherent structure, typically following the pattern of introduction, body, and conclusion. Paragraphs should have a unified focus, be developed with evidence and examples, and have transitions between them. Essays should have appropriate tone and diction, as well as correct spelling and grammar in their final form. Standards for writing apply across the disciplines.

- Expository writing: Write nonfiction essays that describe, narrate, persuade, and compare and contrast.
- Write research essays, with attention to
  asking open-ended questions
  gathering relevant data through library and field research
  summarizing, paraphrasing, and quoting accurately when taking notes
  defining a thesis (that is, a central proposition, a main idea)
  organizing with an outline
  integrating quotations from sources
  acknowledging sources and avoiding plagiarism
  preparing a bibliography

See also English 6 for more guidelines on writing persuasive essays.

B.   SPEAKING AND LISTENING

- Participate civilly and productively in group discussions.
- Give a short speech to the class that is well-organized and well-supported.
- Demonstrate an ability to use standard pronunciation when speaking to large groups and in formal circumstances, such as a job interview.

C.   GRAMMAR

TEACHERS: Students should have a working understanding of the following terms and be able to use them to discuss and analyze writing.

Parts of the Sentence
- Prepositional phrases
  Identify as adjectival or adverbial
  Identify word(s) modified by the prepositional phrase
  Object of preposition (note that pronouns are in objective case)
  Punctuation of prepositional phrases
- Subject and verb
  Find complete subject and complete predicate
  Identify simple subject and simple verb (after eliminating prepositional phrases):
    in statements
    in questions
    in commands (you understood)
    with there and here
  Auxiliary verbs
  Noun of direct address
  Subject-verb agreement:
    with compound subjects
    with compound subjects joined by *or*
    with indefinite pronouns (for example, everyone, anyone, some, all)

- Complements
  - Find direct and indirect objects
  - Review linking vs. action verbs
  - Predicate nominative
  - Predicate adjective
- Appositives
  - Identify and tell which noun is renamed
  - Use of commas with appositive phrases
- Participles
  - Identify past, present participles
  - Identify participial phrases
  - Find the noun modified
  - Commas with participial phrases
- Gerunds and gerund phrases
  - Identify and tell its use in the sentence (subject, direct object, indirect object, appositive, predicate nominative, object of preposition)
- Infinitives and infinitive phrases
  - Adjective and adverb: find the word it modifies
  - Noun: tell its use in the sentence

Clauses
- Review: sentences classified by structure
  - Simple; compound (coordinating conjunctions v. conjunctive adverbs); complex; compound-complex
- Review independent (main) v. dependent (subordinate) clauses
- Kinds of dependent clauses
  - Adjective clauses
    - Identify and tell noun modified
    - Introductory words: relative pronouns, relative adverbs (where, when)
    - Implied "that"
    - Commas with nonrestrictive (nonessential) adjective clause
  - Adverb clauses
    - Identify and tell the word(s) modified
    - Subordinating conjunctions (for example, because, although, when, since, before, after, as soon as, where)
    - Comma after introductory adverbial clause
  - Noun clauses
    - Identify and tell use in the sentence (subject, predicate nominative, direct object, indirect object, object of preposition, appositive, objective complement, noun of direct address)

NOTE: More commonly misspelled words listed in grades 6 and 8.

D. **SPELLING**
- Continue work with spelling, with special attention to commonly misspelled words, including:

achievement	despise	muscular	scholar
address	doesn't	occasionally	shepherd
analysis	environment	offense	sincerely
anonymous	excellent	particularly	sponsor
argument	existence	persuade	succeed
beginning	grammar	politician	surprise
business	hypocrisy	prejudice	tendency
college	immediately	probably	thorough
conscience	interpret	recognize	truly
control	knowledge	remembrance	women
criticism	lieutenant	responsibility	written
definite	medieval	rhyme	
description	muscle	sacrifice	

158

E. VOCABULARY

Students should know the meaning of these Latin and Greek words that form common word roots and be able to give examples of English words that are based on them.

NOTE: More Latin and Greek words and roots are listed in grades 6 and 8. In the listings here, L = Latin, G = Greek. No single form of the Latin or Greek words is consistently used here, but rather the form most similar to related English words.

Latin/Greek Word	*Meaning*	*Examples*
ab [L]	away from	abnormal, absent
ad [L]	to, forward	advocate, advance
amo [L]	love	amiable, amorous
audio [L]	hear	audience, inaudible
auto [G]	self	automobile, autocrat
bene [L]	good/well	beneficial, benefit
circum [L]	around	circulate, circumference
celer [L]	swift	accelerate
chronos [G]	time	chronological
cresco [L]	grow	increase, decrease
cum [L]	with	compose, accommodate
curro [L]	run	current, cursive, course
demos [G]	people	democracy, epidemic
erro [L]	wander, stray	error, erratic
ex [L]	from, out of	exclaim, exhaust
extra [L]	outside	extravagant, extraordinary
facio [L]	make	effect, affect
fero [L]	bring, bear	confer, defer
fragilis [L]	breakable	fragile, fragment
finis [L]	end	confine, finality
homos [G]	same	homogenous
hyper [G]	over, beyond	hypertension, hyperactive
hypo [G]	under, beneath	hypodermic, hypothesis
jacio [L]	throw	eject, interject
judex [L]	a judge	judge, prejudice
juro [L]	swear	jury, perjury
makros [G]	long	macrocosm
malus [L]	bad	malady, malice
manus [L]	hand	manufacture, manuscript
morphe [G]	form	metamorphosis, amorphous
neos [G]	new	neophyte
pan [G]	all	panorama, panacea
pedis [L]	foot	pedal, biped
polis [G]	city	metropolis
pro [L]	before, for	proceed, propose, prodigy
pseudos [G]	a lie	pseudonym
re [L]	back, again	react, reply, revise
scribo [L]	write	scribble, inscribe
sentio [L]	feel (with senses)	sensation, sensual, sentry
sequor [L]	follow	subsequent, sequel
solvo [L]	loosen	solution, dissolve, solvent
specto [L]	look at	inspect, speculate, perspective
strictus [L]	drawn tight	strict, constricted
sub [L]	under	subdue, subject, subtract
super [L]	above	superficial, superlative, supreme
syn [G]	together	synchronize, synthesis
tendo [L]	stretch	tension, intense, detention
teneo [L]	hold, keep	contain, content, maintain
trans [L]	across	transfer, transcontinental
valeo [L]	be strong	prevail, valiant
venio [L]	come	event, advent
voco [L]	call	vocal, voice, vociferous
volvo [L]	revolve	evolve, revolution
zoon, zoe [G]	animal, life	zoology, protozoa

II. Poetry

The poems listed here constitute a selected core of poetry for this grade. You are encouraged to expose students to more poetry, old and new, and to have students write their own poems. Students should examine some poems in detail, discussing what the poems mean as well as asking questions about the poet's use of language.

See also History 7, World War I, *re* Wilfred Owen; and, America in the Twenties, Harlem Renaissance, *re* Langston Hughes and Countee Cullen.

A. POEMS

Annabel Lee (Edgar Allan Poe)
Because I could not stop for Death (Emily Dickinson)
The Charge of the Light Brigade (Alfred Lord Tennyson)
The Chimney Sweeper (both versions from *The Songs of Innocence* and *The Songs of Experience*; William Blake)
The Cremation of Sam McGee (Robert Service)
Dulce et Decorum Est (Wilfred Owen)
Fire and Ice; Nothing Gold Can Stay (Robert Frost)
Heritage (Countee Cullen)
Macavity: The Mystery Cat (T.S. Eliot)
The Negro Speaks of Rivers; Harlem; Life is Fine (Langston Hughes)
This Is Just to Say; The Red Wheelbarrow (William Carlos Williams)

B. ELEMENTS OF POETRY

- Review: meter, iamb, rhyme scheme, free verse, couplet, onomatopoeia, alliteration
- Stanzas and refrains
- Forms
  ballad
  sonnet
  lyric
  narrative
  limerick
  haiku
- Types of rhyme: end, internal, slant, eye

III. Fiction, Nonfiction, and Drama

A. SHORT STORIES

"The Gift of the Magi" (O. Henry)
"The Necklace" (Guy de Maupassant)
"The Secret Life of Walter Mitty" (James Thurber)
"The Tell-Tale Heart"; "The Purloined Letter" (Edgar Allan Poe)

B. NOVELS / NOVELLAS

The Call of the Wild (Jack London)
Dr. Jekyll and Mr. Hyde (Robert Louis Stevenson)

C. ELEMENTS OF FICTION

- Review aspects of plot and setting
- Theme
- Point of view in narration
  omniscient narrator
  unreliable narrator
  third person limited
  first person
- Conflict: external and internal
- Suspense and climax

See also History 7, World War II, *re* Roosevelt's "Declaration of War" and Anne Frank's *Diary of a Young Girl.*

D. ESSAYS AND SPEECHES
"Shooting an Elephant" (George Orwell)
"The Night the Bed Fell" (James Thurber)
"Declaration of War on Japan" (Franklin D. Roosevelt)

E. AUTOBIOGRAPHY
Diary of a Young Girl (Anne Frank)

F. DRAMA
- *Cyrano de Bergerac* (Edmond Rostand)
- Elements of drama
    Tragedy and comedy (review)
    Aspects of conflict, suspense, and characterization
    Soliloquies and asides

G. LITERARY TERMS
- Irony: verbal, situational, dramatic
- Flashbacks and foreshadowing
- Hyperbole; oxymoron; parody

IV. Foreign Phrases Commonly Used in English

TEACHERS: Students should learn the meaning of the following Latin phrases that are commonly used in English speech and writing.

NOTE: In eighth grade students will learn French phrases commonly used in English speech and writing.

ad hoc - concerned with a particular purpose; improvised [literally, "to the thing"]
bona fides - good faith; sincere, involving no deceit or fraud
carpe diem - seize the day, enjoy the present
caveat emptor - let the buyer beware, buy at your own risk
de facto - in reality, actually existing
in extremis - in extreme circumstances, especially at the point of death
in medias res - in the midst of things
in toto - altogether, entirely
modus operandi - a method of procedure
modus vivendi - a way of living, getting along
persona non grata - an unacceptable or unwelcome person
prima facie - at first view, apparently; self-evident
pro bono publico - for the public good
pro forma - for the sake of form, carried out as a matter of formality
quid pro quo - something given or received in exchange for something else
requiescat in pace, R I P - may he or she rest in peace [seen on tombstones]
sic transit gloria mundi - thus passes away the glory of the world
sine qua non - something absolutely indispensable [literally, "without which not"]
sub rosa - secretly

History and Geography: Grade 7

TEACHERS: In earlier grades, the history guidelines in the Core Knowledge Sequence were organized into separate strands on World History and American History. Because the World and American History strands merged chronologically in sixth grade, here in seventh grade the Sequence presents a unified section on History and Geography. Central themes of the history guidelines in grades seven and eight are growth and change in American democracy, and interactions with world forces, particularly nationalism and totalitarianism. Fundamental principles and structure of American government will be reviewed in a civics unit in eighth grade.

The study of geography aims at understanding the spatial relationship between nature and human culture and processes that change environments. Following the main outline of the history curriculum, seventh grade students study the geography of Europe, the United States, and Japan, while eighth graders will study the Middle East, South Asia, China, Canada, Mexico, and post-Cold War changes. Students should learn locations as well as the relationships between physical and human systems.

I.   America Becomes a World Power

- Expansion of the U.S. Navy, Captain Alfred T. Mahan
- U.S. annexation of Hawaii
- The Spanish-American War
    Cuban War for Independence, José Martí
    Teddy Roosevelt and the Rough Riders
    Spain gives the U.S. Guam, Puerto Rico, and the Philippines
- Complications of imperialism: War with the Philippines, Anti-Imperialist League
- Building the Panama Canal: "Roosevelt Corollary" to the Monroe Doctrine, "Speak softly and carry a big stick."

II.   World War I: "The Great War," 1914-1918

A.   HISTORY

- National pride and greed as causes: European nationalism, militarism, and colonialism
    The British Empire: Queen Victoria
    Italy becomes a nation: Garibaldi
    German nationalism and militarism: Bismarck unifies Germany, war against France, France cedes Alsace-Lorraine to Germany
    European imperialism and rivalries in Africa
        Stanley and Livingstone
        British invade Egypt to protect Suez Canal
        French in North Africa
        Berlin Conference and the "scramble for Africa"
- Entangling alliances: Allies vs. Central Powers; Archduke Francis Ferdinand assassinated
- The Western Front and Eastern Front, Gallipoli, Lawrence of Arabia
- War of attrition and the scale of losses: Battle of the Marne (1914), new war technologies (for example, machine guns, tanks, airplanes, submarines), trench warfare
- U.S. neutrality ends: sinking of the Lusitania, "Make the world safe for democracy"
- Armistice Day, Nov. 11, 1918, abdication of Kaiser Wilhelm II
- Treaty of Versailles
    New central European states and national boundaries
    German reparations and disarmament
- Woodrow Wilson's 14 Points
    League of Nations, concept of collective security

B. GEOGRAPHY OF WESTERN AND CENTRAL EUROPE

TEACHERS: Students should regularly consult maps in reference to the following topics.

- Physical features
    - Mountains: Alps, Apennines, Carpathians, Pyrenees
    - Danube and Rhine Rivers
    - Seas: Adriatic, Aegean, Baltic, Black, Mediterranean, North
- Population and natural resources, acid rain damage
- Languages, major religions
- Legacy of Roman Empire: city sites, transportation routes
- Industrial Revolution leads to urbanization (review from grade 6)
- Scandinavia: comprised of Denmark, Norway, Sweden, sometimes also includes Finland and Iceland
    - Cities: Copenhagen (Denmark), Oslo (Norway), Stockholm (Sweden), Helsinki (Finland)
- United Kingdom: comprised of Great Britain (England, Scotland, Wales) and Northern Ireland
    - Irish Sea, English Channel
    - North Sea: gas and oil
    - England: London, Thames River
    - Scotland: Glasgow, Edinburgh
    - Northern Ireland: Ulster and Belfast, Catholic-Protestant strife
    - Ireland: Dublin (review from grade 6: famine of 1840s, mass emigration)
- France
    - Alps, Mont Blanc
    - Seine and Rhone Rivers
    - Bay of Biscay, Strait of Dover
    - Corsica (island)
    - Major cities: Paris, Lyon, Marseilles
- Belgium, Netherlands (Holland), and Luxembourg
    - Cities: Brussels (Belgium), Amsterdam, Rotterdam, The Hague (Netherlands)
- Germany
    - Cities: Berlin, Bonn, Hamburg, Munich
    - Ruhr Valley: mining region, industrial cities including Essen
    - Largest population in Europe, highly urbanized
- Austria and Switzerland
    - Mostly mountainous (the Alps)
    - Cities: Vienna (Austria), Bern, Geneva (Switzerland)
- Italy
    - Apennines
    - Sardinia and Sicily (islands)
    - Cities: Milan, Rome, Venice, Florence
    - Vatican City: independent state within Rome
- Iberian Peninsula: Spain and Portugal
    - Cities: Madrid (Spain), Lisbon (Portugal)

III. The Russian Revolution

A. HISTORY
- Tensions in the Russian identity: Westernizers vs. traditionalists
- Revolution of 1905, "Bloody Sunday," Russo-Japanese War
- The last czar: Nicholas II and Alexandra
- Economic strains of World War I
- Revolutions of 1917
    - March Revolution ousts Czar
    - October Revolution: Bolsheviks, Lenin and revolutionary Marxism
- Civil War: Bolsheviks defeat Czarist counterrevolution, Bolsheviks become the Communist Party, creation of the Soviet Union

B. GEOGRAPHY

TEACHERS: Students should regularly consult maps in reference to the following topics.

- Overview
    - Territorially the largest state in the world
    - All parts exposed to Arctic air masses
    - Little moisture reaches Russia, because of distance from Atlantic Ocean, and because Himalayas block movement of warm, moist air from south
    - Population concentrated west of Ural Mountains
    - Siberia: rich in resources
    - Mongolia: Russian-dominated buffer state with China
    - Few well-located ports
    - Rich oil and natural gas regions
- Physical features:
    - Volga and Don Rivers (connected by canal)
    - Caspian Sea, Aral Sea (being drained by irrigation projects)
    - Sea of Japan, Bering Strait
- Cities: Moscow, Petersburg (formerly Leningrad), Vladivostok, Volgograd (formerly Stalingrad)

IV. America from the Twenties to the New Deal

A. AMERICA IN THE TWENTIES

- Isolationism: restrictions on immigration, Red Scare, Sacco and Vanzetti, Ku Klux Klan
- The "Roaring Twenties": flappers, prohibition and gangsterism, St. Valentine's Day Massacre, Al Capone
- The Lost Generation: Ernest Hemingway, F. Scott Fitzgerald
- Scopes "Monkey Trial"
- Women's right to vote: 19th Amendment
- "New Negro" movement, Harlem Renaissance
    - African American exodus from segregated South to northern cities
    - W. E. B. Du Bois: *The Souls of Black Folk*, NAACP (review from grade 6)
    - Zora Neal Hurston, Countee Cullen, Langston Hughes
    - "The Jazz Age": Duke Ellington, Louis Armstrong
    - Marcus Garvey, black separatist movement
- Technological advances
    - Henry Ford's assembly line production, Model T
    - Residential electrification: mass ownership of radio, Will Rogers
    - Movies: from silent to sound, Charlie Chaplin
    - Pioneers of flight: Charles Lindbergh, Amelia Earhart
    - Decline of rural population

See below, VII. Geography of the United States: New York City.

See also Music 7, American Musical Traditions: Jazz.

B. THE GREAT DEPRESSION

- Wall Street stock market Crash of '29, "Black Tuesday"
- Hoover insists on European payment of war debts, Smoot-Hawley Tariff Act
- Mass unemployment
    - Agricultural prices collapse following European peace
    - Factory mechanization eliminates jobs
    - Bonus Army
    - "Hoovervilles"
- The Dust Bowl, "Okie" migrations
- Radicals: Huey Long, American Communist Party, Sinclair Lewis

C. ROOSEVELT AND THE NEW DEAL

- Franklin Delano Roosevelt: "The only thing we have to fear is fear itself"
  Eleanor Roosevelt
- The New Deal

NOTE: *re* growth of unions,
recall from grade 6, American
Federation of Labor.

  Growth of unions: John L. Lewis and the CIO (Congress of Industrial Organizations),
  A. Philip Randolph, Memorial Day Massacre
  New social welfare programs: Social Security
  New regulatory agencies: Securities and Exchange Commission, National Labor
  Relations Board
  Tennessee Valley Authority
- Roosevelt's use of executive power: "Imperial Presidency", "court packing"

V. World War II

A. THE RISE OF TOTALITARIANISM IN EUROPE

- Italy
  Mussolini establishes fascism
  Attack on Ethiopia
- Germany
  Weimar Republic, economic repercussions of WWI
  Adolf Hitler and the rise of Nazi totalitarianism: cult of the *Führer* ("leader"),
  Mein Kampf
  Nazism and the ideology of fascism, in contrast to communism and democracy
  Racial doctrines of the Nazis: anti-Semitism, the concept of *Lebensraum* (literally, "living
  space") for the "master race," *Kristallnacht*
  The Third Reich before the War: Gestapo, mass propaganda, book burning
- The Soviet Union
  Communist totalitarianism: Josef Stalin, "Socialism in one country"
  Collectivization of agriculture
  Five-year plans for industrialization
  The Great Purge

See also Visual Arts 7,
Picasso's *Guernica*.

- Spanish Civil War
  Franco, International Brigade, Guernica

B. WORLD WAR II IN EUROPE AND AT HOME, 1939-45

- Hitler defies Versailles Treaty: reoccupation of Rhineland, *Anschluss,* annexation
  of Austria
- Appeasement: Munich Agreement, "peace in our time"
- Soviet-Nazi Nonaggression Pact
- *Blitzkrieg:* invasion of Poland, fall of France, Dunkirk
- Battle of Britain: Winston Churchill, "nothing to offer but blood, toil, tears, and sweat"
- The Home Front in America
  American Lend-Lease supplies, Atlantic Charter
  America First movement
  U.S. mobilization for war: desegregation of defense industries, "Rosie the Riveter,"
  rationing, war bonds
  America races Germany to develop the atomic bomb: the Manhattan Project
- Hitler invades Soviet Union: battles of Leningrad and Stalingrad

See also English 7,
Autobiography, Anne Frank's
Diary of a Young Girl.

- The Holocaust: "Final Solution," concentration camps (Dachau, Auschwitz)
- North Africa Campaign: El Alamein
- D-Day: Allied invasion of Normandy, General Dwight Eisenhower
- Battle of the Bulge, bombing of Dresden
- Yalta Conference
- Surrender of Germany, Soviet Army takes Berlin

C. **WORLD WAR II IN THE PACIFIC, AND THE END OF THE WAR**
- Historical background: Japan's rise to power
  - Geography of Japan (review all topics from grade 5)
    - Sea of Japan and Korea Strait
    - High population density, very limited farmland, heavy reliance on imported raw materials and food
  - End of Japanese isolation, Commodore Matthew Perry
  - Meiji Restoration: end of feudal Japan, industrialization and modernization
  - Japanese imperialism: occupation of Korea, invasion of Manchuria, Rape of Nanking
  - Japanese-Soviet neutrality treaty
- Pearl Harbor, Dec. 7, 1941: "A day that will live in infamy."
- Internment of Japanese-Americans
- Fall of the Philippines: Bataan Death March, General Douglas MacArthur, "I shall return."
- Battle of Midway
- Island amphibious landings: Guadalcanal, Iwo Jima
- Surrender of Japan
  - Atom bombs dropped on Hiroshima and Nagasaki, the Enola Gay
  - U.S. dictates pacifist constitution for Japan, Emperor Hirohito
- Potsdam Conference, Nuremberg war crimes trials
- Creation of United Nations: Security Council, Universal Declaration of Human Rights

See also English 7, Essays and Speeches, Roosevelt's "Declaration of War."

VI. Geography of the United States

TEACHERS: **Students should regularly consult maps in reference to the following topics:**

- Physical features
  - General forms: Gulf/Atlantic coastal plain, Appalachian highlands and Piedmont, Midwest lowlands, Great Plains, Rocky Mountains, Intermountain Basin and Range, Pacific coast ranges, Arctic coastal plain
  - Mountains: Rockies, Appalachians, Sierra Nevada, Cascades, Adirondacks, Ozarks
  - Peaks: McKinley, Rainier, Whitney
  - Main water features: Gulf of Mexico, Chesapeake Bay, San Francisco Bay, Puget Sound, Great Salt Lake, Great Lakes (freshwater)—Erie, Huron, Michigan, Ontario, Superior
  - Rivers: Mississippi, Missouri, Ohio, Colorado, Hudson, Columbia, Potomac, Rio Grande, Tennessee
  - Niagara Falls, Grand Canyon, Mojave Desert, Death Valley
- Political, economic, and social features
  - The fifty states and their capitals (review), Washington, D. C., Commonwealth of Puerto Rico, Virgin Islands, Guam
- Cities: Atlanta, Baltimore, Birmingham, Boston, Charlotte, Chicago, Cincinnati, Cleveland, Dallas, Denver, Detroit, Houston, Kansas City, Los Angeles, Memphis, Miami, Milwaukee, Minneapolis, New Orleans, Norfolk, Philadelphia, Phoenix, Pittsburgh, Portland, St. Louis, San Antonio, San Diego, San Francisco, Seattle, Tampa
- Population
  - Expansion of settlement
  - Population density

- Regions
    - New England
    - Mid-Atlantic
    - South: "Dixie," Mason-Dixon Line, Bible Belt
    - Middle West: Rust Belt, Corn Belt
    - Southwest: Sun Belt
    - Mountain States
    - West Coast: San Andreas fault, California aqueduct (water supply) system
    - Coal, oil, and natural gas deposits
    - Agricultural crop regions
- New York City
    - Bronx, Brooklyn, Manhattan, Queens, Staten Island
    - Broadway, Fifth Avenue, Madison Avenue, Park Avenue, Times Square, Wall Street
    - Central Park, Harlem, Greenwich Village

Visual Arts: Grade 7

SEE PAGE 3, "The Arts in the Curriculum."

TEACHERS: In schools, lessons on the visual arts should illustrate important elements of making and appreciating art, and emphasize important artists, works of art, and artistic concepts. When appropriate, topics in the visual arts may be linked to topics in other disciplines. While the following guidelines specify a variety of artworks in different media and from various cultures, they are not intended to be comprehensive. Teachers are encouraged to build upon the core content and expose children to a wide range of art and artists.

In studying the works of art specified below, and in creating their own art, students should review, develop, and apply concepts introduced in previous grades, such as line, shape, form, space, texture, color, light, design, and symmetry.

I. Art History: Periods and Schools

TEACHERS: The guidelines here continue the organizational scheme established in sixth grade, which combined art history with analysis of specific illustrative works. Timelines may help students situate the artists, periods, and schools. Note that the periods and characteristics are not absolute distinctions but generally helpful categories (to which there are always exceptions) often used in discussions of art.

A. IMPRESSIONISM
- Examine characteristics of Impressionism in
    Claude Monet: *Impression: Sunrise, Bridge Over a Pool of Lilies*
    Pierre Auguste Renior, *Luncheon of the Boating Party*
    Edgar Degas, a ballet painting such as *Dancing Class*
    Mary Cassatt, *The Boating Party*

B. POST-IMPRESSIONISM
- Examine characteristics of Post-Impressionism in
    Paul Cezanne: a still life such as *Apples and Oranges*, a version of *Mont Sainte-Victoire*, *The Card Players*
    Georges Seurat and pointillism: *Sunday Afternoon on the Island of the Grande Jatte*
    Vincent van Gogh: *The Starry Night*, one of his *Sunflowers*, a self-portrait such as *Self-Portrait* [1889]
    Paul Gauguin: *Vision After the Sermon, Hail Mary (Ia Orana Maria)*
    Henri Toulouse-Lautrec, *At the Moulin Rouge*
    Art Nouveau as a pervasive style of decoration

C. EXPRESSIONISM AND ABSTRACTION
- Examine representative artists and works, including
    Henri Matisse: *Madame Matisse, The Red Room*, cutouts such as *Beasts of the Sea*
    Edvard Munch, *The Scream*
    Marc Chagall, *I and the Village*
    Pablo Picasso's early works, including *Family of Saltimbanques*
- Cubism
    Pablo Picasso, *Les Demoiselles d'Avignon*
    Marcel Duchamp, *Nude Descending a Staircase*
- Picasso after Cubism: *Girl Before a Mirror, Guernica*
- Other developers of abstraction:
    Vassily Kandinsky, *Improvisation 31 (Sea Battle)*
    Paul Klee, *Senecio* (also known as *Head of a Man*)
    Piet Mondrian, *Broadway Boogie Woogie*
    Salvador Dali and surrealism: *The Persistence of Memory*

D. **MODERN AMERICAN PAINTING**
  - Examine representative artists and works, including
    Edward Hopper, *Nighthawks*
    Andrew Wyeth, *Christina's World*
    Georgia O'Keeffe, *Red Poppies*
  - Regionalists, social realists, and genre painters
    Grant Wood, *American Gothic*
    Diego Rivera [Mexican], *Detroit Industry*
    Norman Rockwell, *Triple Self-Portrait*

Music: Grade 7

SEE PAGE 3, "The Arts in the Curriculum."

I. Elements of Music

TEACHERS: The Music guidelines for grades 6-8 share a basic vocabulary of the elements of music that can inform the discussion, appreciation, and study of selected musical works. Following these guidelines are recommendations in each grade for a core of musical content, broadly organized as a history of music from early to modern times, with attention to specific periods, composers, and genres. While these guidelines focus on musical vocabulary, appreciation, and history, musical performance should be encouraged and emphasized as local resources allow.

- Review as necessary from earlier grades:
  The orchestra and families of instruments (strings, wind, brass, percussion); keyboard instruments
  Vocal ranges: soprano, mezzo-soprano, alto; tenor, baritone, bass
- Recognize frequently used Italian terms:
  grave (very very slow)
  largo (very slow)
  adagio (slow)
  andante (moderate; "walking")
  moderato (medium)
  allegro (fast)
  presto (very fast)
  prestissimo (as fast as you can go)
  ritardando and *accelerando* (gradually slowing down and getting faster)
  crescendo and *decrescendo* (gradually increasing and decreasing volume)
  legato (smoothly flowing progression of notes), *staccato* (crisp, distinct notes)
- Recognize introduction, interlude, and coda in musical selections.
- Recognize theme and variations.
- Identify chords [such as I (tonic), IV (subdominant), V (dominant); V7]; major and minor chords; chord changes; intervals (third, fourth, fifth).
- Understand what an octave is.
- Understand the following notation and terms:

  names of lines and spaces in the treble clef; middle C

  𝄞 treble clef   𝄢 bass clef   𝄚 staff, bar line, double bar line, measure, repeat signs

  𝅝 whole note   𝅗𝅥 half note   𝅘𝅥 quarter note   ♪ eighth notes

  whole rest, half rest, quarter rest, eighth rest

  𝅘𝅥𝅯𝅘𝅥𝅯𝅘𝅥𝅯 grouped sixteenth notes

  tied notes and dotted notes

  ♯ sharps   ♭ flats   ♮ naturals

  Da capo [*D.C.*] *al fine*

  meter signature: $\frac{4}{4}$ or common time $\frac{2}{4}$ $\frac{3}{4}$ $\frac{6}{8}$

  quiet *pp p mp*   loud   *ff f mf*

II. Classical Music: Romantics and Nationalists

TEACHERS: While these guidelines focus on musical vocabulary, appreciation, and history, musical performance should be encouraged and emphasized as resources allow. The focus here combines music history with appreciation of illustrative works, and continues from grade 6 the idea of classifying Western music by periods, with examples of specific composers and works, as well as some associated musical terms. Timelines may help students situate the periods. The periods and their characteristics are not absolute distinctions but generally helpful categories often used in discussions of music. In sixth grade students studied music and composers from the Baroque to the Romantic.

NOTE: In sixth grade, students were introduced to works by Beethoven, Brahms, Chopin, and Schumann.

A. ROMANTIC COMPOSERS AND WORKS
- Composers and works:
  - Johannes Brahms, *Symphony No. 1* (fourth movement)
  - Hector Berlioz, *Symphonie Fantastique*
  - Franz Liszt, *Hungarian Rhapsody No. 2* for piano
  - Richard Wagner, Overture to *Die Meistersinger von Nürnberg*

B. MUSIC AND NATIONAL IDENTITY
- Composers and works:
  - Antonín Dvořák, *Symphony No. 9* (*"From the New World"*)
  - Edvard Grieg, *Peer Gynt Suites Nos. 1 and 2*
  - Peter Ilich Tchaikovsky, *1812 Overture*

III. American Musical Traditions

- Blues
  - Evolved from African-American work songs and spirituals
  - Twelve bar blues form
- Jazz
  - African-American origins
  - Terms: improvisation, syncopation, solo and soloist
  - Ragtime: works of Scott Joplin (such as "The Entertainer" and "Maple Leaf Rag")
  - Louis Armstrong: early recordings such as "Potato Head Blues," "West End Blues," or "St. Louis Blues"
  - Duke Ellington: "Caravan," "Take the 'A' Train" [by Billy Strayhorn]
  - Miles Davis: "So What"
  - Influence of jazz on other music: George Gershwin's *Rhapsody in Blue*

Music

Mathematics: Grade 7

Teachers: In learning the new concepts and procedures, students should use previously acquired mathematics to ensure that the procedures become automatic and habitual. Students should continue to master the use of measuring and drawing instruments, develop their mental arithmetic and their approximating abilities, become more familiar with deductive reasoning, and use calculators and computers in a thoughtful way.

These guidelines are representative of the mathematics typically learned in grade 7 in countries that have strong math traditions and whose students score well in international comparisons. In the United Sates, most teachers of middle-school mathematics follow commercial math textbooks which vary in quality. Because teachers are often selective about the parts of the textbooks they teach, the following guidelines may prove useful as an outline by which the teacher can, regardless of the text-book adopted, make sure the competencies taught in their programs are comparable to the competencies of students in the best-achieving systems.

While teaching methods may vary, it is worth keeping in mind the psychological principle that the most effective method for learning mathematics emphasizes frequent, varied practice, and encourages multiple approaches to solving varied types of problems.

I. Pre-Algebra

A. PROPERTIES OF THE REAL NUMBERS
- Know and use the associative, commutative, and distributive properties by name and in simplifying expressions involving numbers and variables.
- Understand absolute value and evaluate expressions such as $|2x - 3| + 3x$.

B. LINEAR APPLICATIONS AND PROPORTIONALITY
- Know the concept of slope.
- Translate situations of proportionality into equations of the form $y = mx$, where m is the constant of proportionality or slope; specifically know and understand $d = rt$ and $i = prt$.
- Show situations of constant proportionality as a line on the coordinate plane.
- Introduce the concept of a function and determine the equation of a linear function given its slope and intercepts in the form $y = mx + b$.
- Estimate the values of b and m from a given linear graph.

C. POLYNOMIAL ARITHMETIC
- Add, subtract, multiply, and divide monomials and polynomials (divide polynomials by monomials only).
- Factor binomials that have a common monomial factor.

D. EQUIVALENT EQUATIONS AND INEQUALITIES
- Review equality properties for equations.
- Know that addition or subtraction of the same value from both sides of an inequality maintains the inequality.
- Know that multiplying or dividing both sides of an inequality by a positive number maintains the inequality, but multiplying or dividing by a negative number reverses the inequality; be able to show why using a number line.
- Simplify and solve linear equations in one variable such as $3(2x - 5) + 4x = 12(x + 5)$.
- Simplify and graph solutions to linear inequalities in one variable such as $3(2x - 5) + 4x \leq 12(x + 5)$.

E. INTEGER EXPONENTS
- Know the meaning of an exponent n when n is positive or negative.
- Know that a non-zero number to the zero power is one.

- Understand why a negative number to an even power is positive and a negative number to odd power is negative.
- Know the multiplication properties of exponents:
    Product of powers: $(a^m)(a^n) = a^{(m+n)}$
    Power of a power: $(a^m)^n = a^{mn}$
    Power of a product: $(ab)^m = (a^m)(b^m)$.
- Convert decimal numbers to and from scientific notation.
- Know the proper order of operations with exponents.

II. Geometry

A. THREE-DIMENSIONAL OBJECTS
- Describe and construct simple right prisms, cylinders, cones, and spheres using the concepts of parallel and perpendicular; calculate the surface areas and volumes of these objects.
- Know that the section created by the intersection of a plane and a sphere is a circle.
- Calculate the surface area of a sphere using the equation $SA = 4 \pi r^2$.
- Calculate the volume of a sphere using the equation $V = (4/3) \pi r^3$.

B. ANGLE PAIRS
- Construct parallel lines and a transversal using a compass and straight edge.
- Understand congruent angles, vertical angles, complementary angles, supplementary angles, adjacent angles, corresponding angles, and alternate interior and alternate exterior angles.

C. TRIANGLES
- Know that a triangle is determined by its three sides or by two sides and the included angle (SSS and SAS triangle congruence) and solve problems.
- Use SSS to prove that the construction of the bisector of an angle is valid.
- Use SSS to prove that the construction of the perpendicular bisector of a segment is valid.
- Prove that the base angles of an isosceles triangle are congruent.
- Demonstrate that the sum of the interior angles of a triangle equals 180 degrees.
- Know that the shape of a triangle is determined by two (hence all three) of its angles (AA(A) triangle similarity) and solve related problems.
- Construct a circle that circumscribes a triangle using compass and straight edge.
- Know and understand the Pythagorean Theorem and its converse and use it to find the length of the missing side of a right triangle and lengths of other line segments and, in some situations, empirically verify the Pythagorean theorem by direct measurement and a calculator.
- Use the Pythagorean Theorem to determine the exact ratios of the sides in 30-60-right triangles and isosceles right triangles.
- Determine the image of a triangle under translations, rotations, and reflections.

D. MEASUREMENT
- Choose appropriate units of measure and use ratios to convert within and between measurement systems to solve problems.
- Compare weights, capacities, geometric measures, times, and temperatures within and between measurement systems (for example, miles per hour and feet per second, cubic inches to cubic centimeters).
- Use measures expressed as rates (for example, speed, density) and measures expressed as products (for example, person-days) to solve problems; check the units of the solutions; and use dimensional analysis to check the reasonableness of the answer.
- Compute the perimeter, area, and volume of common geometric objects and use the results to find measures of less common objects.
- Know how perimeter, area, and volume are affected by changes of scale.

Mathematics

- Estimate and compute the area of more complex or irregular two- and three-dimensional figures by breaking the figures down into more basic geometric objects.
- Relate the changes in measurement with a change of scale to the units used (for example, square inches, cubic feet) and to conversions between units (1 square foot = 144 square inches of [1 ft² = 144 in²], 1 cubic inch is approximately 16.38 cubic centimeters [1 in³] = [16.36 cm³]).

III. Probability and Statistics

- Show the relationship between two variables using a scatter-plot and describe the apparent relationship informally.
- Find the upper and lower quartiles for a data set.
- Understand that if p is the probability of an event occurring, $1 - p$ is the probability of the event not occurring.
- Understand the difference between independent and dependent events.

Science: Grade 7

TEACHERS: Effective instruction in science requires not only direct experience and observation but also book learning, which helps bring coherence and order to a student's scientific knowledge. Only when topics are presented systematically and clearly can students make steady and secure progress in their scientific learning. The Science sequence for the middle school grades aims for more intensive and selective study of topics, a number of which were introduced in earlier grades. The Sequence continues the practice of studying topics from each of the major realms of science (physical, life, and earth science). Students are expected to do experiments and write reports on their findings.

I. Atomic Structure

- Review (from grade 5): Structure of atoms: protons, neutron, electrons
  Molecules
  Compounds are formed by combining two or more elements and have properties
  different from the constituent elements.
- Early theories of matter
  The early Greek theory of four elements: earth, air, fire, and water
  Later theories of Democritus: everything is made of atoms and nothing else
  ("atom" in Greek means that which can't be cut or divided); atoms of the
  same kind form a pure "element"
  Alchemy in middle ages
- Start of modern chemistry
  Lavoisier and oxygen: the idea that matter is not gained or lost in chemical reactions
  John Dalton revives the theory of the atom.
  Mendeleev develops the Periodic Table, showing that the properties of atoms of
  elements come in repeating (periodic) groups.
  Niels Bohr develops a model of the atom in shells that hold a certain number of
  electrons. Bohr's model, plus the discovery of neutrons, helped explain the
  Periodic Table: atomic number, atomic weight, and isotopes.

See below, Science
Biographies, Lavoisier and
Mendeleev.

II. Chemical Bonds and Reactions

- To get a stable outer shell of electrons, atoms either give away, take on, or
  share electrons.
- Chemical reactions rearrange the atoms and the electrons in elements and compounds
  to form chemical bonds.
- When single atoms combine with themselves or with other atoms, the result is
  a molecule.
  O_2 is a molecule of oxygen. NaCl is a molecule of salt, and because it has more than
  one element is called a compound.
- Ionic bond
  Atoms like sodium that have just one or two extra electrons are very energetic in giving
  them away. Elements with the same number of extra or few electrons can join with
  each other to make an ionic bond. Example: NaCl, table salt.
- Metallic bond
  In the metallic bond, electrons are not given away between elements, but are arranged
  so that they are shared between atoms. Pure metals show this sharing, and the
  atoms can rearrange themselves in different ways, which explains why you can
  pound metals into different shapes.

- Covalent bond

    Some atoms share electrons in a definite way, making them very stable and unreactive. Examples are H_2 and O_2. Carbon, which can take up or give away 4 electrons in covalent bonds, can help make molecules that can adopt almost any shape. It is the basis of life.

- Kinds of reactions

    Oxidation: a chemical reaction that commonly involves oxygen. More generally, oxidation is a reaction in which an atom accepts electrons while combining with other elements. The atom that gives away electrons is said to be oxidized. Examples: rusting of iron, burning of paper. Heat is given off.

    Reduction: the opposite of oxidation. Reduction involves the gaining of electrons. An oxidized material gives them away and heat is taken up.

    Acids: for example, vinegar, HCl, H_2SO_4; sour; turn litmus red

    Bases: for example, baking soda; bitter; turn litmus blue

    pH: ranges from 0-14; neutral = 7, acid = below 7, base = above 7

    Reactions with acids and bases

    In water solution, an acid compound has an H ion (a proton lacking an electron), and the base compound has an OH ion (with an extra electron).

    When the two come together, they form HOH (water) plus a stable compound called a "salt."

- How chemists describe reactions by equations, for example: HCl + NaOH = NaCl + H_2O

- A catalyst helps a reaction, but is not used up.

> NOTE: A useful mnemonic device is "OIL RIG" — "oxidation is loss, reduction is gain."

III. Cell Division and Genetics

- Cell division, the basic process for growth and reproduction

    Two types of cell division: mitosis (growth and asexual reproduction), meiosis (sexual reproduction)

    Asexual reproduction: mitosis; diploid cells (as in amoeba)

    Sexual reproduction: meiosis: haploid cells; combinations of traits

    How change occurs from one generation to another: either mutation or mixing of traits through sexual reproduction

    Why acquired characteristics are not transmitted

- Gregor Mendel's experiments with purebred and hybrid peas

    Dominant and recessive genes

    Mendel's statistical analysis led to understanding that inherited traits are controlled by genes (now known to be DNA).

- Modern understanding of chromosomes and genes

    Double helix (twisted ladder) of DNA coding; how DNA makes new DNA

    How DNA sequence makes proteins; one gene equals one protein

    Genetic engineering

    Modern researchers in genetics: Francis Crick, James Watson, Severo Ochoa, Barbara McClintock

> NOTE: Review from grade 5, Cell Structures and Processes.

IV. History of the Earth and Life Forms

A. PALEONTOLOGY

- Fossils as a record of the Earth's history and past life forms
- How fossils are formed, and types of fossils (mold, cast, trace, true-form)

B. GEOLOGIC TIME

- The age of the earth is about 4.6 billion years, based on geologic evidence and radioactive dating. Life has existed on earth for more than 3 billion years.

    How movements of the earth's plates have affected the distribution of organisms

176

- Organizing geologic time: Scientists have organized the earth's history into four major eras:
  - Precambrian Era (earliest forms of life, such as bacteria and blue-green algae; later in the period, invertebrates such as jellyfish)
  - Paleozoic Era (Pangaea; invertebrate life, such as trilobites, early in this era, followed by development of vertebrates later in the era, including fish; development of insects, amphibians, and the beginnings of reptiles; development of simple plants, such as mosses and ferns)
  - Mesozoic Era (Pangaea separates into continents; "Age of Reptiles"; dinosaurs, flowering plants, small mammals and birds)
  - Cenozoic (Present) Era (Ice Age; mammoths; gradual development of mammals, birds and other animals recognizable today; humans; flowering plants, forests, grasslands)

V. Evolution

A. EVOLUTION

See below, Science Biographies, Charles Darwin.

- Evolution is the change in a population of organisms over time caused by both genetic change and environmental factors.
  Adaptation and mutation
- Charles Darwin: voyages of the *Beagle*; *Origin of Species* (1859)

B. NATURAL SELECTION

- Natural selection as the mechanism of evolution: Darwin's theory that life forms better adapted to their current environment have a better chance of surviving and will pass on their traits to their offspring
  Trait variation and change from generation to generation
- Evidence for the theory of evolution includes comparative anatomy, geology, fossils, and DNA research.

C. EXTINCTION AND SPECIATION

- Extinction occurs when an environment changes and a species is no longer adapted to it.
- New species can develop when part of the population becomes separated and evolves in isolation.
- Life forms have evolved from simple organisms in oceans through amphibians to higher forms such as primates.

VI. Science Biographies

See above, Evolution *re* Darwin; Atomic Structure: Start of modern chemistry, *re* Lavoisier and Mendeleev.

Charles Darwin
Antoine Lavoisier
Lise Meitner
Dmitri Mendeleev

Science

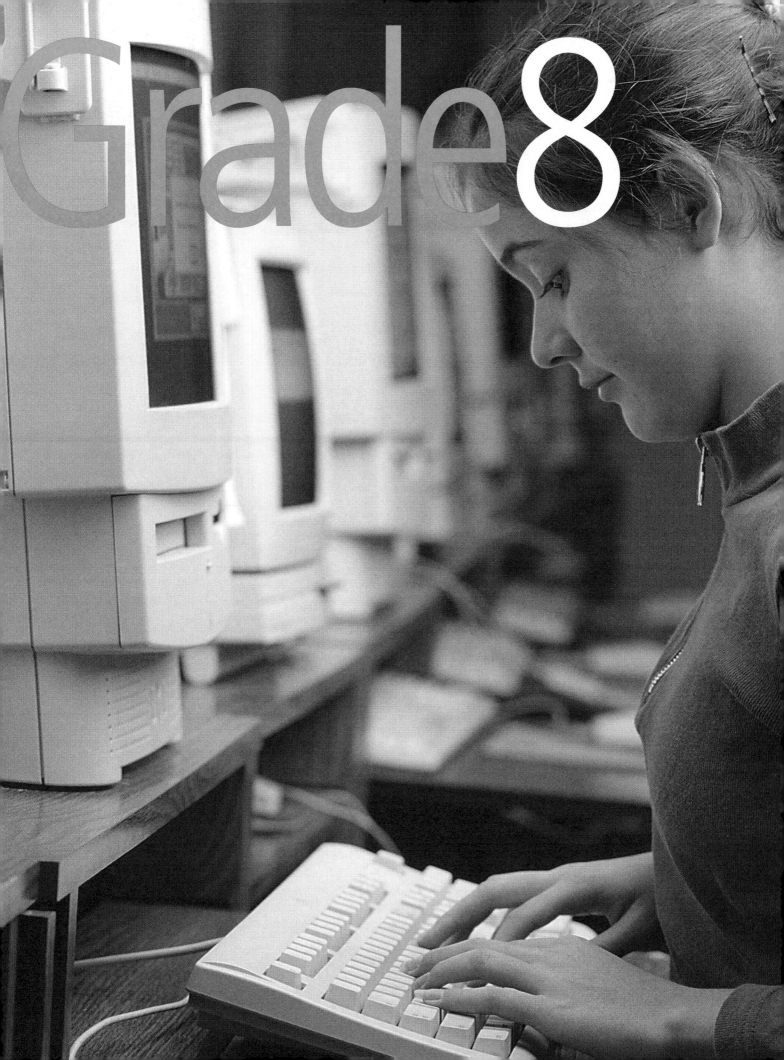

Grade8

Overview of Topics   Grade 8

English
I. Writing, Grammar, and Usage
   A. Writing and Research
   B. Speaking and Listening
   C. Grammar
   D. Spelling
   E. Vocabulary
II. Poetry
   A. Poems
   B. Elements of Poetry
III. Fiction, Nonfiction, and Drama
   A. Short Stories
   B. Novels
   C. Elements of Fiction
   D. Essays and Speeches
   E. Autobiography
   F. Drama
   G. Literary Terms
IV. Foreign Phrases Commonly Used in English

History and Geography
I. The Decline of European Colonialism
   A. Breakup of the British Empire
   B. Creation of the People's Republic of China
II. The Cold War
   A. Origins of the Cold War
   B. The Korean War
   C. America in the Cold War
III. The Civil Rights Movement
IV. The Vietnam War and the Rise of Social Activism
   A. The Vietnam War
   B. Social and Environmental Activism
V. The Middle East and Oil Politics
   A. History
   B. Geography of the Middle East
VI. The End of the Cold War: The Expansion of Democracy
      and Continuing Challenges
   A. The American Policy of Detente
   B. Breakup of the USSR
   C. China under Communism
   D. Contemporary Europe
   E. The End of Apartheid in South Africa
VII. Civics: The Constitution—Principles and Structure of
      American Democracy
VIII. Geography of Canada and Mexico

Visual Arts
I. Art History: Periods and Schools
   A. Painting Since World War II
   B. Photography
   C. 20th-Century Sculpture
II. Architecture Since the Industrial Revolution

Music
I. Elements of Music
II. Non-Western Music
III. Classical Music: Nationalists and Moderns
   A. Music and National Identity
   B. Modern Music
IV. Vocal Music
   A. Opera
   B. American Musical Theater

Mathematics
I. Algebra
   A. Properties of the Real Numbers
   B. Relations, Functions, and Graphs (Two Variables)
   C. Linear Equations and Functions (Two Variables)
   D. Arithmetic of Rational Expression
   E. Quadratic Equations and Functions
II. Geometry
   A. Analytic Geometry
   B. Introduction to Trigonometry
   C. Triangles and Proofs

Science
I. Physics
   A. Motion
   B. Forces
   C. Density and Buoyancy
   D. Work
   E. Energy
   F. Power
II. Electricity and Magnetism
III. Electromagnetic Radiation and Light
IV. Sound Waves
V. Chemistry of Food and Respiration
VI. Science Biographies

English: Grade 8

I. Writing, Grammar, and Usage

A. WRITING AND RESEARCH

TEACHERS: Students should be given opportunities to write fiction, poetry, or drama, but instruction should emphasize repeated expository writing. Students should examine their work with attention to unity, coherence, and emphasis. Expository essays should have a main point and stick to it, and have a coherent structure, typically following the pattern of introduction, body, and conclusion. Paragraphs should have a unified focus, be developed with evidence and examples, and have transitions between them. Essays should have appropriate tone and diction, as well as correct spelling and grammar in their final form. Standards for writing apply across the disciplines.

See also English 6 for more guidelines on writing persuasive essays.

- Expository writing: Write essays that describe, narrate, persuade, and compare and contrast.
- Write research essays, with attention to
    asking open-ended questions
    gathering relevant data through library and field research
    summarizing, paraphrasing, and quoting accurately when taking notes
    defining a thesis (that is, a central proposition, a main idea)
    organizing with an outline
    integrating quotations from sources
    acknowledging sources and avoiding plagiarism
    preparing a bibliography

B. SPEAKING AND LISTENING

- Participate civilly and productively in group discussions.
- Give a short speech to the class that is well-organized and well-supported.
- Demonstrate an ability to use standard pronunciation when speaking to large groups and in formal circumstances, such as a job interview.

C. GRAMMAR

TEACHERS: Students should have a working understanding of the following terms and be able to use them to discuss and analyze writing.

Punctuation
- Review punctuation based on sentence structure, including
    semi-colons
    commas with phrases and clauses
- Review other punctuation, including
    punctuation of quotations, dialogue
    use of parentheses
    hyphens
    dashes
    colons
    italics
    apostrophes

Misplaced modifiers
- Phrases and clauses go as near as possible to the word(s) they modify.
    Dangling modifiers
    Two-way modifiers

Parallelism
- Parallelism is expressing ideas of equal importance using the same grammatical constructions.
- Kinds of parallelism
  coordinate (using coordinating conjunctions *and, but, or, nor, yet*)
  compared/contrasted
  correlative (both . . . and, either . . . or, neither . . . nor, not only . . . but also)
- Correcting faulty parallelism
  repeating words (articles, prepositions, pronouns) to maintain parallelism
  completing parallel construction
  revising sentences using parallel structure (for example, using all gerund phrases, or all noun clauses)

Sentence variety
- Review sentences classified by structure: simple, compound, complex, compound-complex.
- Varying sentence length and structure to avoid monotony
- Varying sentence openings

D. SPELLING

NOTE: More commonly misspelled words listed in grades 6 and 7.

- Continue work with spelling, with special attention to commonly misspelled words, including:

absence	counterfeit	guarantee	permanence
accommodate	courageous	hygiene	physician
analysis	curiosity	independence	prairie
attendance	defendant	laboratory	sergeant
believe	dessert	library	souvenir
bureau	desperate	lightning	straight
capitol	dissatisfied	maintenance	technique
colonel	extraordinary	mileage	temporary
committee	fascinating	necessary	vacuum
correspondence	foreign	occurrence	whether

E. VOCABULARY

TEACHERS: **Students should know the meaning of these Latin and Greek words and be able to give examples of English words that are based on them.**

NOTE: More Latin and Greek words and roots are listed in grades 6 and 7. In the listings here, L = Latin, G = Greek. No single form of the Latin or Greek words is consistently used here, but rather the form most similar to related English words.

Latin /Greek Word	*Meaning*	*Examples*
aequus [L]	equal	equal, equation
ago, acta [L]	do, things done	agent, enact, transact
anthropos [G]	man, human being	anthropology, misanthrope
ars [L]	art	artist, artifact
brevis [L]	short	brevity, abbreviate
canto [L]	sing	chant, cantor
caput [L]	head	captain, decapitate
clino [L]	to lean, bend	incline, decline
cognito [L]	know	cognizant, recognize
copia [L]	plenty	copy, copious
credo [L]	believe	credible, incredulous
culpa [L]	blame	culpable, culprit
dominus [L]	a lord, master	dominate, dominion
duco [L]	lead	abduct, introduce
fido [L]	to trust, believe	confide, infidel
fundo, fusum [L]	pour, thing poured	effusive, transfusion
genus [L]	kind, origin	generic, congenital

182

holos [G]	whole	holistic, catholic
jungo [L]	join	junction, conjugal
lego, lectum [L]	read, thing read	intellect, legible
locus [L]	a place	local, dislocate
loquor [L]	speak	eloquent, loquacious
medius [L]	middle	mediate, mediocrity
missio [L]	a sending	emissary, mission
morior [L]	die	mortal
nego [L]	deny	negate
nihil [L]	nothing	nihilism, annihilate
occido [L]	kill	homicide, suicide
pathos [G]	suffering, feeling	sympathy, apathy
pendo [L]	weigh, hang	depend, pendant
per [L]	through	perceive, persist, persevere
phobos [G]	fear	phobia, claustrophobia
plenus [L]	full	plenty, plenary
positum [L]	placed	position, opposite
porto [L]	carry	transport, export
possum [L]	be able	possible, potent
pugno [L]	to fight	impugn, pugnacious
punctum [L]	point	punctual, punctuation
rego [L]	to rule	regular, regency
sanguis [L]	blood	sanguine
satis [L]	enough	satisfy
scio [L]	know	science, conscious
solus [L]	alone	solo, desolate
sonus [L]	a sound	unison, consonant
sophos [G]	wise	philosophy, sophomore
spiritus [L]	breath	inspire, spirit
totus [L]	whole	totalitarianism
tractum [L]	drawn, pulled	distract, tractor
usus [L]	use	abuse, utensil
vacuus [L]	empty	evacuate, vacuum
verbum [L]	word	verbal
verto [L]	turn	avert, convert, anniversary
via [L]	way, road	deviate, viaduct

II. Poetry

A. POEMS

NOTE: The poems listed here constitute a selected core of poetry for this grade. You are encouraged to expose students to more poetry, old and new, and to have students write their own poems. Students should examine some poems in detail, discussing what the poems mean as well as asking questions about the poet's use of language.

Buffalo Bill's (e.e. cummings)

Chicago (Carl Sandburg)

Do Not Go Gentle into That Good Night (Dylan Thomas)

How do I love thee? (Elizabeth Barrett Browning)

How They Brought the Good News From Ghent to Aix (Robert Browning)

I dwell in possibility; Apparently with no surprise (Emily Dickinson)

The Lake Isle of Innisfree (William B. Yeats)

Lucy Gray (or Solitude); My Heart Leaps Up (William Wordsworth)

Mending Wall; The Gift Outright (Robert Frost)

Mr. Flood's Party (Edward Arlington Robinson)

Polonius's speech from *Hamlet*, "Neither a borrower nor a lender be . . ." (William Shakespeare)

Ozymandias (Percy Bysshe Shelley)

Sonnet 18, "Shall I compare thee. . ." (William Shakespeare)

Spring and Fall (Gerald Manley Hopkins)
A Supermarket in California (Allen Ginsberg)
Theme for English B (Langston Hughes)
We Real Cool (Gwendolyn Brooks)

B. ELEMENTS OF POETRY
- Review: meter, iamb, rhyme scheme, free verse, couplet, onomatopoeia, alliteration, assonance
- Review:
  - forms: ballad, sonnet, lyric, narrative, limerick, haiku
  - stanzas and refrains
  - types of rhyme: end, internal, slant, eye
  - metaphor and simile
    - extended and mixed metaphors
  - imagery, symbol, personification
  - allusion

III. Fiction, Nonfiction, and Drama

A. SHORT STORIES
"The Bet" (Anton Chekov)
"Dr. Heidegger's Experiment" (Nathaniel Hawthorne)
"God Sees the Truth But Waits" (Leo Tolstoy)
"An Honest Thief" (Fyodor Dostoyevsky)
"The Open Boat" (Stephen Crane)

B. NOVELS
Animal Farm (George Orwell)
The Good Earth (Pearl S. Buck)

C. ELEMENTS OF FICTION
- Review:
  - plot and setting
  - theme
  - point of view in narration: omniscient narrator, unreliable narrator, third person limited, first person
  - conflict: external and internal
  - suspense and climax
- Characterization
  - as delineated through a character's thoughts, words, and deeds; through the narrator's description; and through what other characters say
  - flat and round; static and dynamic
  - motivation
  - protagonist and antagonist
- Tone and diction

NOTE: See also History 8: The Kennedy Years, *re* J. F. Kennedy; The Civil Rights Movement, *re* M. L. King, Jr.; and, Emergence of Environmentalism, *re* Rachel Carson.

D. ESSAYS AND SPEECHES
"Ask not what your country can do for you" (John F. Kennedy's Inaugural Address)
"I have a dream"; "Letter from Birmingham Jail" (Martin Luther King, Jr.)
"Death of a Pig" (E. B. White)
"The Marginal World" (Rachel Carson)

E. AUTOBIOGRAPHY
Selections from *I Know Why the Caged Bird Sings* (Maya Angelou)

F. DRAMA
- *Twelfth Night* (William Shakespeare)
- Elements of Drama
    Review:
        tragedy and comedy
        aspects of conflict, suspense, and characterization
        soliloquies and asides
    Farce and satire
    Aspects of performance and staging
        actors and directors
        sets, costumes, props, lighting, music
        presence of an audience

G. LITERARY TERMS
- Irony: verbal, situational, dramatic
- Flashbacks and foreshadowing
- Hyperbole, oxymoron, parody

IV. Foreign Phrases Commonly Used in English

TEACHERS: Students should learn the meaning of the following French words and phrases that are commonly used in English speech and writing.

au revoir - goodbye, until we see each other again
avant-garde - a group developing new or experimental concepts, a vanguard
bête noire - a person or thing especially dreaded and avoided [literally, "black beast"]
c'est la vie - that's life, that's how things happen
carte blanche - full discretionary power [literally, "blank page"]
cause célèbre - a very controversial issue that generates fervent public debate [literally, a "celebrated case"]
coup de grâce - a decisive finishing blow
coup d'état - overthrow of a government by a group
déjà vu - something overly familiar [literally, "already seen"]
enfant terrible - one whose remarks or actions cause embarrassment, or someone strikingly unconventional [literally, "terrible child"]
fait accompli - an accomplished fact, presumably irreversible
faux pas - a social blunder [literally, "false step"]
Madame, Mademoiselle, Monsieur - Mrs., Miss, Mr.
merci - thank you
pièce de résistance - the principal part of the meal, a showpiece item
raison d'être - reason for being
savoir-faire - the ability to say or do the right thing in any situation, polished sureness in society [literally, "to know (how) to do"]
tête-à-tête - private conversation between two people [literally, "head to head"]

NOTE: You are encouraged
to use timelines to help
students place these events
in chronological context
relative to their prior study in
grade 7 of World Wars I
and II.

History and Geography: Grade 8

TEACHERS: In grades K-6, the history guidelines in the Core Knowledge Sequence were organized into separate strands on World History and American History. Because the World and American History strands merged chronologically in sixth grade, the Sequence presents a unified section on History and Geography in grades seven and eight. Central themes of the history guidelines in grades seven and eight are growth and change in American democracy, and interactions with world forces, particularly nationalism and totalitarianism. Fundamental principles and structure of American government are reviewed in a civics unit in this grade.

The study of geography aims at understanding the spatial relationship between nature and human culture and processes that change environments. Following the main outline of the history curriculum, eighth graders study the Middle East, South Asia, China, Canada, Mexico, and post-Cold War changes. Students should learn locations as well as the relationships between physical and human systems.

I. The Decline of European Colonialism

A. BREAKUP OF THE BRITISH EMPIRE
- Creation of British Commonwealth, independence for colonial territories
- Troubled Ireland: Easter Rebellion, Irish Free State
- Indian nationalism and independence
  - Sepoy Rebellion
  - Mahatma Gandhi, Salt March
  - Partition of India into Hindu and Muslim states
- Geography of India and South Asia
  - Overview
    - Legacy of British colonial rule: English language, rail system
    - Himalayas, Mt. Everest, K-2
    - Very high population densities and growth rates, food shortages
    - Monsoons
    - Rivers: Ganges, Indus, Brahmaputra
    - Arabian Sea, Bay of Bengal
    - Pakistan, Karachi
    - Bangladesh
    - Sri Lanka
  - India
    - Second most populous country after China
    - Subsistence agriculture
    - Caste system, "untouchables"
    - Delhi, Bombay, Calcutta, Madras
    - Longstanding tension between Hindus and Moslems

B. CREATION OF PEOPLE'S REPUBLIC OF CHINA
- China under European domination
  - Opium Wars, Boxer Rebellion
  - Sun Yat Sen
- Communists take power
  - Mao Zedong: The Long March
  - Defeat of nationalists led by Chiang Kai-Shek
  - Soviet-Communist Chinese 30-Year Friendship Treaty

- Geography of China
    - Overview
        - One-fifth of world population
        - 4,000-year-old culture
        - Third largest national territory, regional climates
    - Physical features
        - Huang He (Yellow) River, Chang Jiang (Yangtze) River
        - Tibetan Plateau, Gobi Desert
        - Yellow Sea, East China Sea, South China Sea
        - Great Wall, Grand Canal
    - Social and economic characteristics
        - Major cities: Beijing, Shanghai, Guangzhou (formerly Canton), Shenyang
        - World's largest producer of coal and agricultural products, major mineral producer
        - Off-shore oil reserves
    - Multi-dialectal, including Mandarin, Cantonese
    - Hong Kong, special coastal economic zones
    - Taiwan, Taipei

II. The Cold War

A. ORIGINS OF THE COLD WAR
- Post-WWII devastation in Europe, Marshall Plan, Bretton Woods Conference
- Western fear of communist expansion, Soviet fear of capitalist influences
- Truman Doctrine, policy of containment of communism
    - Formation of NATO, Warsaw Pact
    - The "Iron Curtain" (Churchill)
    - Berlin Airlift
    - Eastern European resistance, Hungarian Revolution, Berlin Wall, Prague Spring

B. THE KOREAN WAR
- Inchon, Chinese entry, removal of MacArthur
- Partition of Korea, truce line near the 38th Parallel

C. AMERICA IN THE COLD WAR
- McCarthyism, House Unamerican Activities Committee, "witch hunts"
    - Hollywood Blacklist
    - Spy cases: Alger Hiss, Julius and Ethel Rosenberg
- The Eisenhower Years
    - Secret operations, CIA, FBI counterespionage, J. Edgar Hoover, U-2 incident
    - Soviet Sputnik satellite, "Missile Gap", Yuri Gagarin
    - Eisenhower's farewell speech, the "military-industrial complex"
- The Kennedy Years, "Ask not what your country can do for you . . ."
    - Attack on organized crime, Robert F. Kennedy
    - Cuban Missile Crisis, Fidel Castro, Bay of Pigs invasion
    - Nuclear deterrence, "mutual assured destruction," Nuclear Test Ban Treaty
    - Kennedy assassination in 1963, Lee Harvey Oswald, Warren Commission
- Space exploration, U.S. moon landing, Neil Armstrong
- American culture in the '50s and '60s
    - Levittown and the rise of the suburban lifestyle, automobile-centered city planning
    - Influence of television
    - Baby Boom generation, rock and roll, Woodstock festival, 26th Amendment

See also English 8, III.D, JFK's
Inaugural Address.

III. The Civil Rights Movement

- Segregation
  - *Plessy* v. *Ferguson,* doctrine of "separate but equal"
  - "Jim Crow" laws
- Post-war steps toward desegregation
  - Jackie Robinson breaks color barrier in baseball
  - Truman desegregates Armed Forces
  - Adam Clayton Powell, Harlem congressman
  - Integration of public schools: *Brown* v. *Board of Education* (1954), Thurgood Marshall
- Montgomery Bus Boycott, Rosa Parks
- Southern "massive resistance"
  - Federal troops open schools in Little Rock, Arkansas
  - Murder of Medgar Evers
  - Alabama Governor George Wallace "stands in schoolhouse door"
- Nonviolent challenges to segregation: "We shall overcome"
  - Woolworth lunch counter sit-ins
  - Freedom riders, CORE
  - Black voter registration drives
  - Martin Luther King, Jr.
  - Southern Christian Leadership Conference
  - March on Washington, "I have a dream" speech
  - "Letter from Birmingham Jail"
  - Selma to Montgomery March
- President Johnson and the civil rights movement
  - The Great Society, War on Poverty, Medicare
  - Civil Rights Act of 1964, Voting Rights Act of 1965, affirmative action
- African American militance
  - Malcolm X
  - Black Power, Black Panthers
  - Watts and Newark riots
- Assassinations of Martin Luther King, Jr., and Robert F. Kennedy

See also English 8, III.D, Essays and Speeches, King's "I have a dream" speech and "Letter from Birmingham Jail."

IV. The Vietnam War and the Rise of Social Activism

A. THE VIETNAM WAR
- French Indochina War: Dien Bien Phu, Ho Chi Minh, Viet Cong
- Domino Theory
- U.S. takes charge of the war, Special Forces, Tonkin Gulf Resolution
- Tet Offensive, My Lai Massacre
- Antiwar protests, Kent State, The Pentagon Papers, "hawks" and "doves"
- American disengagement, Nixon's "Vietnamization" policy, Kissinger, War Powers Act
- Watergate scandal, resignation of Nixon
- Vietnam, Hanoi, Ho Chi Minh City (formerly Saigon)

See also Visual Arts 8, 20th Century Sculpture, Vietnam Veterans Memorial.

B. SOCIAL AND ENVIRONMENTAL ACTIVISM
- Feminist movement, "women's liberation"
  - Betty Friedan, National Organization for Women
  - *Roe* v. *Wade*
  - Failure of the Equal Rights Amendment
- Cesar Chavez, United Farm Workers
- American Indian Movement
  - Second Wounded Knee
  - Federal recognition of Indian right to self-determination

- Emergence of environmentalism
    Rachel Carson, *Silent Spring*
    Environmental Protection Agency, Endangered Species Act, Clean Air and Water Acts
    Disasters such as Love Canal, Three Mile Island, Chernobyl, Exxon Valdez

V. The Middle East and Oil Politics

A. HISTORY
- League of Nations' territorial mandates in Middle East
- Creation of Israel in 1948, David Ben-Gurion
- Suez Crisis, Gamal Abal Nasser
- Palestine Liberation Organization, Yasser Arafat
- Arab-Israeli Wars
    Six-Day War, Israel occupies West Bank, Gaza Strip, Golan Heights
    Yom Kippur War, OPEC oil embargo
- Camp David Peace Treaty
- Islamic fundamentalism, Iranian hostage crisis, Iran-Iraq War
- Persian Gulf War

B. GEOGRAPHY OF THE MIDDLE EAST
- Overview
    Heartland of great early civilizations, Nile River, Mesopotamia, "Fertile Crescent"
    Generally hot, arid conditions with thin, poor soils
    Generally speak Arabic, except in Turkey (Turkish), Israel (Hebrew), Iran (Persian)
    Predominant religion is Islam
    Sunni and Shiite sects
    Principal holy places: Makkah (also spelled Mecca) and Medina in Saudi Arabia
- Oil: world's most valuable commodity
    Greatest known oil reserves concentrated around the Persian Gulf
    Strait of Hormuz, shipping routes and national imports
    Extraction of Arab oil required Western technology, which introduced competing
        cultural influences to Islam
- Egypt
    Most populous Arab country
    Nile River and delta, surrounded by inhospitable deserts
    Aswan Dam, Lake Nasser
    Cairo (largest city in Africa), Alexandria
    Suez Canal, Sinai Peninsula, Red Sea
- Israel
    Formed by the United Nations in 1948 as homeland for Jewish people
    Jerusalem: Holy city for Judaism (Wailing Wall, Temple Mount), Christianity (Church of
        the Holy Sepulcher), and Islam (Dome of the Rock)
    Tel Aviv, West Bank, Gaza Strip, Golan Heights
    Jordan River, Sea of Galilee, Dead Sea (lowest point on earth), Gulf of Aqaba
- Middle East states and cities
    Lebanon: Beirut
    Jordan: Amman
    Syria: Damascus
    Iraq: Baghdad
        Kurdish minority population (also in Turkey and Iran)
    Iran: Tehran
    Kuwait
    Saudi Arabia: Riyadh, Makkah
- Turkey
    Istanbul (formerly Constantinople)
    Bosporus, Dardanelles
    Ataturk Dam controls upper Euphrates River

NOTE: Review from grade 4,
World History III.A, Islam.

NOTE: It is recommended
that you examine with
students a map of the
world's oil reserves.

VI. The End of the Cold War: The Expansion of Democracy and Continuing Challenges

A. THE AMERICAN POLICY OF DETENTE
- Diplomatic opening to China
- Strategic Arms Limitation Talks
- Jimmy Carter's human rights basis for diplomacy

B. BREAKUP OF THE USSR
- History
  - Arms race exhausts USSR economy, Afghanistan War
  - Helsinki Accord on human rights, Andrei Sakharov
  - Mikhail Gorbachev
  - Solidarity labor movement, Lech Walesa
  - Reunification of Germany, demolition of the Berlin Wall
- Geography
  - Consequences of the breakup of the Soviet Union
    - New European states from former Soviet Union:
      - Belarus, Latvia, Lithuania, Moldova, Ukraine
    - Newly independent Muslim states in Asia (with ethnic Russian minorities):
      - Kazakstan, Kyrgyzstan, Turkmenistan, Uzbekistan
    - Caucasus, mountainous region where Western and Islamic cultures meet:
      - Armenia, Azerbaijan, Georgia
- Legacies of Soviet policies
  - Numerous internal republics, many language distinctions
  - Forced relocation of large numbers of ethnic minorities
  - Environmental poisoning from industrial and farm practices

C. CHINA UNDER COMMUNISM
- The Cultural Revolution
- Tiananmen Square

D. CONTEMPORARY EUROPE
- Toward European unity
  - European Economic Community, "Common Market"
  - European Parliament, Brussels, Maastricht Treaty on European Union
  - France linked to Britain by the Channel Tunnel ("Chunnel")
- Conflict and change in Central Europe
  - Geography of the Balkan region
    - Ethnically fragmented, mixture of languages and religions
    - Mountainous region, Danube River
    - Seas: Adriatic, Ionian, Black, Aegean, Mediterranean
  - Romania, Bulgaria, Greece, Albania
  - Countries that emerged from the breakup of Yugoslavia: Slovenia, Croatia, Bosnia and Herzegovina, Macedonia
  - "Balkanization"

E. THE END OF APARTHEID IN SOUTH AFRICA
- Background
  - British and Dutch colonialism in South Africa, Cecil Rhodes, Afrikaners
  - African resistance, Zulu wars, Shaka
  - Boer Wars
  - Union of South Africa, majority nonwhite population but white minority rule
  - Apartheid laws
- African National Congress
  - Nelson Mandela
- Internal unrest and external pressures (such as economic sanctions) force South Africa to end apartheid, Mandela released

VII. Civics: The Constitution—Principles and Structure of American Democracy

- Overview of the U.S. Constitution
  - James Madison
  - Founders' view of human nature
  - Concept of popular sovereignty, the Preamble
  - Rule of law
  - Separation of powers
  - Checks and balances
  - Enumeration of powers
  - Separation of church and state
  - Civilian control of the military
- Bill of Rights
  - Amendments protecting individual rights from infringement (1-3)
  - Amendments protecting those accused of crimes (5-8), Miranda ruling
  - Amendments reserving powers to the people and states (9 and 10)
  - Amendment process
  - Amendments 13 and 19
- Legislative branch: role and powers of Congress
  - Legislative and representative duties
  - Structure of the Congress, committee system, how a bill is passed
  - Budget authority, "power of the purse"
  - Power to impeach the president or federal judge
- Executive branch: role and powers of the presidency
  - Chief executive, cabinet departments, executive orders
  - Chief diplomat, commander-in-chief of the armed forces
  - Chief legislator, sign laws into effect, recommend laws, veto power
  - Appointment power, cabinet officers, federal judges
- Judiciary: Supreme Court as Constitutional interpreter
  - Loose construction (interpretation) vs. strict construction of U.S. Constitution
  - Concepts of due process of law, equal protection
  - *Marbury* v. *Madison*, principle of judicial review of federal law, Chief Justice John Marshall

VIII. Geography of Canada and Mexico

- Canada
  - The ten provinces and two territories, Nunavut (self-governing American Indian homeland), Ottawa
  - St. Lawrence River, Gulf of St. Lawrence, Grand Banks, Hudson Bay, McKenzie River, Mt. Logan
  - Two official languages: English and French, separatist movement in Quebec
  - Montreal, Toronto, Vancouver, most Canadians live within 100 miles of U.S.
  - Rich mineral deposits in Canadian Shield, grain exporter
  - U.S. and Canada share longest open international boundary, affinities between neighboring U.S. and Canadian regions
  - North American Free Trade Agreement (NAFTA)
- Mexico
  - Mexico City: home of nearly one-quarter of population, vulnerable to earthquakes
  - Guadalajara, Monterrey
  - Sierra Madre mountains, Gulf of California, Yucatan Peninsula
  - Oil and gas fields
  - Rapid population growth rate
  - North American Free Trade Agreement (NAFTA), Maquiladoras

Visual Arts: Grade 8

SEE PAGE 3, "The Arts in the Curriculum."

T̲E̲A̲C̲H̲E̲R̲S̲: In schools, lessons on the visual arts should illustrate important elements of making and appreciating art, and emphasize important artists, works of art, and artistic concepts. When appropriate, topics in the visual arts may be linked to topics in other disciplines. While the following guidelines specify a variety of artworks in different media and from various cultures, they are not intended to be comprehensive. Teachers are encouraged to build upon the core content and expose children to a wide range of art and artists.

In studying the works of art specified below, and in creating their own art, students should review, develop, and apply concepts introduced in previous grades, such as line, shape, form, space, texture, color, light, design, and symmetry.

I. Art History: Periods and Schools

T̲E̲A̲C̲H̲E̲R̲S̲:   The guidelines here continue the organizational scheme established in sixth and seventh grades, which combined art history with analysis of specific illustrative works. Timelines may help students situate the artists, periods, and schools. Note that the periods and characteristics are not absolute distinctions but generally helpful categories (to which there are always exceptions) often used in discussions of art.

A. PAINTING SINCE WORLD WAR II
* Examine representative artists and works, including
  Jackson Pollock and Abstract Expressionism: *Painting, 1948*
  Willem de Kooning, *Woman and Bicycle*
  Mark Rothko, *Orange and Yellow*
  Helen Frankenthaler, *Wales*
  Andy Warhol and Pop Art: *Campbell's Soup Can, Marilyn*
  Roy Lichtenstein, *Whaam*
  Romare Bearden, *She-Ba*
  Jacob Lawrence, a work from his *Builder* series or *Migration of Negroes* series

B. PHOTOGRAPHY
* Examine representative artists and works, including
  Edward Steichen, *Rodin with His Sculptures "Victor Hugo" and "The Thinker"*
  Alfred Steiglitz, *The Steerage*
  Dorothea Lange, *Migrant Mother, California*
  Margaret Bourke-White, *Fort Peck Dam*
  Ansel Adams, *Moonrise, Hernadez, New Mexico*
  Henri Cartier-Bresson, *The Berlin Wall*

C. 20TH-CENTURY SCULPTURE
* Examine representative artists and works, including
  Auguste Rodin: *The Thinker, Monument to Balzac*
  Constantin Brancusi, *Bird in Space*
  Pablo Picasso, *Bull's Head*
  Henry Moore, *Two Forms*
  Alexander Calder, *Lobster Trap and Fish Tail*
  Louise Nevelson, *Black Wall*
  Claes Oldenburg, *Clothespin*
  Maya Lin, *Vietnam Veterans Memorial*

II. Architecture Since the Industrial Revolution

- Demonstrations of metal structure: Crystal Palace, Eiffel Tower
- First skyscrapers: "Form follows function"
    Louis Sullivan: Wainwright Building
    Famous skyscrapers: Chrysler Building, Empire State Building
- Frank Lloyd Wright: Fallingwater, Guggenheim Museum
- The International Style
    Walter Gropius, Bauhaus Shop Block
    Le Corbusier: Villa Savoye, Unite d'Habitation, Notre Dame du Haut
    Ludwig Mies van der Rohe and Philip Johnson: Seagram Building

Music: Grade 8

SEE PAGE 3, "The Arts in the Curriculum."

I. Elements of Music

<small>TEACHERS:</small> The Music guidelines for grades 6-8 share a basic vocabulary of the elements of music that can inform the discussion, appreciation, and study of selected musical works. Following these guidelines are recommendations in each grade for a core of musical content, broadly organized as a history of music from early to modern times, with attention to specific periods, composers, and genres. While these guidelines focus on musical vocabulary, appreciation, and history, musical performance should be encouraged and emphasized as local resources allow.

- Review as necessary from earlier grades:
  The orchestra and families of instruments (strings, wind, brass, percussion);
    keyboard instruments
  Vocal ranges: soprano, mezzo-soprano, alto; tenor, baritone, bass
- Recognize frequently used Italian terms:
  grave (very very slow)
  largo (very slow)
  adagio (slow)
  andante (moderate; "walking")
  moderato (medium)
  allegro (fast)
  presto (very fast)
  prestissimo (as fast as you can go)
  ritardando and *accelerando* (gradually slowing down and getting faster)
  crescendo and *decrescendo* (gradually increasing and decreasing volume)
  legato (smoothly flowing progression of notes), *staccato* (crisp, distinct notes)
- Recognize introduction, interlude, and coda in musical selections.
- Recognize theme and variations.
- Identify chords [such as I (tonic), IV (subdominant), V (dominant); V7]; major and minor chords; chord changes; intervals (third, fourth, fifth).
- Understand what an octave is.
- Understand the following notation and terms:

  names of lines and spaces in the treble clef; middle C

  𝄞 treble clef   𝄢 bass clef   ≡ staff, bar line, double bar line, measure, repeat signs

  ○ whole note   ♩ half note   ♩ quarter note   ♪ eighth notes

  whole rest, half rest, quarter rest, eighth rest

  ♬ grouped sixteenth notes

  tied notes and dotted notes

  ♯ sharps   ♭ flats   ♮ naturals

  Da capo [*D.C.*] *al fine*

  meter signature: $\frac{4}{4}$ or common time $\frac{2}{4}$ $\frac{3}{4}$ $\frac{6}{8}$

  quiet *pp   p   mp*   loud *ff   f   mf*

II. Non-Western Music

- Become familiar with scales, instruments, and works from various lands, for example: 12-tone scale, sitar from India, Caribbean steel drums, Japanese koto.

III. Classical Music: Nationalists and Moderns

TEACHERS: While these guidelines focus on musical vocabulary, appreciation, and history, musical performance should be encouraged and emphasized as resources allow. The focus here combines music history with appreciation of illustrative works, and continues from grades 6 and 7 the idea of classifying Western music by periods, with examples of specific composers and works, as well as some associated musical terms. Timelines may help students situate the periods. The periods and their characteristics are not absolute distinctions but generally helpful categories often used in discussions of music.

A. MUSIC AND NATIONAL IDENTITY

NOTE: In seventh grade, students were introduced to works by Dvořák, Grieg, and Tchaikovsky.

- Composers and works:
  Jean Sibelius, *Finlandia*
  Bela Bartók, folk-influenced piano music such as *Allegro barbaro*, selections from *Mikrokosmos* or *For Children*
  Joaquin Rodrigo, *Concierto de Aranjuez*
  Aaron Copland, *Appalachian Spring (Suite)*

B. MODERN MUSIC

- Composers and works:
  Claude Debussy, *La Mer,* first movement, "De l'aube à midi sur la mer"
  Igor Stravinsky, *The Rite of Spring*, first performed in Paris, 1913

IV. Vocal Music

A. OPERA

- Terms: overture, solo, duet, trio, quartet, chorus, aria, recitative
- Composers and works:
  Gioacchino Rossini, from *The Barber of Seville*: Overture and "Largo al factotum"
  Giuseppe Verdi, from *Rigoletto*: aria, "Questa o quella"; duet, "Figlia! . . . Mio padre!"; aria, "La donna è mobile"; quartet, "Bella figlia dell'amore"

B. AMERICAN MUSICAL THEATER

- Composers and popular songs:
  Irving Berlin, "There's No Business Like Show Business," "Blue Skies"
  George M. Cohan, "Give My Regards to Broadway," "Yankee Doodle Dandy"
  Cole Porter, "Don't Fence Me In," "You're the Top"
- Broadway musicals: selections including
  Jerome Kern, *Showboat*: "Ole Man River"
  Rodgers and Hammerstein, *Oklahoma!*: "Oh What a Beautiful Mornin'," "Oklahoma"
  Leonard Bernstein and Stephen Sondheim, *West Side Story*: "Maria," "I Feel Pretty"

Music

Mathematics: Grade 8

TEACHERS: These guidelines are representative of the mathematics typically learned at this grade level in countries that have strong math traditions and whose students score well in international comparisons. Concepts that were in the Grade 7 specifications are generally not repeated here but they are assumed.

In learning the new concepts and procedures, students should use previously acquired mathematics to ensure that the procedures become automatic and habitual. Students should continue to master the use of measuring and drawing instruments, develop their mental arithmetic and their approximating abilities, become more familiar with deductive reasoning, and use calculators and computers in a thoughtful way. The work in eighth grade requires some minimal use of a scientific calculator.

Appropriate preparation for algebra is critical for success in that subject and some students, particularly students who have not been in a Core Knowledge school, may simply not be ready for the content described herein. Most schools will need to spend a limited time reviewing prerequisite concepts, but those students for whom that is insufficient may well require a year in a program that is closer to the Grade 7 specifications.

I. Algebra

A. PROPERTIES OF THE REAL NUMBERS
- Be able to raise a positive number to a fractional power and simplify appropriately, including rationalizing the denominator of a simple radical expression.
- Know and use of the rules of exponents extended to fractional exponents.
- Use the definition of absolute value to solve equations such as $|2x - 3| + 3x = 4x - 2$ and understand why "extraneous solutions" are not solutions at all.

B. RELATIONS, FUNCTIONS, AND GRAPHS (TWO VARIABLES)
- Be able to plot a set of ordered pairs and surmise a reasonable graph of which the points are a part.
- Be able to make a reasonable table of ordered pairs from a given function rule, plot the points, and surmise its graph.
- Know that the points of intersections of two graphs are simultaneous solutions of the relations that define them and indicate approximate numerical solutions.

C. LINEAR EQUATIONS AND FUNCTIONS (TWO VARIABLES)
- Graph linear equations by finding the x- and y-intercepts; for example, know that $2x + 3y = 4$ is linear and graph it using its intercepts.
- Be able to convert between slope-intercept form ($y = mx + b$) and standard form ($ax + by = c$).
- Write an equation for a line given two points or one point and its slope.
- Know lines are parallel or perpendicular from their slopes.
- Find the equation of a line perpendicular to a given line that passes through a given point.
- Understand and be able to graph the solution set of a linear inequality.
- Solve a system of two linear equations in two variables algebraically and interpret the answer graphically.
- Solve a system of two linear inequalities in two variables and sketch the solution set.
- Solve word problems (including mixture, digit, and age problems) that involve linear equations.

D. ARITHMETIC OF RATIONAL EXPRESSION
- Factor second- and higher-degree polynomials when standard techniques apply, such as factoring the GCF out of all terms of a polynomial, the difference of two squares, and perfect squares trinomials.
- Add, subtract, multiply, and divide rational expressions and express in simplest form.

E. QUADRATIC EQUATIONS AND FUNCTIONS
- Solve quadratic equations in one variable by factoring or by completing the square.
- Complete the square to write a quadratic expression as the difference of two squares.
- Graph quadratic functions by completing the square to find the vertex and know that their zeros (roots) are the x-intercepts.
- Know the quadratic formula and be familiar with its proof by completing the square.
- Know how to clear fractions to solve equations that lead to linear or quadratic equations.
- Know how to use squaring to solve problems that lead to linear or quadratic equations.
- Solve word problems, including physical problems such as the motion of an object under the force of gravity, and combined rate (work) problems.

II. Geometry

A. ANALYTIC GEOMETRY
- Reinforce the knowledge of algebra with geometry and vice versa.
- Know that the midpoint of a line segment of any slope, projected perpendicularly onto the horizontal x-axis or vertical y-axis, will be the midpoint of its projection.
- Know the similar triangles connection (AA Similarity) with slope and that this is the tangent of the angle the line makes with the x-axis.

B. INTRODUCTION TO TRIGONOMETRY
- Know that in a right triangle the cosine of an angle is the ratio of the adjacent side to the hypotenuse and the sine is the ratio of the opposite side to the hypotenuse.
- Know the values of the sine, cosine, and tangent of 0, 30, 45, 60, and 90 degrees and use a scientific calculator to determine the approximate value of any acute angle.
- Use a scientific calculator to determine the approximate value of an acute angle of a given sine, cosine, or tangent.

C. TRIANGLES AND PROOFS
- Prove that the bisector of an angle is the set of all points equidistant from both sides.
- Prove that any triangle inscribed in a circle with one side as the diameter is a right triangle.
- Prove the Pythagorean Theorem.
- Know that a line tangent to a circle is perpendicular to the radius at the point of tangency.
- Taking geometry as a model, understand the concept of a mathematical proof, as distinct from an opinion, an approximation, or a conjecture based on specific cases.
- In geometry and elsewhere, understand that a single-counter example suffices to disprove a general assertion.

Mathematics

Science: Grade 8

TEACHERS: Effective instruction in science requires not only direct experience and observation but also book learning, which helps bring coherence and order to a student's scientific knowledge. Only when topics are presented systematically and clearly can students make steady and secure progress in their scientific learning. The Science sequence for the middle school grades aims for more intensive and selective study of topics, a number of which were introduced in earlier grades. The Sequence continues the practice of studying topics from each of the major realms of science (physical, life, and earth science). Students are expected to do experiments and write reports on their findings.

I. Physics

A. MOTION
- Velocity and speed
  The velocity of an object is the rate of change of its position in a particular direction.
  Speed is the magnitude of velocity expressed in distance covered per unit of time.
  Changes in velocity can involve changes in speed or direction or both.
- Average speed = total distance traveled divided by the total time elapsed
  Formula: Speed = Distance/Time (S = D/T)
  Familiar units for measuring speed: miles or kilometers per hour

B. FORCES
- The concept of force: force as a push or pull that produces a change in the state of motion of an object
  Examples of familiar forces (such as gravity, magnetic force)
  A force has both direction and magnitude.
  Measuring force: expressed in units of mass, pounds in English system, newtons in metric system
- Unbalanced forces cause changes in velocity.
  If an object is subject to two or more forces at once, the effect is the net effect of all forces.
  The motion of an object does not change if all the forces on it are in balance, having net effect zero.
  The motion of an object changes in speed or direction if the forces on it are unbalanced, having net effect other than zero.
  To achieve a given change in the motion of an object, the greater the mass of the object, the greater the force required.

C. DENSITY AND BUOYANCY
- When immersed in a fluid (i.e. liquid or gas), all objects experience a buoyant force.
  The buoyant force on an object is an upward (counter-gravity) force equal to the weight of the fluid displaced by the object.
  Density = mass per unit volume
  Relation between mass and weight (equal masses at same location have equal weights)
- How to calculate density of regular and irregular solids from measurements of mass and volume
  The experiment of Archimedes
- How to predict whether an object will float or sink

D. WORK
- In physics, work is a relation between force and distance: work is done when force is exerted over a distance.
    Equation: Work equals Force x Distance (W = F x D)
    Common units for measuring work: foot-pounds (in English system), joules (in metric system; 1 joule = 1 newton of force x 1 meter of distance)

E. ENERGY
- In physics, energy is defined as the ability to do work.
- Energy as distinguished from work
    To have energy, a thing does not have to move.
    Work is the transfer of energy.
- Two main types of energy: kinetic and potential
    Some types of potential energy: gravitational, chemical, elastic, electromagnetic
    Some types of kinetic energy: moving objects, heat, sound and other waves
- Energy is conserved in a system.

F. POWER
- In physics, power is a relation between work and time: a measure of work done (or energy expended) and the time it takes to do it.
    Equation: Power equals Work divided by Time (P = W/T), or Power = Energy/Time
    Common units of measuring power: foot-pounds per second, horsepower (in English system); watts, kilowatts (in metric system)

II.   Electricity and Magnetism

A. ELECTRICITY
- Basic terms and concepts (review from grade 4):
    Electricity is the flow of electrons in a conductor.
    Opposite charges attract, like charges repel.
    Conductors and insulators
    Open and closed circuits
    Short circuit: sudden surge of amperage due to the reduction of resistance in a circuit; protection from short circuits is achieved by fuses and circuit breakers
    Electrical safety
- Electricity as the flow of electrons
    Electrons carry negative charge; protons carry positive charge
    Conductors: materials like metals that easily give up electrons
    Insulators: materials like glass that do not easily give up electrons
- Static electricity
    A static charge (excess or deficiency) creates an electric field.
    Electric energy can be stored in capacitors (typically two metal plates, one charged positive and one charged negative, separated by an insulating barrier). Capacitor discharges can release fatal levels of energy.
    Grounding drains an excess or makes up a deficiency of electrons, because the earth is a huge reservoir of electrons. Your body is a ground when you get a shock of static electricity.
    Lightning is a grounding of static electricity from clouds.
- Flowing electricity
    Electric potential is measured in volts.
    Electric flow or current is measured in amperes: 1 ampere = flow of 1 coulomb of charge per second (1 coulomb = the charge of 6.25 billion billion electrons).
    The total power of an electric flow over time is measured in watts.
    The unit of electrical resistance is the ohm. Ohm's Law: watts = amps x volts. And the corollaries: amps = watts/volts; volts = watts/amps.

Science

B. MAGNETISM AND ELECTRICITY

- Earth's magnetism

  Earth's magnetism is believed to be caused by movements of charged atoms in the molten interior of the planet.

  Navigation by magnetic compass is made possible because the earth is a magnet with north and south magnetic poles.

- Connection between electricity and magnetism

  Example: move a magnet back and forth in front of wire connected to a meter, and electricity flows in the wire. The reverse: electric current flowing through a wire exerts magnetic attraction.

  Spinning electrons in an atom create a magnetic field around the atom.

  Unlike magnetic poles attract, like magnetic poles repel.

  Practical applications of the connection between electricity and magnetism, for example:

  An electric generator creates alternating current by turning a magnet and a coil of wire in relation to each other; an electric motor works on the reverse principle.

  A step-up transformer sends alternating current through a smaller coil of wire with just a few turns next to a larger coil with many turns. This induces a higher voltage in the larger coil. A step-down transformer does the reverse, sending current through the larger coil and creating a lower voltage in the smaller one.

III. Electromagnetic Radiation and Light

- Waves and electromagnetic radiation

  Most waves, such as sound and water waves, transfer energy through matter, but light belongs to a special kind of radiation that can transfer energy through empty space.

- The electromagnetic spectrum

  From long waves, to radio waves, to light waves, to x-rays, to gamma rays

  Called "electromagnetic" because the radiation is created by an oscillating electric field which creates an oscillating magnetic field at right angles to it, which in turn creates an oscillating electric field at right angles, and so on, with both fields perpendicular to each other and the direction the wave is moving.

  The light spectrum: from infrared (longest) to red, orange, yellow, green, blue, violet (shortest)

  Speed in a vacuum of all electromagnetic waves including light: 300,000 km per second, or 186,000 miles per second; a universal constant, called c

- Refraction and reflection

  Refraction: the slowing down of light in glass causes it to bend, which enables lenses to work for television, photography, and astronomy

  How Isaac Newton used the refraction of a prism to discover that white light was made up of rays of different energies (or colors)

  Reflection: concave and convex reflectors; focal point

IV. Sound Waves

- General properties of waves

  Waves transfer energy by oscillation without transferring matter; matter disturbed by a wave returns to its original place.

  Wave properties: wavelength, frequency, speed, crest, trough, amplitude

  Two kinds of waves: transverse (for example, light) and longitudinal (for example, sound)

  Common features of both kinds of waves:

  Speed and frequency of wave determine wavelength.

  Wave interference occurs in both light and sound.

  Doppler effect occurs in both light and sound.

- Sound waves: longitudinal, compression waves, made by vibrating matter, for example, strings, wood, air

    While light and radio waves can travel through a vacuum, sound waves cannot. Sound waves need a medium through which to travel.

    Speed

    Sound goes faster through denser mediums, that is, faster through solids and liquids than through air (gases).

    At room temperature, sound travels through air at about 340 meters per second (1,130 feet per second).

    Speed of sound = Mach number

    Supersonic booms; breaking the sound barrier

    Frequency

    Frequency of sound waves measured in "cycles per second" or Hertz (Hz)

    Audible frequencies roughly between 20 and 20,000 Hz

    The higher the frequency, the higher the subjective "pitch"

    Amplitude

    Amplitude or loudness is measured in decibels (dB).

    Very loud sounds can impair hearing or cause deafness.

    Resonance, for example, the sound board of a piano, or plates of a violin

IV. Chemistry of Food and Respiration

- Energy for most life on earth comes from the sun, typically from sun, to plants, to animals, back to plants.
- Living cells get most of their energy through chemical reactions.

    All living cells make and use carbohydrates (carbon and water), the simplest of these being sugars.

    All living cells make and use proteins, often very complex compounds containing carbon, hydrogen, oxygen, and many other elements.

    Making these compounds involves chemical reactions which need water, and take place in and between cells, across cell walls. The reactions also need catalysts called "enzymes."

    Many cells also make fats, which store energy and food.

- Energy in plants: photosynthesis

    Plants do not need to eat other living things for energy.

    Main nutrients of plants: the chemical elements nitrogen, phosphorus, potassium, calcium, carbon, oxygen, hydrogen (some from soil or the sea, others from the air)

    Photosynthesis, using chlorophyll, converts these elements into more plant cells and stored food using energy from sunlight.

    Leafy plants mainly get their oxygen dissolved in water from their roots, and their carbon mainly from the gas CO_2.

    Plant photosynthesis uses up CO_2 and releases oxygen.

- Energy in animals: respiration

    Animal chemical reactions do the opposite of plants—they use oxygen and release CO_2 and water.

    In animals the chief process is not photosynthesis but respiration, that is, the creation of new compounds through oxidation.

    Animals cannot make carbohydrates, proteins, and fats from elements. They must eat these organic compounds from plants or other animals, and create them through respiration.

    Respiration uses oxygen and releases CO_2, creating an interdependence and balance between plant and animal life.

- Human nutrition and respiration

  Humans are omnivores and can eat both plant and animal food.

  Human respiration, through breathing, gets oxygen to the cells through the lungs and the blood.

  The importance of hemoglobin in the blood

- Human health

  While many other animals can make their own vitamins, humans must get them from outside.

  A balanced diet: the food pyramid for humans (review); identification of the food groups in terms of fats, carbohydrates, proteins, vitamins, and trace elements

VI. Science Biographies

Albert Einstein
Dorothy Hodgkin
James Maxwell
Charles Steinmetz

appendices

Overview
of Topics

APPENDICES

Appendix A: Sample Phoneme Sequence

In kindergarten through second grade, the most common phonemes and letter-sound patterns should be taught in a systematic fashion that builds logically and sequentially, with plenty of practice and review. While there is no single universally accepted sequence of phonemes, a sequence representative of reliable scientific research on beginning reading is offered here. Decisions as to the order in which certain phonemes are taught (for example, short vowels vs. long vowels) are arbitrary. Other sequences for teaching phonemes may be as reliable as the one we list here, as long as they are founded in solid linguistic and pedagogical understanding.

As children proceed, they should be presented with simple, decodable stories written in a controlled vocabulary that corresponds to the letter-sound patterns taught so far. Any child capable of reading more complex texts should of course not be held back, but should still take part in phonemic activities, since explicit and conscious knowledge of letter-sound patterns is one of the tools children will need when later they confront more challenging tasks in reading and writing. Practice with decodable texts is separate from the equally important act of listening to read-aloud works of poetry, fiction, and non-fiction.

Kindergarten

- Vowel sounds:

/a/ as in cat	/e/ as in net	/i/ as in rip
/o/ as in mop	/u/ as in nut	

- Consonant sounds:

/b/ as in big	/k/ as in kid	/s/ as in sun
/d/ as in dog	/l/ as in log	/t/ as in top
/f/ as in fun	/m/ as in man	/v/ as in van
/g/ as in got	/n/ as in not	/w/ as in win
/h/ as in hot	/p/ as in pig	/ks *spelled* x/ as in fox
/j/ as in jet	/r/ as in red	/z/ as in zip

- Adjacent consonant clusters in VCC, CCVC, and CVCC words with short vowel sounds.

Note: In abbreviations such as VCC, V stands for vowel and C stands for consonant. For example, "ant," "elf," and "and" are VCC words. "Frog," "stop," and "flag" are CCVC words. "Milk," "tent," and "desk" are CVCC words. It is recommended that in words with adjacent consonant clusters, children be taught the two adjacent consonants not as a "blend" with a single sound but as two sounds, that is, in "trap," /t/ /r/, not /tr/; in "frog," /f/ /r/, not /fr/. Adjacent consonant clusters in VCC, CVCC, and CCVC words with short vowel sounds may be introduced and practiced in the later term of the kindergarten year, though mastery is not expected until further review and practice in first grade.

First Grade

- Vowel sounds:
  /a/ /e/ /i/ /o/ /u/
  (as in cat, net, rip, mop, nut)

- Consonant sounds (see Kindergarten guidelines above for sample words):
  /b/ /d/ /f/ /g/ /h/ /j/ /k/ /l/ /m/ /n/ /p/
  /r/ /s/ /t/ /v/ /w/ /ks *spelled* x/ /z/

- Double letters that stand for only one sound:
  ff as in stuff
  ll as in full
  ss as in glass
  zz as in buzz

- Adjacent consonant clusters in CCVC, CVCC, and CCVCC words

Note: In abbreviations such as CCVC, C stands for consonant and V stands for vowel. For example, "frog," "stop," and "flag" are CCVC words. "Milk," "tent," and "desk" are CVCC words. "Blast" and "plant" are CCVCC words. It is recommended that in words with adjacent consonant clusters, children be taught the two adjacent consonants not as a "blend" with a single sound but as two sounds, that is, in "trap," /t/ /r/, not /tr/; in "frog," /f/ /r/, not /fr/.

- Common initial adjacent consonant clusters, such as:

Note: The consonant clusters listed here are not meant to be comprehensive but to illustrate the kinds of letter-sound correspondences that should be given attention.

bl and *br* as in blot and brim

fl and *fr* as in flat and from   *dr* and *tr* as in drop and trip

gl and *gr* as in glad and grab   *sk* as in skip

cl and *cr* as in clap and crab   *sl, sm,* and *sn* as in slam, smell, and snap

pl and *pr* as in plan and prop   *sp, st,* and *sw* as in spin, stop, and swim

- Common final adjacent consonant clusters, such as:

ft as in left

ld, lf, lp, lt, lk as in old, elf, help, melt, milk

mp as in bump, lamp

nt, nd, nk as in tent, hand, ink

sk, st as in desk, fast

- Single sounds represented by more than one letter (digraphs):

INITIAL DIGRAPHS:		FINAL DIGRAPHS:	
/ch/	as in chin	/ng/	as in sing
/kw/	spelled *qu* as in queen	/ch/	spelled *tch* as in witch
/sh/	as in ship		
/th/	as in thin; /th/ as in that		

- Vowel sounds commonly spelled as vowel + *e*:

Note: Children may benefit from recognizing these common spelling patterns: that the spelling *a - e* is always split (gate); *i - e, o - e,* and *u - e* are very often split (as in fine, tone, cute); and that *ee* is rarely split (as in feet).

/ā/   spelled *a-e* as in gate

/ē/   spelled *ee* as in feet

/ī/   spelled *i-e* as in fine

/ō/   spelled *o-e* as in bone

/ū/   spelled *u-e* as in cute

TEACHERS: The following may be introduced and practiced in the later term of the first grade year, though mastery is not expected until further review and practice in second grade.

- More vowel sounds and their common spellings:

/o͞o/	spelled *oo* as in boot	/oi/	spelled *oi* as in boil
	spelled *ue* as in blue		spelled *oy* as in toy
	spelled *ew* as in new		
	spelled *u-e* as in tune	/ar/	spelled *ar* as in star
	spelled *u* as in super		
		/er/	spelled *er* as in her
/oo/	spelled *oo* as in book		spelled *ir* as in girl
	spelled *u* as in put		spelled *ur* as in turn
			spelled *or* as in work
/ou/	spelled *ou* as in shout		
	spelled *ow* as in cow	/or/	spelled *or* as in for

- Final adjacent consonant clusters with *-r* such as *rk, rm, rn, rt* (as in fork, worm, torn, fort)

Note: Final adjacent consonant clusters with -r are best taught after children have practiced vowel + *r* spellings.

- Consonant sounds that can be spelled in more than one way:

INITIAL CONSONANT SOUNDS:

/k/ spelled *c* as in coat   /h/ spelled *wh* as in whole
/s/ spelled *c* as in cent   /r/ spelled *wr* as in write
/hw/ spelled *wh* as in whale [distinguish from /w/ spelled *w* as in wash]

FINAL CONSONANT SOUNDS:

/k/ spelled *ck* as in duck
/l/ spelled *le* as in apple
/z/ spelled *s* as in is

- Other consonant sounds:

/j/ spelled *j* as in jet   /f/ spelled *ph* as in phone
   spelled *g* as in magic   spelled *gh* as in tough
   spelled *ge* as in page
   spelled *dge* as in fudge   /n/ spelled *n* as in no
       spelled *kn* as in know

- Vowel sounds that can be spelled in more than one way:

/ā/ spelled *a-e* as in cape   /ō/ spelled *o-e* as in hope
   spelled *ai* as in rain   spelled *o* as in most
   spelled *a* as in paper   spelled *oa* as in coat
   spelled *ay* as in day   spelled *oe* as in toe
   spelled *eigh* as in weigh   spelled *ow* as in blow
   spelled *ey* as in they
   spelled *ea* as in break   /ū/ spelled *u-e* as in cute
       spelled *u* as in unit
/ē/ spelled *ee* as in feet   spelled *ew* as in few
   spelled *ea* as in team
   spelled *y* as in bunny   /e/ spelled *e* as in bed
   spelled *ie* as in chief   spelled *ea* as in head
   spelled *e* as in she

                  /u/ spelled *u* as in cut
/ī/ spelled *i-e* as in kite   spelled *o* as in mother
   spelled *ie* as in cried   spelled *o-e* as in done
   spelled *i* as in child
   spelled *y* as in fly
   spelled *igh* as in night

Second Grade

<u>TEACHERS:</u>   Second grade instruction should consist primarily of review and reinforcement of the phonemes introduced in first grade, as well as practice with a few new letter-sound patterns.   By the end of second grade, decoding should (with grade-level appropriate texts) become almost automatic and effortless, and so allow the child to focus attention instead on meaning.

Most of the following phonemes should have been introduced in first grade. In second grade, review and reinforce as necessary to ensure fluent decoding. *Letter-sound correspondences introduced here in second grade are marked by an asterisk (*).*

- More vowel sounds and their common spellings:

/o͞o/	spelled *oo* as in boot	/oi/	spelled *oi* as in boil
	spelled *ue* as in blue		spelled *oy* as in toy
	spelled *ew* as in new		
	spelled *u-e* as in tune	/ar/	spelled *ar* as in star
	spelled *u* as in super		
	spelled *ou* as in soup*	/er/	spelled *er* as in her
	spelled *ui* as in suit*		spelled *ir* as in girl
			spelled *ur* as in turn
/oo/	spelled *oo* as in book		spelled *or* as in work
	spelled *u* as in put		spelled *ear* as in learn*
	spelled *oul* as in would*		
		/or/	spelled *or* as in for
/ou/	spelled *ou* as in shout		spelled *ore* as in more*
	spelled *ow* as in cow		spelled *oar* as in soar*
			spelled *our* as in four*

- Consonant sounds that can be spelled in more than one way:

INITIAL CONSONANT SOUNDS:
/k/	spelled *c* as in coat
/s/	spelled *c* as in cent
/h/	spelled *wh* as in whole
/r/	spelled *wr* as in write
/hw/	spelled *wh* as in whale [distinguish from /w/ spelled *w* as in wash]

FINAL CONSONANT SOUNDS:
/k/	spelled *ck* as in duck
/f/	spelled *ff* as in stuff
/l/	spelled *ll* as in full, spelled *le* as in apple
/s/	spelled *ss* as in glass
/z/	spelled *s* as in is

- Other consonant sounds:

/j/	spelled *j* as in jet	/f/	spelled *ph* as in phone
	spelled *g* as in magic		spelled *gh* as in tough
	spelled *ge* as in page		
	spelled *dge* as in fudge	/n/	spelled *n* as in no
			spelled *kn* as in know

- Vowel sounds that can be spelled in more than one way:

/ā/	spelled *a-e* as in cape	/ū/	spelled *u-e* as in cute*
	spelled *ai* as in rain		spelled *u* as in unit*
	spelled *a* as in paper		spelled *ew* as in few*
	spelled *ay* as in day		
	spelled *eigh* as in weigh	/e/	spelled *e* as in bed*
	spelled *ey* as in they		spelled *ea* as in head*
	spelled *ea* as in break		
		/o/	spelled <u>o</u> as in mop
/ē/	spelled *ee* as in feet		spelled <u>a</u> as in father
	spelled *ea* as in team		spelled <u>ah</u> as in shah
	spelled *y* as in bunny		
	spelled *ie* as in chief	/ô/	spelled *o* as in dog*
	spelled *e* as in she		spelled *a (ll)* as in fall*
/ī/	spelled *i-e* as in kite	/aw/	spelled *aw* as in lawn*
	spelled *ie* as in cried		spelled *au* as in author*
	spelled *i* as in child		spelled *ough* as in fought*
	spelled *y* as in fly		spelled *augh* as in taught*
	spelled *igh* as in night		
		/u/	spelled *u* as in cut
/ō/	spelled *o-e* as in hope		spelled *o* as in mother
	spelled *o* as in most		spelled *o-e* as in done
	spelled *oa* as in coat		
	spelled *oe* as in toe		
	spelled *ow* as in blow		
	spelled *ough* as in though *		

- Triple consonant clusters:

Note: The consonant clusters listed here are not meant to be comprehensive but to illustrate the kinds of letter-sound correspondences that should be given attention.

INITIAL CLUSTERS, SUCH AS:	FINAL CLUSTERS, SUCH AS:
spl as in split *	*nch* as in bench *
spr as in spring *	*nth* as in tenth *
str as in strong *	*rch* as in porch *
shr as in shrink *	*rth* as in worth *

Appendix B: **Supplement on Biblical Literacy**

The Core Knowledge Foundation provides this appendix in response to many requests for a more comprehensive selection of topics from the Bible than is provided in the Core Knowledge Sequence. The topics listed below are not an integral or required part of a Core Knowledge school program. This list of Biblical topics that are widely alluded to in speech and writing has an educative purpose: it is designed to help students understand these allusions when they encounter them. No reasonable person will interpret this list as intending religious indoctrination.

A distinction needs to be made between teaching the Bible and teaching about the Bible. Teaching the Bible as a guide to faith is the job of the home (if the home so chooses) or church, not the schools. Teaching about the Bible in historical context is something schools can do to help produce literate and historically informed citizens.

Thus, the topics below are suggested for those who want to offer children some familiarity with the Bible as part of their overall cultural literacy. As E. D. Hirsch, Jr. explains in *The Dictionary of Cultural Literacy* (2nd edition, Boston: Houghton Mifflin, 1993),

> *No one in the English-speaking world can be considered literate without a basic knowledge of the Bible. … All educated speakers of American English need to understand what is meant when someone describes a contest as being between David and Goliath, or whether a person who has the "wisdom of Solomon" is wise or foolish, or whether saying "My cup runneth over" means the person feels fortunate or unfortunate. Those who cannot understand such allusions cannot fully participate in literate English.*

SUGGESTED TOPICS FOR GRADE 1:

FROM THE HEBREW BIBLE (OLD TESTAMENT):
Noah's Ark
Moses in the bulrushes, saved by Pharaoh's
    daughter
Moses and the burning bush
The parting of the Red Sea
The Promised Land

FROM THE NEW TESTAMENT:
Mary and Joseph; the birth of Jesus; Bethlehem;
    the three wise men (Magi) and their gifts
The parable of the good Samaritan
The "Golden Rule": "Do unto others. . ." [from the
    Sermon on the Mount: "All things
    whatsoever ye would that men should do to
    you, do ye even so to them."]

SUGGESTED TOPICS FOR GRADE 2:

FROM THE HEBREW BIBLE (OLD TESTAMENT):
The Tower of Babel
Joseph and his coat of many colors
How Joseph saved his family

FROM THE NEW TESTAMENT:
The loaves and fishes

SUGGESTED TOPICS FOR GRADE 3:

FROM THE HEBREW BIBLE (OLD TESTAMENT):
David and Goliath
Jonah and the whale

FROM THE NEW TESTAMENT:
The parable of the prodigal son
The parable of the lost sheep

SUGGESTED TOPICS FOR GRADE 4:

FROM THE HEBREW BIBLE (OLD TESTAMENT):
Joshua conquers Jericho
The story of Ruth ("Whither thou goest, I will go")
Samson and Delilah
The judgment of Solomon
Daniel:
    the handwriting on the wall
    in the lion's den

FROM THE NEW TESTAMENT:
Choosing the disciples; "fishers of men"
Familiar phrases:
    the blind leading the blind [Jesus on the
    Pharisees: "Can a blind man lead a blind
    man?"]
    walk on water

SUGGESTED TOPICS FOR GRADE 5:

King James Bible

What it means, literally and figuratively, to cite "chapter and verse"

FROM THE HEBREW BIBLE (OLD TESTAMENT):

Creation (Genesis 1-3) "In the beginning"; "Let there be light"; Garden of Eden; "Be fruitful and multiply"

Adam and Eve; tree of knowledge of good and evil, forbidden fruit; fall from Eden; "Dust thou art, and unto dust shalt thou return"

Cain and Abel: "Am I my brother's keeper?"; mark of Cain

FROM THE NEW TESTAMENT:

The Annunciation; Mary and the angel Gabriel

The Nativity: Luke 2:1-20

John the Baptist

The temptation; "Man shall not live by bread alone"; "Get thee behind me, Satan"

Raising Lazarus from the dead

Palm Sunday

The Last Supper

Judas

Pilate; washing hands (as a way of disclaiming responsibility)

Calvary

Crucifixion

Resurrection and appearance to the disciples

Ascension

SUGGESTED TOPICS FOR GRADE 6:

FROM THE HEBREW BIBLE (OLD TESTAMENT):

Noah and the flood (review)

God tests Job

The destruction of Sodom and Gomorrah; Lot's wife

The covenant with Abraham: the Promised Land, Canaan

Abraham and Isaac

Jacob; Esau sells his birthright for "a mess of pottage"

Joseph

    his coat of many colors (review from grade 1)

    his brothers sell him into slavery

    Potiphar's wife

    he interprets Pharaoh's dreams

    he saves his family

Moses and the burning bush (review from grade 1)

The plagues of Egypt

Passover

The Exodus

The parting of the Red Sea (review from grade 1)

Manna from Heaven

The Ten Commandments

The 23rd Psalm

Ecclesiastes 3:1-8 ("To everything there is a season")

The message of the prophets [such as Isaiah, Jeremiah, Ezekiel, Amos]

Familiar phrases:

    "an eye for an eye, tooth for a tooth" [Mosaic law, Deuteronomy 19:21]

    "Physician, heal thyself"

    Philistine

    "love thy neighbor as thyself" [Leviticus 19:18]

FROM THE NEW TESTAMENT:

The Sermon on the Mount; the Beatitudes ("Blessed are . . .")

Familiar phrases and precepts, such as:

    "turn the other cheek"

    "Ask, and it shall be given you"

    "Cast not pearls before swine"

    "go the extra mile"

    "Wolves in sheep's clothing"

    "No man can serve two masters . . . Ye cannot serve God and Mammon"

    "the salt of the earth"

    "Consider the lilies of the field"

    "Love your enemies"

    "Judge not, that ye be not judged"

    "Lay not up for yourselves treasures upon earth, where most and rust doth corrupt"

OTHER FAMILIAR PHRASES:

"Render to Caesar the things that are Caesar's, and to God the things that are God's"

the straight and narrow [see Matthew 7:14]

cast the first stone [John 8:7]

"Faith hope and charity"; "through a glass, darkly" [Paul, I Corinthians 13:1-13]

"the love of money is the root of all evil" [1 Timothy 6:10]

"swords into plowshares"

"wolf also shall dwell with the lamb"

Appendix C:
Common
Misconceptions
About
Core
Knowledge

Appendix C: Common Misconceptions About Core Knowledge

Before people become informed about what the Core Knowledge Sequence is and what's going on in Core Knowledge schools, they sometimes ask questions or make objections based on misconceptions or lack of accurate information. These pages offer responses to the most common questions and objections.

Our school already has a curriculum. We don't need to replace it with something else.

Does the school's curriculum state any specific knowledge goals? In most schools, the curriculum is defined in terms of very general processes and skills. Core Knowledge does not replace the skills-based curriculum; rather, it complements it by providing carefully sequenced and challenging knowledge in which to ground skills instruction. Core Knowledge is meant to comprise about half of a school's curriculum, thus leaving ample freedom for local requirements and variations. Schools already using the Core Knowledge Sequence have welcomed its ready accommodation to existing state or local requirements.

A common core of knowledge will make schools into cookie cutters that turn out the same product everywhere.

Other countries teach a common core of knowledge: are all French, Japanese, and German children alike? A common core of knowledge that makes up only about half of American schooling will be no threat to children's individuality. A body of shared knowledge will be taught in a variety of ways by different teachers, and responded to in a variety of ways by different students. And, influential as schools are, children are shaped by a great deal outside of school as well.

Students are unique individuals and can't be expected all to learn the same material. Schooling should respond to the unique learning styles of each individual child.

There is no incompatibility between teaching a core curriculum and adapting instruction to the needs of individual students. Moreover, even as we look to teachers to bring out the best in each child as a learner, we also ask them to recognize the needs of each child as part of a larger community. All communities require some common ground. The community of the classroom requires, in particular, that its members share some common knowledge, because this knowledge makes communication and progress possible.

Specific academic content is not developmentally appropriate for young children.

What exactly does "developmentally appropriate" mean? Who is to decide what is "developmentally appropriate" for particular children? Are the topics recommended in existing curricula "developmentally appropriate"? For example, to cite one state's Social Studies curriculum framework, is it "developmentally appropriate" for second graders to "learn about the community and its components—stores, recreational facilities, protective and educational services," or to "explore components of the community such as shopping centers or community services"? Must children in the second grade have their horizons bounded by the local mall, as opposed to the much greater reach of the Core Knowledge Sequence for second grade, which has children learning about China and India, ancient Greece, and the Civil War?

The question of "developmental appropriateness" applies less to content than to methods of instruction. That is, within reason, specific content is itself neither developmentally appropriate nor inappropriate. Given specific content guidelines, teachers are generally aware of how to deliver the content in developmentally appropriate ways: for example, not lecturing to kindergartners about the seven continents, but singing songs, making paper-mache globes, cutting out and coloring continent-shaped patterns, and making charts with animals characteristic of different continents.

A curriculum that specifies what is to be taught at each grade level takes away the creative freedom of teachers.

Some educators argue that curricular decisions should be left up to the individual classroom teacher. They say that it is part of a teacher's "professional autonomy" to decide what should be taught. Yes, the individual teacher should have significant freedom to decide how to teach, and some say in what to teach as well. But to leave all decisions about what to teach up to the individual teacher is to place too great a burden on the teacher, to remove the opportunity for professional cooperation among teachers, and to lose sight of what schools need to be fair and effective. Teaching a common core of knowledge, such as that articulated in the Core Knowledge Sequence, is compatible with a variety of instructional methods and additional subject matters. Teachers in Core Knowledge schools report that making the commitment to teach a shared body of specific knowledge is not confining but liberating. Given specific content guidelines, teachers can fashion a variety of creative lessons and teaching approaches, and collaborate by sharing ideas and resources. In general, teachers in Core Knowledge schools report a sense of empowerment, both personal and professional.

Knowledge is changing so fast that the best approach is not to teach specific knowledge but to teach children to "learn how to learn."

"Learning how to learn" is an admirable aim but a misleading slogan. If learning is to proceed on any principle besides random chance, then schools need to follow a carefully sequenced body of knowledge. Why? Because children learn new knowledge by building upon what they already know. It's important to begin building foundations of knowledge in the early grades because that's when children are most receptive, and because academic deficiencies in the first six grades can permanently impair the quality of later schooling. The most powerful tool for later learning is not an abstract set of procedures (such as "problem solving") but a broad base of knowledge in many fields. The idea that "knowledge is changing" is only partly true, and, as it pertains to schools, mostly misleading. It is true that some

ideas and terms—such as sub-atomic particles, software, Internet, or the Commonwealth of Independent States—did not exist or were not widely known even as recently as a couple of generations ago. But the obvious fact that the modern world is changing in no way leads to the conclusion that "knowledge is changing so fast that we can't keep up with it" or that "what we learn today will be obsolete by the year 2000." The basic principles of science and constitutional government, the important events of world history, the essential elements of mathematics and of oral and written expression—all of these are part of a solid core that does not change rapidly, but instead forms the basis for true lifelong learning.

In curriculum, "less is more"; schools should not try to cover a lot of content but instead should help students master a few areas in depth and detail.

Many among us perhaps share grim memories of, for example, the high school history course as a superficial blitz through a heavy textbook crammed with facts, names, and dates. Courses like this are what make many people respond warmly to the idea that "less is more." Surely, we think, we would have learned more if we had been confronted with less, if we had been allowed to investigate specific issues and questions in depth and detail. Does it follow, then, that when it comes to knowledge, less is more? Like most slogans in education, there is some truth to "less is more," but also some danger when the slogan is wrongly construed or thoughtlessly applied. It is hard to disagree with the view that deep knowledge is better than shallow. But—particularly in the elementary years—it does not follow that deep knowledge of a few things is better

than broad knowledge of many things. In fact, one needs both deep knowledge and broad knowledge. To help children gain breadth of knowledge is to help them lay the foundation on which they can build new knowledge, including more in-depth, specialized knowledge. The best time to acquire broad general knowledge is in the early years, when children are most curious and receptive. In these early years, the idea of "less is more" does not apply, and is especially irrelevant, even potentially damaging, to students from disadvantaged backgrounds, who may be left behind while some advantaged students learn a desirable breadth of knowledge at home.

The idea of "less is more" is also misleading because it flatters a strain in some educational theory that disparages challenging content and focuses instead on feelings, attitudes, and "self-esteem." But there is one sense in which "less is more" applies even to the early years. This sense is not in opposition to broad and rich knowledge, but in encouraging selectivity about the way in which broad and rich knowledge is chosen. Educational planners need to take on the responsibility of selecting a rich core of important knowledge, defined in an explicit sequence. It is this particular sense of "less is more" that informs the process of selection and consensus-building that went into the Core Knowledge Sequence.

The content of the Core Knowledge Sequence was arbitrarily decided by a few people who have no right to tell others what they should know.

The content specified in the Core Knowledge Sequence represents a broad consensus of diverse groups and interests, including parents, teachers, scientists, professional curriculum organizations, and experts on America's multicultural traditions. Provisional versions of the curriculum were reviewed and revised by panels of teachers. In March1990, the curriculum was further revised by almost 100 people, of diverse backgrounds and interests, attending a national conference sponsored by the Core Knowledge Foundation. As more schools teach Core Knowledge, teachers participate in occasional updates of the Sequence. In short, Core Knowledge, far from being arbitrary, is more democratic and broadly representative than any current alternative we know of. Certainly the consensus behind the Core Knowledge Sequence is more diverse and democratic than the de facto curricular decisions made by a small group of educational specialists and commercial publishers who issue the textbooks that often drive curriculum in schools today.

It is elitist to specify a body of content.

A central motivation behind the Core Knowledge initiative is *anti-elitist*. The goal is to guarantee equal access for all to knowledge necessary for higher literacy and learning. Such knowledge is currently possessed only by the educated elite—and that's the problem. Our aim is to make that knowledge available to all through the institution available to all: universal public schooling. Core Knowledge is critically important for children from disadvantaged backgrounds. As Albert Shanker, past president of the American Federation of Teachers, has written, as long as curriculum remains completely a matter of local choice, "schools and school districts are free to hold students up to high standards or, as often happens in the case of disadvantaged children, to decide the kids can't do the work and give

them a watered-down curriculum. The trouble with this is that it virtually guarantees these children will fall behind their more advantaged peers—and never catch up" (*New York Times*, Dec. 16, 1991). In a Core Knowledge school, however, all children are taught a core of challenging, interesting knowledge that provides a foundation to build on year by year.

Our population is changing, and schooling needs to change to meet the needs of an increasingly diverse population. What we need is a curriculum that is more multicultural.

Schools should foster respect for diversity, and a curriculum should include the study of many cultures. Typically, however, state and district curriculum guidelines do not define specific multicultural content. Rather, they prescribe a set of nice-sounding but vague goals and attitudes, such as the following from one state's "Curricular Framework for Social Studies":
• Understand the characteristics and development of cultures throughout the world.
• Understand that societies reflect contributions from many cultures.
• Understand and appreciate various dimensions of world interdependence.
• Understand historic and current events from the perspective of diverse cultural and national groups.

These are admirable goals that nod in the direction of multiculturalism—but where is the specific multicultural content? Without some specificity, the door is open to repetition and gaps. How many times will children study the Woodland Indians, and yet perhaps never examine the different ways of life of the Anasazi or the Cheyenne? Will children study

Mexico but not Japan, Kenya but not China? Or Kenya in second grade then again in fourth? If we truly want our children to know about and appreciate many cultures, then we need to specify which cultures, and teach them in a way that broadens their perspective on the world and its diversity, rather than bores them with repetition or leaves them unaware of people and places that most educated people know about.

The job of the teacher is to teach children, not subject matter.

There's something warm and appealing in that slogan. After all, it gives top priority to children—and don't we all want the highest priority of teachers to be the best interests of our children? But there's something disconcerting in the way the imperative to "teach children, not subject matter" is phrased. It suggests an either-or situation: either you teach children, or you teach subject matter. The implication is that teachers who teach "subject matter" are somehow not teaching children! But what exactly does it mean to "teach children"? Are we in fact teaching children if we do not teach subject matter? What a strange pass American education has come to when many educators assume that between children and subject matter there is some fundamental incompatibility, as though they were, as the old saying goes, like east and west, and never the twain shall meet. One would have thought, rather, that the challenge for the teacher is to link east and west—that is, to bring children and subject matter together, through practice, hard work, and imaginative and creative endeavors that kindle in children the love of subject matter that the teacher herself or himself feels (or should feel).

Students don't learn from rote memorization of isolated facts. What children need is not a bunch of facts but critical thinking skills.

Those who think that the only way to teach specific content is through rote memorization need to observe the many imaginative, resourceful, and creative ways that teachers in Core Knowledge schools have found to engage their students in active learning of important knowledge: through dramatizations, art projects, writing workshops, collaborative learning groups, research projects, etc. Yes, children may occasionally memorize a poem or the Preamble to the Constitution—but these are valid learning experiences, which, in fact, children enjoy, and from which they get a sense of pride and achievement. Behind the outcry against "rote memorization" lies a deep prejudice—a prejudice against fact. Many educators object to any curriculum that says, for example, that children should learn the seven continents, because that is "mere fact." To teach facts, they say, is to reduce education to "Trivial Pursuit." Granted, some facts are trivial. Who starred in "Car 54 Where Are You"? That's trivial. But, who was Dred Scott and what was the significance of the Supreme Court's Dred Scott decision? That's worth knowing: it gives you insight into the causes of the Civil War as well as historical perspective on race relations in the United States.

No one wants schools to think of curriculum solely in terms of facts. We also want—and students need—opportunities to use the facts, to apply them, question them, discuss them, doubt them, connect them, analyze them, verify or deny them, solve problems with them. All these activities, however, rely upon having some facts to work with. Without factual knowledge about an issue or problem, you can't think critically about it—you can only have an uninformed opinion.

Many teachers may not have learned much about Ancient Egypt or the Industrial Revolution or photosynthesis. So how can you put such content in a curriculum? You can't expect teachers to teach what they don't know.

Educators are fond of talking about preparing children to be "lifelong learners." Why don't we have equal confidence in our teachers as lifelong learners? In schools that build a program on the Core Knowledge Sequence, many teachers express initial anxiety about having to prepare to teach topics they're unfamiliar with. But, once they make the effort (and it does take hard work), they often express tremendous enthusiasm and a rekindled love of learning, which carries over to their students. A second-grade teacher at a Core Knowledge school in the South Bronx wrote to tell us that

Core Knowledge has made a major difference to my students and myself. I am very excited about teaching interesting subjects. The content is thrilling and fascinating for me as a person and a teacher. I feel that my interest and energy rub off on my students. They are "turned on" because I am "turned on." In addition, I have also developed a close working relationship with other teachers. There is congruence and unity among us. My students are learning high level concepts. They are being challenged and they love it!

Core Knowledge is just another passing educational fad.

There are plenty of educational fads around, with no grounding in solid research or real scholarship. Core Knowledge is not one of them. The idea behind Core Knowledge is supported by the top reading researchers in the nation: in the recent report called *Becoming a Nation of Readers*, they observe, "Even for beginners, reading should not be thought of simply as a 'skill subject.' It is difficult to imagine, for instance, that kindergartners could be called literate for their age if they did not know Goldilocks and the Three Bears or Peter Rabbit" (p. 61). Perhaps the most important research attesting to the power of Core Knowledge is the long experience of educational systems in other countries—all of which teach a common core of knowledge— consistently rated as the best in the world both for excellence and fairness.

The following papers of related interest are available from the Core Knowledge Foundation:

• Toward a Centrist Curriculum: Two Kinds of Multiculturalism in Elementary School
• Fairness and Core Knowledge

Appendix D: **The Four S's of Core Knowledge**

For any curriculum to be both excellent and fair, it must demonstrate four qualities that we at the Core Knowledge Foundation refer to as the four S's:
> **(1) shared,**
> **(2) solid,**
> **(3) sequenced, and**
> **(4) specific.**

SHARED KNOWLEDGE

It is important for our children to share a body of knowledge for reasons that have to do with literacy, Americans' high mobility, and social cohesion.

Literacy: The connection between shared knowledge and literacy is a main focus of E. D. Hirsch's *Cultural Literacy*. In that book, Mr. Hirsch examined the role that shared knowledge plays in literacy. Part of literacy is the basic and essential ability to decode the signs on the page, to associate the letters with their corresponding speech sounds. But beyond that functional literacy–which needs to be taught early and well–to be fully literate one must also have a broad range of background knowledge. To be "culturally literate" is to possess this shared background knowledge.

For example, on a broadcast of the evening news, the newscaster might refer to a "threatened presidential veto" or "an appellate court decision." The newscaster doesn't stop to define the three branches of government or explain how checks and balances work in the Constitution. Rather, all this background knowledge is taken for granted, because that is the nature of communication: we cannot stop to spell out and define every term, so we assume some–in fact, a great deal–of shared knowledge. One function of schooling is, or should be, to ensure that our children grow up sharing such knowledge.

Student mobility: Every year millions of Americans move. Our current school system, in which content varies from one locality to another, is unfair to the many students who change schools. When children move into a new school, they are often bored by familiar material or baffled by new material that assumes background knowledge they have never been taught. But in a system in which the curriculum is based upon a shared core of knowledge, students who move from school to school are treated more fairly because they remain on a more equal footing with their classmates, since all have been taught the shared core.

Social cohesion: In our diverse society, differences should be recognized and celebrated. At the same time, there needs to be a complementary emphasis on what we share. Shared, multicultural knowledge makes for effective classroom learning and for cooperation and respect among students, both within the limited community of the classroom and the extended community of American society.

SOLID KNOWLEDGE

Solid knowledge is knowledge that persists from generation to generation, indeed, that makes it possible for one generation to communicate with another. This solid core of knowledge is too often left out of school materials. For example, the near disappearance from the elementary curriculum of traditional history, myth, and literature is a great mistake. Basal reading programs constantly update the content that young children are taught, under the theory that modern, "relevant" materials will be of greater interest than older stories and myths. But such programs are based on the mistaken premise that reading, writing, and oral communication are formal skills that can be perfected without regard for specific literate content. Publishers and schools need to abandon this mistaken theory and instead enhance the effectiveness with which a solid core of literate knowledge is presented.

SEQUENCED KNOWLEDGE

Extensive research in learning theory has proven that children learn new knowledge by building on what they already know. In our current educational system, however, in which content varies greatly from school to school, often from classroom to classroom, it is difficult for teachers to predict what their students already know. This causes teachers to spend a great deal of time reviewing and repeating. Even so, many children who lack the necessary background knowledge are left behind. But if a school follows a clearly sequenced curriculum, which allows, for example, a third grade teacher to know what her students were taught in first and second grades, then the teacher can more effectively and efficiently help students build new knowledge on their old knowledge.

For example, if second graders learn some basic geography about the continents and major oceans, then as third graders they can build on that knowledge to learn about early explorers and their encounters with the "new world." It is important to build such foundations in the early grades because that is when children are most receptive, and because academic deficiencies in the first six grades can permanently impair the quality of later schooling.

SPECIFIC KNOWLEDGE

Many state and district curricular guidelines are phrased in vague and general terms. A typical curriculum guideline reads, "Students will demonstrate knowledge of people, events, ideas, and historical movements that contributed significantly to the development of the United States." Which people and events? What ideas and movements?

In contrast, the elementary core curricula of countries with systems more fair than ours are more specific. Only by specifying a core of knowledge that all children should share can we guarantee equal access to that knowledge. In our current system, disadvantaged children often suffer from low expectations that translate into a watered-down curriculum. But in schools that build their curriculum upon specific content such as that outlined in the Core Knowledge Sequence, disadvantaged children, like all children, learn a core of challenging knowledge that they can build on grade by grade.

The Core Knowledge Sequence is designed to provide schools with the core of a shared, solid, sequenced, and specific curriculum. In Core Knowledge schools, teaching and learning are more effective as teachers help students build upon prior knowledge and make more efficient progress from one year to the next. All students enjoy more equal educational opportunities as they are motivated by consistently challenging content. And all children are prepared to become members of the wider national community, respectful of diversity while strengthened by the shared knowledge that helps unite us on common ground.

217

Core Knowledge at a Glance: Major Topic Headings, K-8

	Kindergarten	First Grade
Language Arts/English	I. Reading and Writing II. Poetry III. Fiction IV. Sayings and Phrases	I. Reading and Writing II. Poetry III. Fiction IV. Sayings and Phrases
History and Geography	**World:** I. Spatial Sense II. Overview of the Seven Continents **American:** I. Geography II. Native Americans III. Early Exploration and Settlement (Columbus; Pilgrims; Independence Day) IV. Presidents, Past and Present V. Symbols and Figures	**World:** I. Geography II. Early Civilizations (Mesopotamia; Ancient Egypt; History of World Religions) III. Mexico **American:** I. Early People and Civilizations (Maya, Inca, Aztec) II. Early Exploration and Settlement III. American Revolution IV. Early Exploration of American West V. Symbols and Figures
Visual Arts	I. Elements of Art II. Sculpture III. Looking at and Talking About Art	I. Art from Long Ago II. Elements of Art III. Kinds of Pictures: Portrait and Still Life
Music	I. Elements of Music II. Listening and Understanding III. Songs	I. Elements of Music II. Listening and Understanding (Composers; Orchestra; Opera; Ballet; Jazz) III. Songs
Mathematics	I. Patterns and Classification II. Numbers and Number Sense III. Money IV. Computation V. Measurement VI. Geometry	I. Patterns and Classification II. Numbers and Number Sense III. Money IV. Computation V. Measurement VI. Geometry
Science	I. Plants and Plant Growth II. Animals and Their Needs III. Human Body (Five Senses) IV. Introduction to Magnetism V. Seasons and Weather VI. Taking Care of the Earth VII. Science Biographies	I. Living Things and Their Environments II. Human Body (Body Systems) III. Matter IV. Properties of Matter: Measurement V. Introduction to Electricity VI. Astronomy VII. The Earth VIII. Science Biographies